Working with German corpora

Working with German corpora

Edited by Bill Dodd

With a foreword by John Sinclair

First published in the United Kingdom by The University of Birmingham Press, Edgbaston, Birmingham, BI5 2TT, UK.

ISBN 0-902459-05-9

British Library Cataloguing in Publication data
A CIP catalogue record for this book is available from the British Library

Printed in Great Britain by Redwood Books Limited

Contents

Foreword

This book marks a new stage in the rapid development of its subject, and I am very pleased to have been asked to write a foreword.

The study of language corpora held on computers developed slowly from around 1960 until the mid-1980s, in the shadow of mentalist linguistic theories which taught that language data was of little importance. In the 1990s more and more attention has been paid to the evidence of usage, so conveniently made available by ever more powerful and flexible computers, and it can no longer be ignored or dismissed.

Furthermore, the findings of this early research are unexpected and pose questions of some theoretical importance. It was natural for researchers to expect that the systematic examination of a large amount of evidence would largely confirm what was already 'known', because it had been established by careful research using traditional methods. However, it soon became clear that there were very considerable areas of language patterning that had received little attention from researchers; as well as complementing many of the established facts, the corpora showed that there was a lot more ordering to linguistic choices than had been suspected.

Because of this, corpus linguists have recently been making a case for their work being treated as a sub-discipline and not just a source of information or an innovative methodology. Corpus linguistics lays claim to its own emerging theories, to descriptions that use novel categories and cut across even fundamental categorizations of traditional linguistics, and gives new thrust to many important applications of linguistic knowledge in fields such as translation and lexicography.

This book marks a stage in the maturation of corpus linguistics and its transformation into a component discipline within linguistics. The English language has dominated linguistics for many years now, especially in relation to computers. While this may be understandable in economic and political terms, it is unhelpful from a linguistic perspective. It is often conceded that English is by no means a reliable exemplar even of the languages around it, and yet much of the software that is available for processing corpora is guided by assumptions that apply mainly to English. To many, the inclusion of German texts is only a small step towards the provision of multilingual resources, but to a computer there is a lot of difference between English texts and German ones.

While energetic individual scholars have built their own special corpora for their chosen studies, several of which are reported in this book, the Institut für Deutsche Sprache in Mannheim has led the way in the provision of generic corpus data and appropriate software for German, and its support is acknowledged in many places. Both large and small corpora are consulted, using a range of investigative tools.

Indeed, once it is noted that all the papers in this book concern the German language, the next impression that one gets is the variety of approaches taken, giving an idea of the versatility of corpus techniques and the variety of research projects in which corpora play a central role. Literary texts are analysed, in a tradition directly descending from the earliest computer applications in linguistic study – the studies of authorship and style. Some papers feature the re-examination of grammatical patterns, the phraseological choices and the distribution of language varieties, and these make us aware of the complexity and geographical spread of the German language. The historical dimension and the contribution of corpora to the teaching of German are also addressed.

Finally, I am very pleased to see how much of this work centres on the University of Birmingham – evident in the contributions, the editorial work and the publisher. Since the mid-1960s there has been research activity in corpus linguistics in Birmingham, first concentrating on English and blossoming into the Cobuild project and – just established – a special Chair in Corpus Linguistics. From an early stage, enthusiasts in other departments, notably Modern Languages, grouped together and began work in parallel. I would like to pay tribute to Tim Johns, much referred to in this book, for his supportive work in linking the various groups and inspiring them to pursue corpus research. In the Department of German the leader has been the editor of this volume, Bill Dodd, who has gradually established corpus linguistics in his department and fostered it in the work of many others. The diversity of contributions to this volume shows how far-reaching his interests are.

This volume is fascinating in itself in presenting a range of different types of corpus research. It is especially important for scholars of German, both in the research findings that are reported and the development of reusable resources for other scholars. It points the way for researchers in other languages to gather material for similar volumes. In my view it shows how pervasive corpus research can be, and makes me wonder once again how we ever managed to do linguistic and literary research without the benefit of corpora.

John Sinclair
Professor of Modern English Language, University of Birmingham
President, Tuscan Word Centre
April 2000

Editor's preface

As a relative newcomer to the field of corpus linguistics I am aware of being fortunate in having such good neighbours in the Department of English at the University of Birmingham, who are both leading practitioners in this new and exciting discipline, and generous of their time in sharing their knowledge and enthusiasm through seminars and personal contacts. I am indebted to John Sinclair, Tim Johns and Philip King for their early proselytizing work which first convinced me of the importance of corpora, and to Ramesh Krishnamurthy, with whom I have had the privilege of working closely over the past year. The Press's reader provided invaluable criticism at various stages of the book's gestation. I would like to thank the School of Humanities at Birmingham for supporting the proposal for this book, and Vicki Whittaker at the Press for her professionalism in preparing it for publication. As usual, any remaining blemishes are the responsibility of the contributors and in particular the editor. Finally, I would like to thank the contributors for managing to produce their contributions despite the increasingly hectic demands of academic (and non-academic) life.

Every attempt has been made to ensure that information contained in this book is accurate, though it is extremely difficult at times to keep up with the fast-changing Internet. Website addresses (given in this book between <angled brackets>) were correct at the time the book went into production.

Bill Dodd
Birmingham 2000

Note on language corpora and software

Ramesh Krishnamurthy and Bill Dodd

Given the rapid developments in both these areas it is likely that any survey of the field will quickly become outdated. The following overview, while making no claims to being exhaustive, is intended to provide a basic orientation and give information on the main sources of corpora and types of software currently available, and to indicate where further information might be sought.[1]

1 Language corpora

1.1 Information and access

The easiest way to get information about corpora, and access to them, is via the Internet. The following sites give information about corpora, software, courses in corpus linguistics, bibliographies, etc. and provide links to related sites: the Corpus Research Group at the University of Birmingham (<http://www-clg.bham.ac.uk>), the British National Corpus (or BNC) (<http://info.ox.ac.uk/bnc/corpora.html>), and Michael Barlow's Corpus Linguistics page (<http://www.ruf.rice.edu/~barlow/corpus.html>). There are two major corpus distribution agencies, one in the USA (Linguistic Data Consortium or LDC: <http://www.ldc.upenn.edu>) and one in Europe (European Language Resources Association or ELRA: <http://www.icp.grenet.fr/ELRA/home.html>), which offer corpora and linguistic software for a fee. ICAME (International Computer Archive of Modern and Medieval English: <http://

www.hit.uib.no/icame.html>) offers a smaller range. Each corpus, archive, or text may have copyright restrictions on its use.

1.2 German corpora

There are fewer corpora of German than of English, but the number is growing rapidly.

1.2.1

The Institut für Deutsche Sprache (IDS), Mannheim, is the main centre of corpus construction and exploitation for German. Its various corpora of written and spoken German run to some 220 million words, some 63 million of which (known as the Publikcorpus, and containing only written German) can be viewed without charge via a Telnet connection or, more conveniently, via the IDS website. Further information on access to these corpora can be obtained from the IDS website, as can a detailed description of each of the separate corpora (see <http://www.ids-mannheim.de/kt/corpora.html>). The IDS corpora are interrogated using COSMAS, a specially designed set of software tools. (Contributions in this book which use IDS corpora are those by Dodd, Gupta, Kenny, Lawson and Witton. A link to the *Frühneuhochdeutsches Wörterbuch* project reported on by West can be found at <http://www.ids-mannheim.de/lexik>.)

1.2.2

There are also an unknown number of *ad hoc* corpora of German compiled by researchers all over the world – a trend which is almost certainly increasing exponentially with the arrival of the Internet. Some of these are 'one-off' corpora constructed for a specific research project, while others are intended to grow into substantial specialist corpora. Six contributions to this book report on work on such corpora: Jones (600 000-word corpus of spoken German, Brigham Young University) (Jones 1997); Kenny (German-English Parallel Corpus of Literary Texts, GEPCOLT, University of Manchester Institute of Science and Technology) (Kenny 1999); Mackison (one million word corpus of business and management periodicals, University of Birmingham); Roe (100 000-word corpus of A-level and undergraduate texts, University of Aston);

West (part of the ENHG corpus being developed in conjunction with the IDS, University of Newcastle-upon-Tyne);[2] and Wichmann and Nielsen (25 000-word marked-up corpus of legal documents, University of Central Lancashire, this being part of a projected one million word corpus of contract law).

1.2.3

The LDC (see 1.1) offers five German corpora: CALLFRIEND (German, German Lexicon, German Speech, and German Transcripts) and CELEX2.

1.2.4

The Project Gutenberg (<http://gutenberg.aol.de/gutenb.htm>) is an enormous and expanding online text archive (partly available on CD-ROM), comprising major German literary and philosophical texts, and German translations of classical Greek, Latin, English, and French literature (over 300 authors, 150 000 pages, and 370 Mb of text and pictures). Current German authors seeking publishers can also send in their own works.

1.2.5

The NEGRA corpus (<http://www.coli.uni-sb.de/sfb378/negra-corpus/>) is a syntactically annotated corpus of 10 000 sentences from the *Frankfurter Rundschau*, created at Saarland University, Saarbrücken, and is available free for research.

1.2.6

ELRA (see 1.1) offers four German corpora: the ECI-ELSNET fine-grained morphosyntactically tagged corpus of 50 000 words (from the *Frankfurter Rundschau*) which has its own DBT software; the Multilingual Corpora for Cooperation (MLCC), which contains a thirty-three million word German sub-corpus of samples from *Handelsblatt* (1986–88); the MTP morphosyntactically annotated 500 000 word corpus of texts from the *Frankfurter Allgemeine Zeitung* and *Die Zeit* (1990–92), with a suite of software tools; and the Karl-May-Korpus, about 1.6 million words of the works of Karl May (1993–97), tagged with word class and lemma.

1.3 English corpora

1.3.1

The COBUILD Bank of English corpus (<http://www.cobuild.collins.co.uk/>) built by HarperCollins and the University of Birmingham contains over 329 million words of text. There is a free demonstration at the website. Fifty million words are publicly available for a fee, using the in-house *Lookup* software. The data is mainly British, American, and Australian, and predominantly post-1990. The corpus is frequently updated and expanded.

1.3.2

The BNC (see 1.1) is a 100 million word collection of samples of written and spoken language from a wide range of sources, designed to represent a wide cross-section of current British English, both spoken and written. It is available online and on CD-ROM, with its SARA software, but use is currently restricted to users within the EU.

1.3.3

ICAME (see 1.1) offers eighteen corpora on a CD-ROM, with several software tools. The corpora include written, spoken, and parsed corpora; British, American, Indian, Australian and New Zealand varieties of English; the Brown and LOB corpora; the Freiburg corpora FROWN and FLOB; and Historical English. This website also hosts the *corpora-list*, the main e-mail discussion list for all corpus-related activities.

1.3.4

Michael Barlow (see 1.1) mentions numerous resources: the Oxford Text Archive; the Susanne Corpus; Project Gutenberg (English); and various others.

1.3.5

The LDC (see 1.1) offers numerous English language resources.

1.3.6

ELRA (see 1.1) offers numerous English language resources.

1.4 Multilingual/parallel corpora

This is a fairly new and rapidly developing area. The Canadian Hansard (parallel English and French versions of parliamentary debates) was one of the earliest publicly available resources. Various European Union documents are now available electronically in parallel multilingual versions.

1.4.1

The Parallel Texts Library (<http://web.bham.ac.uk/johnstf/multdata.htm>), created at the University of Birmingham, offers an expanding collection of texts (currently, European Parliament debates 1996, and European Parliament financial regulations) that can be used with Multiconcord software.

1.4.2

Michael Barlow's Parallel Corpora page (<http://www.ruf.rice.edu/~barlow/para.html>) is a useful source.

1.4.3

LDC (see 1.1) offers ECI Multilingual Text; European Language Newspaper Text; and OGI Multilanguage Corpus.

1.4.4

ELRA (see 1.1) offers a Multilingual Parallel Corpus of translated data in nine European languages, comprising two sub-corpora from the *Official Journal of the European Communities* ('Written Questions' 1993, and 'Debates of the European Parliament' 1992–94); and the MULTEXT JOC Corpus, one million words each for five languages from the 'Written Questions and Answers' of the *Official Journal of the European Community*.

1.5 Future developments

There is no sign of a let-up in corpus activities. Many academic and commercial research institutions, computer and telecommunications companies, and publishing and broadcasting organizations are involved.

There is a growing concern at conferences of the natural language processing and computational linguistics communities (e.g. <http://ceres.ugr.es/~rubio/elra/program.html>) for evaluation and standardization (e.g. the use of Unicode for dealing with character sets, and SGML for typographical and text-structural information) of resources. Corpora are beginning to be annotated for semantics, pragmatics, and discourse markers. The use of corpora in language learning and teaching is increasing. Specialized corpora for business, healthcare, and other domains are being built, as well as terminological databases. Lexicons such as WordNet (Princeton University's English lexical database: <http://www.cogsci.princeton.edu/~wn/>) and EuroWordNet (a multilingual database with basic semantic relations between words for several European languages: <http://www.hum.uva.nl/~ewn/>) are being widely used. More languages are being incorporated (e.g. the TELRI research archive of computational tools and resources for central and east European languages: <http://solaris3.ids-mannheim.de/telri/main.html>). Advances in speech recognition will make spoken data more accessible. Audio (not just written transcriptions) and video materials are being collected and assembled into corpus systems. Corpus sizes are continuing to increase. The Internet itself is being seen and used as a vast corpus.

2 Software

Corpus software has also developed very rapidly in the 1990s, and various functions are now regarded as fairly standard. Most corpus programs should be able to provide: **frequency lists** (a list of words in the corpus, with their number of occurrences) of various kinds, **concordances** (every occurrence of a given word with some of the surrounding text, usually displayed in a KWIC (Key Word In Context) format, with the selected word at the centre of the screen), **concordance sorting** (the ability to arrange the concordances alphabetically by the word one to the left or right of the key word, two to the left or right, etc.), and **concordance editing** or **selection** (the ability to discard or select all concordance lines that contain a particular word or other feature). More advanced software will add **lemmatization** (the ability to group words according to their notional 'root' or 'base' form), the use of **grammar**

tags (the part-of-speech label assigned to each word in the corpus) and/or **parse tags** (the syntactic or clause-functional label assigned to each word in the corpus), analysis of **collocation** (the tendency of some words to occur with certain other words at a rate significantly above random), **distribution** (the occurrence of words in particular genres or domains, or in particular parts of a text), and so on.

2.1 Early corpus software programs

The programs of the 1970s and 1980s, such as COCOA, CLOC, OCP, the Longman Miniconcordancer (which cannot handle German special characters), Microconcord (which does not give corpus frequencies), Micro-OCP, and Wordcruncher, were all deficient in some or all of the functions listed above, or could not handle the large corpora that are now available.

2.2 Current software

1990s programs such as Mike Scott's WordsmithTools (<http://www.liv.ac.uk/~ms2928/index.htm>), Oliver Mason's Qwick (<http://www-clg.bham.ac.uk/QWICK/>), or Michael Barlow's Monoconc (<http://www.ruf.rice.edu/~barlow/mono.html>) are robust, sophisticated, and easily available. Longer lists of software (with links) are provided at the sites mentioned in 1.1 above. The BNC sampler CD (<http://info.ox.ac.uk/bnc/getting/sampler.html>) contains versions of Corpus Work Bench, Qwick, SARA, and WordSmith Tools. COSMAS (Corpus Storage, Access and Maintenance System, see 1.2.1) was introduced in 1992 as the in-house set of software tools used by the IDS in Mannheim. The current version is R2.4-6.

2.3 Multilingual software

Multilingual software is rapidly developing, including Michael Barlow's ParaConc (<http://www.ruf.rice.edu/~barlow/parac.html>) and David Woolls' Multiconcord (<http://web.bham.ac.uk/johnstf/lingua.htm>).

2.4 Specialist programs

Specialist software for grammarians, translators, or language teachers, such as taggers, parsers, text aligners, automatic translation and translation memory programs, automatic text selection, and testing and marking programs are also becoming widely available, and many are listed at the sites mentioned in 1.1 above and at the main CALL (Computer Assisted Language Learning) sites (e.g. <http://web.bham.ac.uk/johnstf/>). One recent area of specialist applications is the use of corpus tools in forensic linguistics,[3] including plagiarism detection programs (Woolls and Coulthard 1998).

2.5 Future developments

The developments of the 1990s have been nothing short of spectacular: the academic discipline of corpus linguistics, its teaching at universities, the availability of resources, the advances in technology and software, and (above all) the growth of the Internet have all been important factors. The next decade is likely to prove even more fruitful, if that is conceivable. More work will undoubtedly be done in looking at user needs and software design (possibly incorporating some of the excellent graphics and user-friendly interfaces used in computer games), in standardization and evaluation of software (e.g. platform-independence and benchmarking), and in methods of delivery (hand-held devices; combining TV, phone, and computer facilities; constantly updated satellite downloads).

Notes

1 Detailed surveys can be found in Kennedy (1998: chs 2, 4), Biber et al. (1998: 281–7) and Wichmann et al. (1997: 311–22).

2 See also note 13 in the Introduction to this book.

3 See *Forensic Linguistics: The International Journal of Speech, Language and the Law* (also at <http://www.bham.ac.uk/forensiclinguistics>).

References

Biber, Douglas, Susan Conrad and Randi Reppen (1998), *Corpus Linguistics. Investigating Language Structure and Use*. Cambridge University Press: Cambridge.

Jones, Randall (1997), 'Creating and using a corpus of spoken German', in Anne Wichmann, Steven Fligelstone, Tony McEnery and Gerry

Knowles (eds) (1997), *Teaching and Language Corpora*. Longman: London and New York, pp. 146–56.

Kennedy, Graeme (1998), *An Introduction to Corpus Linguistics*. Longman: London and New York.

Kenny, Dorothy (1999), 'The German-English parallel corpus of literary texts (GEPCOLT): a resource for translation scholars', *Teanga* 18: 25–42.

Wichmann, Anne, Steven Fligelstone, Tony McEnery and Gerry Knowles (eds) (1997), *Teaching and Language Corpora*. Longman: London and New York.

Woolls, David and Malcolm Coulthard (1998), 'Tools for the trade', *Forensic Linguistics: The International Journal of Speech, Language and the Law* 5(1): 33–57.

Notes on contributors

Gordon J. A. Burgess studied German at the Universities of London and Freiburg i.Br., before joining the Department of German at the University of Aberdeen in 1976, where he currently holds the position of Reader in German. His main interests lie in two areas: (a) German literature from the seventeenth to the twentieth centuries, with special emphasis on the German Baroque, German Classicism, and post-1945 writings; and (b) Computer-Assisted Language Learning (CALL), particularly in the fields of hypertext and multimedia applications, and parallel concordancing. He is a founder member of the International Wolfgang Borchert Society, Hamburg (President since 1992); and a founder member of EuroCALL.

Bill Dodd is Reader in German Studies at the University of Birmingham. His research interests range across modern German literature, language description, and critical linguistics. He has published on Franz Kafka, Heinrich Böll, and Dolf Sternberger, and is co-author of *Modern German Grammar* (Routledge 1996) and *Reading German* (OUP 1997). He has recently been awarded a Leverhulme Major Research Fellowship.

Piklu Gupta teaches German language and linguistics to undergraduates and information technology and natural language processing to postgraduates at the University of Hull. His first degree in German is from the University of London and he also has an MSc in Machine Translation from UMIST. Before coming to Hull he held posts at the

University of Manchester and UMIST. He has previously published on valency lexicography and is currently conducting research on corpus-based means of semi-automatically acquiring the lexicon, using *be*-verbs as a case study for a more general methodology.

Randall Jones is a Professor of German and former Dean of the College of Humanities at Brigham Young University. He holds a BA and MA in German from Brigham Young University and an MA and Ph.D in Linguistics from Princeton University. He teaches courses in the history of the German language, the structure of modern German, German dialects, and German phonetics. His research interests include the structure of modern spoken German, corpus linguistics, and computer-assisted language learning and research. He is the editor of the Brigham Young University Corpus of Spoken German and the author of numerous papers and articles relating to corpus-based research in colloquial German.

Dorothy Kenny studied translation in Dublin and Quebec, and machine translation at UMIST in Manchester. Her doctoral research, also conducted at UMIST, focused on using corpus linguistic techniques to investigate lexical creativity in original German writing and translations into English. She is author of *Lexis and Creativity in Translation* (forthcoming), and co-editor of *Unity in Diversity: Current Trends in Translation Studies* (1998) and the *Bibliography of Translation Studies* (1998, 1999), all published by St. Jerome, Manchester. She lectures at Dublin City University and specializes in corpus linguistics, translation technology, and corpus-based translation studies.

Ramesh Krishnamurthy was born in Madras, India, in 1948 and brought up in England. He has a degree from Cambridge University in French and German, and from London University in Sanskrit and Tamil. He worked full time for the University of Birmingham and Cobuild from 1984 to 1997 and contributed to many Cobuild publications, as well as developing corpora and software for Collins dictionaries. Ramesh continues to work on the Bank of English corpus at Cobuild as a freelance consultant on language corpora, linguistics and lexicography, and also

undertakes work for major publishers (CUP, Helicon, Bloomsbury, HarperCollins), the BBC, and various European and international language projects (NERC, TELRI, SENSEVAL, SELECT, VerbNet, ELDA). He is a Research Fellow at the universities of Birmingham and Wolverhampton, and teaches on undergraduate, postgraduate, and professional courses, and supervises research.
(<http://www-clg.bham.ac.uk/ramesh>) or (<http://www.wlv.ac.uk/~in6052>).

Ann Lawson was born in Scotland in 1969. Upon graduation from the Department of German Studies at the University of Birmingham, she went on to complete a Ph.D on Thomas Mann's tetralogy *Joseph und seine Brüder*. Her thesis discussed the relationship between Mann's political essays and literary work between the World Wars. A period as Research Fellow in the Corpus Research Group of the School of English at Birmingham followed, during which she worked on corpus-based lexicographic projects. She then worked in the Department of Lexicology of the Institut für Deutsche Sprache in Mannheim on several European research and infrastructure projects in the field of language engineering, with the emphasis on corpus linguistics. She now works as Data Licensing Manager for Collins dictionaries, facilitating the use of dictionary material and language resources in electronic form. Her particular interests lie in collocation, translation equivalence, and the development and exploitation of corpus and lexicon resources. She is also a freelance lexicographer.

April Mackison is a postgraduate student in the Department of German Studies at the University of Birmingham. She has taught German at Birmingham for three years and at the University of the West of England for one year. She is currently employed by CLS Corporate Language Services AG in Zurich as a translator, specializing in insurance.

Jane Nielsen currently works as a consultant for a London-based IT consultancy, coordinating the training of end users as part of large-scale international projects to implement integrated business system solutions.

Peter Roe is currently Research Director in the Languages Studies Unit (<http://www.les.aston.ac.uk/lsu>) in Aston University's School of Languages and European Studies, where, in addition to teaching the Lexical Studies and Corpus Analysis modules on the distance learning masters degree in TEFL/TESOL, he is very active in the doctoral research programme (<http://www.les.aston.ac.uk/~roepj/research/lsrsmenu.htm>), with a special interest in language policy and language medium in tertiary education. He designs his own software for exploring natural language (<http://www.les.aston.ac.uk/~roepj/guide/guide.htm>) and programs in Unix and Perl. He is the Chief Coordinating Examiner for Business English with the International Certificate Conference in Frankfurt.

Jonathan West was born and educated in Yorkshire and graduated at the universities of Manchester and Dublin (Trinity College). He has taught at university level since 1979, first at the University of Bonn, then in Dublin, and from 1988 at the University of Newcastle upon Tyne, where he is now Senior Lecturer in German. Dr West's research interests are primarily in German and Germanic linguistics (see <http://www.ncl.ac.uk/sml/staff/west.htm>).

Anne Wichmann is Reader in Speech and Language at the University of Central Lancashire, Preston. Her main research interests lie in the analysis of speech corpora, and in particular the intonation of spoken discourse. She has worked for many years on spoken corpus data, mainly English. She has published comparative intonation studies (English and Dutch) and many studies of English intonation. Other publications have covered the use of corpus data for teaching German and a corpus-based study of modal expressions in English and German legal texts (with Jane Nielsen). Her major publication is *Intonation in Text and Discourse* (Addison Wesley Longman 2000).

Nic Witton has over thirty years' experience of teaching German language, philology and applied linguistics in Australia. A related area of interest is computer-assisted language learning on which he has published as well as designing and writing his own programs. Over the last few years he has been working on applications of machine-readable corpora and concordancing software. Early in 1999, because of government funding cut-backs in the university sector, he was offered and accepted a redundancy package and is now working in an honorary capacity using Australian corpora as a contributor to Australia's national dictionary, the *Macquarie*.

Introduction
The relevance of corpora to German studies

Bill Dodd

This volume presents examples of recent work in German studies by English-speaking scholars working on computerized text corpora of German. To my knowledge, this is the first volume of essays in English devoted to corpus work in German studies. By and large, monographs and collections of essays on language corpora today are dominated by work on English.[1] The essays collected here would not normally be found between the same covers. In traditional academic terms, they make rather unusual bed-fellows. However, the traditional compartments into which we are accustomed to put the different aspects of what we collectively do as Germanists have been set aside in this book in order to focus on the rapidly expanding applications of computerized German-language corpora across the spectrum of the discipline as a whole. The common ground for these essays lies in their exploitation of machine-readable text and their commitment to a set of methods and principles which have come to be associated with 'corpus linguistics'. All the essays in this book are concerned with empirically examining authentic texts or collections of texts, including literary prose, medieval texts, newspaper articles, and texts belonging to a particular register (such as legal documents) or realm of discourse (such as the language of business and management). Some are specifically concerned with language-learning applications, whilst others have a more traditional research orientation. The majority, perhaps inevitably, deal with written language; one, however, reports on a corpus of spoken German. Together, they illustrate the wide range of corpus-related work now being done across the spectrum of German studies, and the growing importance of text corpora to teaching and research. Ten years ago a book such as this would have been unthinkable. In 2000, no one can seriously doubt that corpora of German will play an increasingly influential role as computer-readable texts of all kinds become widely available.

Constructing large corpora is still beyond the means of most individuals and indeed most institutions. The main source for several of the contributions in this volume are the large text corpora of German held at the Institut für Deutsche Sprache (IDS) in Mannheim, which currently run to more than two hundred million words. The intensive work for most of the studies in this book which use the IDS corpora has been done by scholars visiting the excellent research facilities in Mannheim, and a selection of these corpora can be browsed free via the World Wide Web or, by arrangement with the IDS, the full set can be investigated via Telnet, in both cases using the IDS in-house software COSMAS.[2] However, doing corpus-based work does not necessarily mean that one is restricted to corpora created by large research institutions. Four of the studies in this book are based on relatively small corpora specially constructed by academics and/or postgraduate students at universities in the United Kingdom and the United States (Aston, Birmingham, Central Lancashire, and Brigham Young). These have been created either by scanning in text, entering transcribed spoken text, or transferring text which was already electronically stored. Major developments in corpus construction, however, are often joint enterprises, for example the collaboration between Collins and the University of Birmingham to create the Cobuild[3] project, and the parallel corpus of European languages constructed by an EU-funded consortium under the LINGUA initiative, which runs to several hundred thousand words.[4]

'Corpus linguistics', not surprisingly, has been taken up mainly by colleagues with a background in linguistics, and because of this there may be a perception that it has little in common with, or, worse, is somehow inimical to the critical research traditions in literary and cultural studies. In English Studies, where much of the pioneering work in text processing has been done, such attitudes can still be found, so it would be surprising if they were not also common amongst Germanists. And yet some of the early applications of this technology were in the field of literary studies. 'Paper-form' concordances of German literary works began to appear in the late 1960s (e.g. Wisbey 1968), and cover, for example, the Luther Bible (*Große Konkordanz*, 1979), Wittgenstein's *Philosophische Untersuchungen* (McKinnon 1972), Trakl's poetry (Wetzel 1971), and Kafka's *Der Prozeß* (Speidel 1978). Few literary scholars would dispute that these early concordances provided a valuable research tool. A new generation of interactive editions of literary 'classics' on CD-ROM is now extending the possibilities offered by these early concordances – for example, Goethe's *Die Leiden des jungen Werther* (1995) and Kafka's *Die Verwandlung* (Kafka 1997). Texts on CD-ROM usually have some kind of keyword search facility for finding the next occurrence of a particular word, and a text-export facility enabling marked text to be exported to a text file which can be investigated by a concordancer.[5] The increasing availability of literary works in electronic form provides a research tool much more versatile and therefore more powerful than the early paper-form concordances.

Some key terms

In this Introduction I will outline some of the main implications of language corpora, and in particular the importance of work already done on English. There are now several helpful introductions to the field, and I will focus here on the work of John Sinclair and Michael Stubbs, who has also done some work on German.[6] (For a more detailed set of definitions see, for example, Sinclair (1991: 169–76)).

A **corpus** is a 'body' of naturally produced language, selected according to some design and stored in machine-readable form. It can be investigated by software programs such as concordancers, which typically produce a **KWIC** (key word in context) file or **concordance** in which the key word (or **node**) appears in the centre of the line, as Figure 1 shows. The stretch of language preceding the node is its left **co-text**, the stretch following the node is its right co-text. These co-texts contain the immediate and less immediate **collocates** of the node, enabling the study of **collocation**, 'the occurrence of two or more words within a short space of each other within a text' (Sinclair 1991: 170). Sinclair places collocation, in terms of rank, between 'independent' word-meaning and 'dependent' phrase-meaning: 'In between these two fixed points is collocation, where we see a tendency for words to occur together though they remain largely independent choices' (Sinclair 1991: 71). The KWIC file in Figure 1, taken – like all the KWIC files used in this Introduction – from the IDS Bonner Zeitungskorpus (BZK),[7] has been sorted alphabetically by the first word to the right of the node. In this particular file, a distinctive patterning also appears one to the left of the node. With a single exception (line 12), the distinction between *Vergleich mit* and *Vergleich zu* correlates with the class of word preceding the noun. The fact that the phrase *im Vergleich zu* is found thirty-four times in three million words, and *im Vergleich mit* only once, tells us that both forms are attested but that their **distribution** is very different.

```
MicroConcord search SW: vergleich
90 characters per entry
Sort : 1R/SW unshifted.
1 n Italienern waren es 25,7 Prozent (im Vergleich dazu die Ergebnisse der Gruppe der Spani
2 etrug 680 Mill. DM oder 18 Prozent. im Vergleich dazu sind die Kommunaldarlehen in der Ze
3  einer Übergangszeit leben, die keinen Vergleich mit ähnlichen Zeiten aushält ... Die Ver
4 genannten Entwicklungsländern, und ein Vergleich mit dem Durchschnittseinkommen eines wes
5 it einem Jahresüberschuß von 2,28. Ein Vergleich mit dem Rumpfgeschäftsjahr 1962 ist schw
6 ergrößerten Produktionssteigerung. Der Vergleich mit 6,8 Prozent Produktions- und rund ze
7 ßenordnungen sind, zeigt am besten ein Vergleich mit dem vielbeschriebenen Hochdamm von A
8 ieses Bootes zu schaden. Immerhin, der Vergleich mit dem mitteldeutschen Vierer, der 20 M
9 eigentlich interessiert, ist nicht ein Vergleich mit Farbigen in anderen Ländern, sondern
10 e Farbabstufung angeht, sehr wohl den Vergleich mit den Bildteppichen der berühmteren Wo
11 er (in Nimes) war. Hier wäre also ein Vergleich mit dem Beispiel Herbergers möglich. Dar
12 ann es offen und nüchtern aus, daß im Vergleich mit dem Tempo der Entwicklung zur faschi
13  äußeren Verhältnisse in Südafrika im Vergleich zu anderen noch so herrlich sein. Sie mü
14 ten Ihnen alle Fluggesellschaften. Im Vergleich zu allen anderen Economy-Preisen können
15 onald Bunting begünstigt zu haben, im Vergleich zu denen, die nun außer Strafverfolgung
16 r Gesamtumsatz 240 Millionen Mark (im Vergleich zu 197 Millionen in der vorangegangenen
17 eweglich im Keller. Sie sind heute im Vergleich zu 1959/60 bei Thomas-Güten im Inland no
18 dlichen Nachbarn einzuräumen. Auch im Vergleich zu anderen Investitionsgebieten führt Eu
19 Kommunisten und Sozialisten hatten im Vergleich zu den Wahlen im Vorjahr einen erheblich
20 e, Wissenschaft und Industrie, die im Vergleich zu Amateurgeräten ungemein starke Absatz
21 eugpark von 85 Millionen Einheiten im Vergleich zu seiner Bevölkerung an der Spitze Kont
22 r Linie angesprochen werden, liegt im Vergleich zu den anderen Ausländern verhältnismäßi
23 blik die inflatorische Entwicklung im Vergleich zu Italien und Frankreich am wenigsten b
24 t nicht sehr groß, schon gar nicht im Vergleich zu der kommunistischen Hilfe für Kuba. I
25 r Linie angesprochen werden, liegt im Vergleich zu den anderen Ausländern verhältnismäßi
26 blik die inflatorische Entwicklung im Vergleich zu Italien und Frankreich am wenigsten b
27 fungen der Ost-BVG waren seit 1950 im Vergleich zu Westberlin lediglich für das Ausrangi
28 eld dazu fehlt, sagte Martens. Die im Vergleich zu anderen Ländern niedrigen Toleranzgr
29 aßenbahnnetz in Ostberlin hat sich im Vergleich zu Westberlin keineswegs verringert. Die
30 ie ausgewiesenen 75,8 Mill. D-Mark im Vergleich zum Vorjahresergebnis lediglich eine Zun
31 um nur sieben Prozent zeigt jedoch im Vergleich zum Umsatzzuwachs, daß die Verwaltung mi
32 . Das mitteldeutsche Boot war also im Vergleich zum süddeutschen Vierer auf der zweiten
33 xemburgischen und deutschen Werken im Vergleich zum Monatsdurchschnitt 1968 einen Produk
34 mit zwar ein Rückgang eingetreten, im Vergleich zum März 1963 wurden jedoch rund 223000
35  habe. Der Zimmerpreis ist dagegen im Vergleich zum Vorjahr nur unerheblich gestiegen. D
36 den Erwartungen. Der Umsatz konnte im Vergleich zum entsprechenden Zeitraum des Vorjahre
37 n um 2,5 beziehungsweise 6 Prozent im Vergleich zum Vorjahr. In Bremen und Hamburg haben
38 mit zwar ein Rückgang eingetreten, im Vergleich zum März 1963 wurden jedoch rund 223000
39 n Zigarren, Stumpen und Zigarillos im Vergleich zum entsprechenden Vorjahreszeitraum um
40 n um durchschnittlich neun Prozent im Vergleich zum Vorjahr gestiegen. Das geht aus eine
41 . 1963 Hatte sich der Gesamtumsatz im Vergleich zum Vorjahr um 4,2 Prozent erhöht. Die B
42  September 1,5 Prozent der Stimmen im Vergleich zur vorigen Wahl verloren, während die S
43 munique 597000 Besucher, das wären im Vergleich zur Frühjahrsmesse 1968 knapp 19000 Besu
44 gleichmäßiger Bodenbeschaffenheit. Im Vergleich zur Arbeit mit anderen, von flüssigem Br
45  ist die Stahlerzeugung rückläufig im Vergleich zur gleichen Zeit im Jahre 1948; die Koh
46 reditieren sind. Daraus ergab sich im Vergleich zur Normalfinanzierung, bei der die Kred
47 r schließlich in seinem Referat einen Vergleich zwischen der Situation der gegenwärtigen
```

Figure 1 A Key Word in Context (KWIC) file, sorted alphabetically by the first word on the right of the key word

We cannot ignore the existence of the marginal pattern, but we can quantify the frequency of its occurrence relative to the more frequent, 'normal' pattern. We might be tempted to say that we have discovered a general feature of the language; however, we would need to look in other, and larger corpora, before we could be reasonably confident of such a statement. At the very least, the concordancer has enabled us, or obliged us, to consider empirical evidence.

The computer can sort the file in various ways, for example alphabetically by the first or second word to the right. In this way, recurring patterns of collocation can be captured and made visible. The computer can also record the **frequency** of occurrence of a given item as a node or as a collocate of a node, as well as the relative frequency of two collocating items with respect to one other. The number of words to the left or right which are considered to contain significant collocations is known as the **span**. A span of about four words either side of the node is commonly used for English, though there is no reason for this orthodoxy to be taken over in work on German, and indeed a larger span is used on occasions for English. Although corpora are commonly described as consisting of so many 'words', corpus linguists distinguish between **types** and **tokens**. For example, fifty instances of *und* in a text are counted as fifty tokens of the same type. Modern software can calculate **type-token ratios** in a given text or corpus (for the above example, the type-token ratio is 1:50, or 2 per cent). This information can provide an insight into the characteristics of a particular text or set of texts, particularly when we compare the findings with those from another text or set of texts. Some corpora, especially those built for grammatical analysis, are **tagged**, that is to say some or all items are assigned to a computer-readable category, most typically according to a part-of-speech classification. This exercise, now increasingly automated, makes possible the study of **colligation**, the patterns in which grammatical categories combine. Software for personal computers is constantly being developed, and a modern corpus tool like Mike Scott's Wordsmith can perform many sophisticated tasks such as generating word frequency lists and collocation frequency lists.[8] An example of a word frequency list can be found in Peter Roe's contribution to this volume.

A corpus is not a random collection of texts.[9] Its construction is planned according to some design to produce a body of texts which are in some way representative of, for example, a particular field and/or time. A corpus which aims to reflect the range of usage in English, or German, must not only be very large but be designed to reflect, for example, different kinds of spoken and written language, and regional varieties, in a controlled proportion. Corpora can be historical or contemporary. Having more than one corpus of a language makes it possible to examine the frequency and distribution of particular words, collocations, or other features across different corpora as well as within the same corpus. Comparing a large, general **control corpus**, for example, with a corpus drawn from a particular register of the language, will help to highlight the specific features of that register (as well as the extent of shared patterning). **Parallel corpora** contain, in separate compartments, or sub-corpora, original texts and their translations. By aligning the source text and its translation, it is possible to study translation techniques (see below). **Comparable corpora**, on the other hand, contain texts in different languages which are related in subject matter or genre, for example, but are not translations (see Teubert 1996).[10] Much work has gone into developing **specialized** or **domain-specific corpora**, which are used for investigating the language of particular defined discourse areas (such as microbiology, European legislation, or learners' output in a foreign language). This kind of corpus work, focused on language for specific purposes (LSP), is perhaps the most important area not to be represented in this volume.

Adopting and adapting work on English

As I have already noted, the major theoretical and practical advances in harnessing the text-processing power of the computer have been made by scholars and teachers working on English, and in particular on English as a second or foreign language – though the pioneering work of the Germanist Roy Wisbey deserves special mention here (e.g. Wisbey 1971). Today, Germanists need to ask whether the features and positions which have been elaborated by the international 'English language corpus community' can be taken over ready-made for work on German. I would suggest that the current state of knowledge regarding the 'large' issues of a methodological and theoretical nature can largely be adopted when transferring from English to German, though clearly, differences in grammatical structure need to be acknowledged and practical solutions sought for the specific difficulties these raise for analysing a corpus of German. Here, new procedures need to be devised by corpus analysts and, in particular, software designers. The most immediate problems are posed by the fact that German has a more complex morpho-syntactic system than English. Searching for all occurrences (singular and plural) of a noun or all the grammatical forms of a verb is a relatively straightforward matter in English (where a verb can have as few as three grammatical forms: *hit*, *hits*, *hitting*), but a much more complicated task in German. Designing lemmatization software, which will, for example, group the forms *Haus*, *Hause*, *Häuser* and *Häusern*, or *schlaf*, *schlafe*, *schlafen*, *schlaft*, *schläfst*, *schläft*, *schlief*, *schliefst*, *schlieft*, *schliefen*, *schliefe*, and *geschlafen* as different grammatical forms of the same lexeme, is a complex but necessary task for a language like German. (For an example of such software in use, see Pik Gupta's contribution to this volume.) The discontinuous realization of some important grammatical constituents, evident in word forms such as *ge+schlaf+en*, *be+gnad+ig+en*, also poses problems at clause and sentence level, most obviously in the distance which frequently separates the constituents of the verbal group in longer clauses and sentences. A span of four words will rarely be enough to capture these important syntactic relationships, and the same is true of complex structures such as the extended adjectival attribute, where important adjectival collocates may be several words removed from the noun they qualify. In such cases, it may be necessary to cast the net wider when looking for collocational evidence in German. And there are other problems. Average word length and sentence length in German texts are reputedly greater than for the equivalent text-type in English. (This is actually an impressionistic statement, which could be tested for different types of text.) Such differences could present a problem if we want to align a text in one language with a translation of this text into the other language, especially if the translation uses more, or fewer, sentences than the original. The use of the definite article to mark case/gender relations in German means that we have a problem if we want to examine the use of definiteness/indefiniteness in German, since abstract, non-count nouns such as *Zeit*, *Geld* and *Liebe*, unlike their English equivalents *time*, *money* and *love*, are typically accompanied by a definite article even when they are semantically abstract. Where a concordance of English *time* would quickly isolate uses of *time* from those of *the time*, *this time*, *the times* and so on, one would not expect an equivalent file for *Zeit* in German to reflect these sense distinctions so clearly. Seemingly minor differences in grammatical structure can have large implications. For example, the fact that English *it* has no direct equivalent in German (which generally insists on grammatical (gender) rather than semantic agreement, using *er*, *sie*, and *es*) means that while it is relatively easy to get an impression of how often an English text or corpus contains pronominal reference to things rather than to people, this is a daunting task for German. Yet such information can be important for the study of text-types and registers (Biber 1998: 73–5).[11] Clearly, for some purposes, language-specific strategies (and software) need to be devised for German. However, important though the differences between the languages are, they should perhaps not be exaggerated. 'Wildcard' searches (typically using the 'asterisk' or 'ampersand' operator) will find morphemes and other strings at sub-word level just as easily in German as in English, and a great deal of important collocational evidence in German can be found using the kind of collocational spans commonly used for English. On the whole, then, and without wishing to understate the importance of these differences, the news for the late arrivals from languages other than English is generally positive: much important practical and theoretical work has already been done and much of the time Germanists will not need to invent their own wheel. Today, the debates within the corpus community are a sophisticated and many-faceted reflection of modern thinking about the nature of language, literature, and society, which will be readily recognized by Germanists interested in these same broad questions.

Semantic prosody

The study of collocation has led to new insights into the existence of a particular kind of collocational behaviour characteristic of some words. The concept of semantic prosody goes back to observations by Sinclair, for example on the tendency of the verb HAPPEN to be associated with 'unpleasant things' (1991: 112). Stubbs demonstrates that the English lemma CAUSE (verb and noun) has 'a strongly negative prosody': 'The most characteristic [collocates] include *accident*, *concern*, *damage*, *death*, *trouble*'. He continues:

> It only rarely occurs with 'positive' collocates: *cause for concern* is very much more common than *cause for confidence*. Although many words seem to have such negative prosodies, some words, such as PROVIDE, have positive prosodies. For example, *causing work* usually means bad news, whereas *providing work* is usually a good thing. Typical collocates of PROVIDE are from the semantic fields of care, food, help, money and shelter. The most frequent object nouns are *aid*, *assistance*, *care*, *employment*, *facilities*, *food*, *funds*, *housing*, *jobs*, *money*, *opportunities*, *protection*, *relief*, *security*, *services*, *support*, *training*. (Stubbs 1996: 173–4)

Other English expressions discovered to have a similar profile include the phrasal verb *set in* (Sinclair 1991: 73–5) and *utterly* (Louw 1993). It is not unknown for sceptical native speakers of English to object that they knew this already. They are almost certainly not being quite honest with themselves. What Stubbs describes may be recognizably English usage, but it is doubtful whether a native speaker could volunteer such information, or, if asked, would come up with such a detailed list of the most frequent or representative patterns. Only a quantitative approach to a record of naturally occurring language can tell us such information with a degree of objectivity not available to our native-speaker intuitions. The observation and description of such prosodic features has only really become possible with the advent of corpora. Louw decribes a semantic prosody as 'an aura of meaning with which a form is imbued by its collocates' (Louw 1993: 157), and argues that this phenomenon, where it is found, is so strong that breaks in the prosody are indicative either of irony or of an unsuccessful attempt by speakers and writers to conceal their true feelings.

This raises some fascinating questions. Do semantic prosodies really exist? The evidence from English strongly suggests they do. So do they exist in German? If so, do they correspond to those found in English or are they language-specific? The first fifty lines from a concordance of *verursach** (Figure 2) suggest that at least some semantic prosodies do 'translate' across language divides. Although some of the KWIC lines do not contain enough context to show the object of the verb (underlined), all those that do suggest that this German verb has a strong, perhaps exclusive, tendency to be used when we want to indicate a consequence which is perceived as unpleasant. Line 29, however, appears to be a counter-example; but if we ask the concordancer to show the whole context it turns out that the cloud-free skies in this instance are harbingers of unwelcome weather conditions:

> Eine Hochdruckzone, die vom Ostatlantik über Mitteleuropa zum Schwarzen Meer reicht, bestimmt weitgehend unser Wetter. Ein zunächst auch in höheren Luftschichten wirksamer Hochkeil verursacht größtenteils wolkenfreies Wetter. In der Folge werden jedoch schwache Störungen den Norden der DDR streifen. Die Lufttemperaturen erreichen vielfach Werte um 30 Grad Celsius, beim Übergreifen der Störungen gehen sie vorübergehend auf 25 Grad zurück. Infolge des trockenen Wetters nimmt die Waldbrandgefahr zu.

The 'span' needed here to comprehend the full implications of the prosody 'wolkenfreies Wetter verursachen' is actually several sentences. This particular textual relationship would probably pass unnoticed were it not for the data-driven formulation of a theory which prompts the analyst to search for more contextual information. Once again, work on English provides the impetus for parallel work on German. An obvious starting point would be to investigate German equivalents of English words which have been shown to behave in this way.[12] Further questions suggest themselves: To what extent are semantic prosodies language-specific? Are they 'universal'? Where they occur, do they tend to be negative rather than positive? How strong is their presence? Are there absolute, exceptionless prosodies, or are we dealing with (strong) tendencies in collocation which can in principle be quantified? In what kind of contexts are such prosodies 'violated'? Evidently, there is a cultural phenomenon here which is so ingrained in our use of language that we barely notice it until we are confronted by the empirical evidence.

```
MicroConcord search SW: verursach*
90 characters per entry
Sort : 1L/SW unshifted.
1 muß, dann wehe denen, die das Ärgernis verursachen. (Acheson spielte hiermit auf ein Wor
2 d von Weber registrierten Abweichungen verursacht sein. Michael Globig. Mehr Mitbestimmun
3 Grenzkommandos beträchtliche Aufregung verursacht. Bei Redaktionsschluß war lediglich ino
4 Prozent einen Verlust von 5504 DM aus, verursacht durch erhöhte Steuerzahlungen. Dadurch
5 m Teil durch die schärfere Besteuerung verursacht. Die HV soll am 6. Mai eine auf 18 (17)
6 den und Verluste unter der Bevölkerung verursacht haben. (Reuter - dpd - AP - UP). Nürnbe
7 sie sonst noch darunter? Messer? Damit verursachte man weniger Lärm als mit einem Schuß;
8 ab der Münchener Rundfunk bekannt. Der verursachte Sachschaden beträgt 4,8 Millionen D-Ma
9 nommenen Rentenposten von 135 Mill. DM verursacht wurden. Dieser riesige Verlust wurde ko
10 n kann. den durch die Drei-Tage-Woche verursachten volkswirtschaftlichen Verlust beziffe
11 inute - hätte Zmuda fast ein Eigentor verursacht. Er konnte von Glück sagen, daß sein To
12 brocken an den Rändern der Eisscholle verursachten durch ihr ständiges Aneinanderreiben
13 welcher durch das Hochwasser der Elbe verursacht werden sollte, ist nicht eingetreten. D
14 mir die Kolonie seit ihrer Entstehung verursacht, nur den Schädel der gemeinsamen Mutter
15 ngeblich Ausfälle bei der neuen Ernte verursacht haben sollen. Es steht jedoch fest, daß
16 nerscheinungen, Existenzunsicherheit, verursacht Feierschichten, Kurzarbeit und Entlassu
17 zungen gerettet werden. Die Explosion verursachte einen Stollenbruch, durch den 60 Berga
18 ollegen durchgeführt wird, die Fehler verursachen. Bisher wurden die betreffenden Kolleg
19  im Bett geraucht und damit das Feuer verursacht hatte. Im Nebel wurde am Donnerstagmorg
20 faschistischen Krieg und seine Folgen verursachten Zerschlagung unseres Betriebes, insbe
21 Feld, während Lauck, der den Freistoß verursacht hatte, seinen Platz räumen mußte. Und d
22 rücke und durch den anhaltenden Frost verursacht wurden. Alle Kumpel stimmten zu. Die We
23 ndes und die Stadt Flensburg gehören, verursachten im August einen Sachschaden von 11000
24 berg u. Co. - jetzt AEROPA - Hamburg, verursacht seien, erklärt Krukenberg, unmittelbare
25 kstoff. Das Gemisch Helium-Sauerstoff verursacht während der ersten Zeit in der Kabine e
26 lauf der westalliierten Herbstmanöver verursachten Flurschäden werden die Bauern Schaden
27 cht nur die von den Hitler-Faschisten verursachten schweren Zerstörungen überwunden, son
28 die Plünderungen der Hitlerokkupanten verursacht war. Heute ist unser Land von Neubauge
29 eren Luftschichten wirksamer Hochkeil verursacht größtenteils wolkenfreies Wetter. In de
30 ckstand. Böhlen holt durch Hochwasser verursachte Produktionsausfälle auf /. Kampfmonat
31 veredeln, um den durch das Hochwasser verursachten Produktionsausfall im Textilwerk Grei
32 en zur Beseitigung der vom Hochwasser verursachten Schäden organisiert. Dabei zeigte sic
33  nicht so schroff, daß eine Inflation verursacht würde. Dollar-Textilkredit für Spanien.
34  Bankenkundschaft und Investmentfonds verursacht wurde, auch als ein Strohfeuer erweisen
35 ien von Ägyptern und sechs von Israel verursacht worden. Feisal: befreit Jerusalem! AP,
36 der Altersgruppe sechs bis zehn Jahre verursachte Verkehrsunfall auf vorschriftswidriges
37  Stellungswechsel, der Komplikationen verursacht. Die Betriebsruhe der Firma Salvarani i
38 der Regierung in Tokio Kopfzerbrechen verursacht, dann steht jetzt das Problem im Vorder
39 tatistik, die 1,9 Mill. D-Mark Kosten verursachen wird, soll Aufschluß über die Ertrags-
40 bsatz dieser Mengen werde hohe Kosten verursachen, die in erster Linie von der Bundesrep
41 dungsplätze würden noch höhere Kosten verursachen. Außerdem müßten fast 500000 zusätzlic
42 er Alkoholeinfluß stehende Kranfahrer verursachten, wurden drei Personen getötet, und ac
43 stehen, daß die Lücken, die der Krieg verursacht hat, ungemein groß und daher auch nur s
44  Tapies befindet sich in einer Krise, verursacht, wer weiß, durch den weltweiten Einfluß
45 rderungen insolvent gewordener Kunden verursacht; vor allem durch die Pleiten von Gebhar
46  ausgeschlossen, weil sie zuviel Lärm verursachen. Karst stellt Europarekord ein. DW. Os
47 g unmittelbar benötigten Lebensmittel verursachen würde. (Dpd - eig. Ber.). Deutsche Gen
48 s Jahrhunderts so unendlich viel Leid verursacht hatte, zu bannen? Heute können wir fest
49 m durch mangelhafte Leitungstätigkeit verursachten höheren Arbeitsaufwand ausgegangen. U
50 o Ihrer Familie keine Verwirrung mehr verursachen. Dann blickte sie zur Ikeda hinüber.
```

Figure 2 KWIC file of *verursachen*, revealing the extent of the negative semantic prosody

Descriptive language studies: lexicography and grammar

The advent of corpus-based studies of English has led, in Sinclair's words, to 'the demise of cherished methods and the wholesale revision of many cherished publications' (1991: 5). This process is already well advanced in English studies, where large corpora such as the COBUILD

Bank of English and the British National Corpus at Oxford have revolutionized reference works of English. Almost certainly, the present situation in English presages the not-too-distant future in related disciplines. Corpus evidence is consulted in Durrell's revised editions of *Hammer's German Grammar and Usage* (Durrell 1996: xv and xvii), probably the most enlightened English-language reference work of German to date in this respect,[13] and a new generation of reference works is beginning to use corpus evidence.[14] The use made of corpora is a matter for debate: some corpus theorists (such as Sinclair) appear to want to banish intuited examples altogether, whilst others aim to strike a judicious balance between attested and intuited examples. This debate between 'purists' and 'pragmatists' will doubtless have an impact on future generations of reference works. Also, although good monolingual and bilingual dictionaries of German already offer 'idiomatic' contextual information, this is typically implicit rather than explicit. As long as this is the case the evidence provided in dictionaries, for example, will be regarded by some corpus linguists as in principle incomplete and suspect. Does it really reflect the typical, the most frequent, the most probable usage of the word?

The shortcomings of the introspective approach are exposed by Luise Pusch in her entertaining analysis of the entries for the letter 'A' in the 1970 edition of the Duden *Bedeutungswörterbuch* (Pusch 1984). The title of her essay, 'Sie sah zu ihm auf wie zu einem Gott' ('she looked up to him as if to a god'), is one of the example sentences in the entry for *aufsehen*, and one of scores of examples of sexist bias implicit in the collocations and contexts created in these (invented) example sentences. Pusch goes so far as to characterize the dictionary as a clichéd novel in which the male characters play the dominant roles while the female characters either play out domestic roles or act as temptresses and tomboys. Her principal charge against the lexicographical team is misogyny ('Frauenverachtung'), but her indictment also specifies: 'Mief, Spießigkeit, Männlichkeitswahn, Pennälermentalität, Obrigkeits- und Schubladendenken' ('small-mindedness, bourgeois complacency, obsession with masculinity, schoolboy mentality, hierarchical and stereotyped thinking', p. 144). Pusch makes a strong case for the dictionary's underlying bias, citing many examples of sexist stereotyping (e.g. *ab-*

kehren: ‘Sie kehrte den Schmutz von der Treppe ab’; *auskleiden*: ‘Sie kleidete sich aus’; *Angst*: ‘Mit großer Angst erwartete sie seine Rückkehr’; *ängstlich*: ‘Sie war schon immer sehr ängstlich’). The underlying stereotyping is traced further in the entries for words with no ostensible connection to sexism (e.g. *abpressen*: ‘Die Angst preßte ihr den Atem ab’). How representative or typical such collocations are of actual language in use can now be tested against corpus evidence. A quick search of the BZK produces nineteen instances of *ängstlich**, for example, none of which collocates with the verb *sein* to produce the structure *X ist ängstlich.* Only two contexts clearly refer to a female being or appearing anxious (e.g. *lächelte sie ängstlich*), but then there are two with male referents (e.g. *er sah sich ängstlich um).* There seems to be a pattern with the word used adverbially, as in *ängstlich bemüht/bestrebt/verfolgt*, and examples of institutions (e.g. *Mitgliedsstaat*, *Gericht*, *Gewerkschaften*) being or acting *ängstlich*. These findings can hardly be regarded as definitive, but they already reveal the rather arid fictional character of the invented example *Sie war schon immer sehr ängstlich*. As Pusch demonstrates, such ‘intuited’ examples also come with their own undeclared ideological baggage. Modern lexicography, increasingly informed by empirical principles, is better equipped to avoid such pitfalls, though equally the same principles dictate that where sexist collocations are attested, these should also be recorded.

Of course, collocation is not a completely new concept in German linguistics. The principles underlying the Duden *Stilwörterbuch* are collocational and empirical (Drosdowski 1970: v–xiv), in contrast to the ‘ossification’ (‘Erstarrung’, p. v) of traditional dictionaries. Nevertheless, the formal and semantic constraints on combinatorial possibilities, and the criteria for selecting examples, are generally not made explicit. The entry for *Vergleich*, for example, includes the following examples:

> [...] dieser Roman hält keinen Vergleich mit den früheren Werken des Schriftstellers aus; im V. zu/(auch:) mit seinem Bruder ist er unbegabt.

The KWIC file in Figure 1 actually bears out the information given here, but provides much more detail, not least that the phrase *im Ver-*

gleich zu/mit accounts for the majority of all instances of the word, in one corpus at least, and in quantifying the preference for *zu* over *mit*. The fact that *zwischen* also collocates with *Vergleich* is not covered in the *Stilwörterbuch* but is captured in the concordance. Turning to the verb *verursachen*, we find that the *Stilwörterbuch* captures its semantic prosody, though implicity:

> **verursachen** <etwas v.>: *hervorrufen, bewirken*: das Unwetter verursachte große Schäden; Kosten, viel Arbeit, Lärm v.; er verursachte durch seine Bemerkung große Aufregung, Verdruß, Ärger; es verursachte große Schwierigkeiten, seinen Wohnsitz ausfindig zu machen; <jmdm. etwas v.> dieses Problem hat mir manches Kopfzerbrechen verursacht.

If we compare the information in this entry with the concordance for *verursach** (Figure 2), we find that once again it is essentially accurate. The subject nouns *Unwetter* and *Problem* imply a negative semantics, as do the object nouns *Schäden*, *Kosten*, etc. That these nouns are well-chosen as typical subjects/objects of the verb is confirmed by our concordance. But the information in the *Stilwörterbuch* could be improved in three respects.[15] First, a list of the most frequent subject and object collocates could be given, in descending order. On the limited evidence of the BZK this would promote *Verlust/e* (four occurrences) to the list of typical collocates. Second, an important generalization could be made with explicit reference to the existence and strength of the prosody, so that even apparently 'positive' collocations (such as *wolkenfreies Wetter*) can be predicted and explained. And third, the equivalence between *verursachen* and the verbs *hervorrufen* and *bewirken* could be qualified to point up the differences as well as the similarities in meaning and usage. An initial search of corpus evidence suggests that whilst negative prosodies are associated with both these verbs, they also occur with semantically neutral and even with semantically positive object nouns (see Figure 3) in a way not attested for *verursachen*. Eight of the forty-one instances of *bewirk** in the BZK appear on the face of it to collocate with semantic positives, as do four of the twenty instances of *hervorruf**.[16]

```
MicroConcord search SW: bewirk*
90 characters per entry
Sort : 1L/1R unshifted.
5 edite zur Verfügung stellte. Der dadurch bewirkte Produktivitätsfortschritt scheint wesent
11 en wiederherzustellen. Das durch Genuol bewirkte Gefühl der jugendlichen Ausstrahlung und
24 0000 Mark. Ein anderes Neuererkollektiv bewirkte materialsparende Veränderungen an den Sc
27 Besserung in dem Befinden des Patienten bewirken kann, deutet in diese Richtung. Selbstve
30 die das Funktionieren der Schutzleitung bewirken. Kürzlich erst ist der Hersteller eines
31 inung, daß Überläufer verdächtig seien, bewirkt im Fall Rehs Hoffnung bei der SPD und Zur
33 slohn. Der Leistungslohn im Sozialismus bewirkt die größte Interessiertheit des Werktätig
35 auf, leise. Die elektronische Steuerung bewirkt, daß zahlreiche Meßdaten des Motors von e

MicroConcord search SW: hervorruf*
90 characters per entry
Sort : 1L/SW shifted 6 characters.
5 und schwarze Tönungen wohl attraktive Effekte hervorrufen sollten. Als sich die beiden ken
7  Leser unwillkürlich ein freundliches Lächeln hervorruft: Valentina Gaganowa schenkte eine
14 ch und selbstgefällig, daß er fast Sympathie hervorruft: Was jenseits des Kanals geschieh
20 en muß, was das Vertrauen und die Zuversicht hervorrufen könnte, die für die Planung in b
```

Figure 3 Examples of semantic positives as grammatical objects of *bewirken* and *hervorrufen*

Especially where the prosodic evidence is not clear cut, there is need of a quantitative element in our descriptions of the language. Corpus data could enable a reference work such as the *Stilwörterbuch* to be developed into a more rigorous dictionary of collocations.[17] (A new generation of corpus-based reference works for English, including dictionaries of collocations, descriptions of grammatical categories such as phrasal verbs, and 'bridge-bilingual' dictionaries, is already with us.[18]) In the meantime, the collocational ranges found in the *Stilwörterbuch* and other dictionaries, and in works on German semantics like Ernst Leisi's classic study *Der Wortinhalt* (1975), provide excellent starting points for corpus-based, contextually sensitive lexical research which could include research into semantic prosody, irony, and metaphor.

Language teaching and learning

The principle of data-driven description and analysis leads naturally to the pedagogic concept of data-driven learning (Johns 1991, 1993). For Tim Johns, the leading exponent of this approach, the distinguishing feature is 'the attempt to ... give the learner direct access to the data, the underlying assumption being that effective language learning is a form of linguistic research, and that the concordance printout offers a unique way of stimulating inductive learning strategies' (Johns 1991). A variation on this idea is 'reciprocal learning', in which native speakers of two languages use each other as a resource in studying corpus-based data from both languages (Johns, forthcoming). What is innovative about this methodology is that it transforms the role of the teacher into that of a facilitator and adviser who is also a student and researcher of the language – even if he or she is a native speaker – and shifts the focus in the classroom from 'language teaching' to 'language learning'. From a pedagogical perspective it is not necessarily the quality of the results obtained, but 'the conscious process of framing and testing our theoretical assumptions' that is formative (Jappy 1996: 148). Fernandez-Villanueva comments that the advantage of using of a corpus of spoken language (the Freiburg Corpus at the IDS) to study the use of modal particles is that 'it enables students to concentrate on an interpretative phase during which they get to perceive the function of these elements ... without having to confront their productive use immediately' (Fernandez-Villanueva 1996: 92–3). One problem is of course the 'chaotic', uncontrolled nature of unedited data, which is suitable perhaps for only very advanced learners. For this category of student one can, for example, devise high-level research tasks moving backwards and forwards between data and reference works (Dodd 1997). For beginning and intermediate levels, however, the customization of corpus data (mainly involving careful selection of examples) requires great patience and skill of the teacher, but produces worthwhile materials. The kind of gapped exercise illustrated in Figure 4, based on the *Contexts* program developed by Tim Johns (Johns 1997), is in principle easy to produce from concordance files and is probably educationally more productive than a session of teacher-led instruction:

```
1 ärt. Die Gewerkschaft wandte sich scharf _____ Äußerungen aus Arbeitgeberkreisen, die de
2 enutzte, wird von dem Herrn, der in Hamm _____ 11 Uhr zustieg und den Zug in Düsseldorf v
3 elt. Berlin, 20. Februar. Mit 31 Stimmen _____ 13 Enthaltungen wurde am Donnerstagabend d
4  des Bundesstaates New York nahm mit 147 _____ 2 Stimmen einen Gesetzentwurf an, der Mitg
5 den deutschen Vorsprung und den 13. Sieg _____ Österreich nicht mehr gefährden. Tore: Öst
6  Wochenende nicht so leicht fallen. Erst _____ Abend, nach fünf Stunden, kehrte der Kraft
7 . Aus dem gleichen Grund müßten wir auch _____ das Besatzungsstatut kämpfen. Der Wiederau
8 it den Kommunisten ablehne und den Kampf _____ den Bolschewismus als erste Aufgabe ansehe
9 zu setzen und verlängerte den Haftbefehl _____ ihn bis zur neuen Verhandlung am kommenden
10 in großer Erregung. Sie haben sich alle _____ mich verschworen, schrie er in den Saal.
11 eiten DIN A5 Punkte DM 2,-. Postversand _____ Vorkasse 2,15 DM, Postschekkonto Hannover
12 s Kartellamtesfinden zum Teil im Gesetz _____ Wettbewerbsbeschränkungen (Kartellgesetz)
```

Figure 4 Example of a *Contexts*-style application for language-learning purposes, with the key word blanked

Students can be shown this file and asked to work out which word has been omitted from all contexts. In the process they can find out about the semantics and case government of the preposition *gegen*, and also the range of English equivalents for such contexts (e.g. *against*, *(at) about*, *over*, *towards*, *on*, *compared with*, and *in exchange for*). In addition to the semantic and grammatical information which can be gleaned or reinforced from working on such data, the student also encounters authentic contexts and collocational patterns. This, of course, can be a problem. As Brian Farrington remarks in his review of data-driven learning, 'it is not uncommon to find that you have concocted an exercise that is so hard that you cannot do it yourself' (Farrington 1996). The job of the teacher or materials designer is to ensure that the data are not too 'raw' for the level of ability of the student. If the context contains too many unfamiliar words, or too many complex or incomplete syntactic structures, the danger is that the student will not have sufficient knowledge to use the contextual information adequately. Customization is time-consuming, but necessary. A program such as Tim Johns's *Contexts* provides an authoring frame to do precisely this.

Translation studies

The nature and status of translation as a (sub-)discipline is changing fast under the influence of corpus-based methods, as a recent collection of essays (Laviosa 1998) demonstrates. For example, it no longer sees itself as merely a 'sub-field of applied linguistics', as Mona Baker explains:

> translation is a unique form of linguistic and cultural communication, because it involves much more than simply getting to grips with the subtleties and patterning of source and target languages. Indeed, it is so unique and distinct a phenomenon as to merit being the object of an independent discipline: what we now know as translation studies. (Baker 1998: 480)

The relevance of corpora to translation studies is surveyed by Dorothy Kenny in her article on this topic in a recent encyclopedia of translation studies (Baker 1998a: 50–3), in which she observes that whereas other areas of corpus linguistics have traditionally been data-driven, 'bottom-up' in their approach, much recent work in corpus-based translation studies proceeds 'top-down'. In this field, she notes, 'theorists are interested in finding evidence to support abstract hypotheses'. Amongst hypotheses to be tested against corpus evidence one might mention the **simplification hypothesis** (that translations tend to simplify the propositional and structural complexity of the original), the **explicitation hypothesis** (that translations tend to add additional explanatory material, making explicit what was implicit in the source text), and what might be termed the **normalization hypothesis** (that translations exhibit a tendency towards the norm, for example by avoiding the extremes of register in lexical choices, or even 'sanitizing' the original). As a consequence of this theory-driven work, Kenny believes, 'ongoing research in translation studies may lead to new ways of looking at corpora, just as corpora are already leading to new ways of looking at translation'. Kenny outlines a somewhat different corpus typology in this area from that outlined earlier in this Introduction, in that the term **comparable corpus** is used to denote 'a collection of texts originally written in a language, say English, alongside a collection of texts translated (from one or more languages) into English'. A **multilingual corpus**, as defined by Baker (1995), is composed of 'sets of two or more monolingual corpora in different languages, built up in either the same or different institutions on the basis of similar design' (see also Lewis 1998). The definition of a **parallel corpus** is as explained above; it 'consists of texts originally written in language A alongside their translations into a language B'. Kenny herself is engaged in a study of sanitization in literary translations from English to German (Kenny 1998), using a parallel corpus of English literary texts and their German translations (at the University of Manchester Institute of Science and Technology). Using the British National Corpus and the IDS corpora as control corpora, she focuses in particular on the translation challenges of semantic prosodies.

For translation between German and English, various types of corpus can be envisaged which would be a useful tool to research: a corpus of L1 texts and their translation (or translations) into the L2; separate sets of L1 texts from each language, which share some common features, e.g. in respect of text-type and historical context; a corpus of 'natural' L1 texts and an accompanying corpus of texts translated into the L1. There are important questions which such corpora could help us to answer (or formulate more adequately). These include: How do good translators do translation? Are there any specific or typical characteristics of translated texts, as opposed to 'natural' texts? How do two translations of a given text differ? The availability of large amounts of data in English and German in a suitable form (whether in 'parallel' or 'comparable' or 'multilingual' corpora) promises to transform translator training and research into translation, and indeed the experience of translation in many undergraduate programmes. There are now several alternatives to the traditional 'grammar-translation' approach, unchanged and unchallenged for decades in many university German departments, an approach which in practice more often than not focuses on a narrow range of privileged text-types and treats them as collections of grammatical and lexical features of the language, for whose explanation students are often reliant on an expert reader who is already well-versed in the text's various (inter)textual, social, and historical particulars. There may be good reasons for retaining this model, but there is no good reason why it should continue to enjoy an unquestioned monopoly when technology gives us so many ways of accessing banks of 'natural' and translated texts across a variety of genres.

Critical language studies

Corpus techniques can contribute usefully to what might loosely be termed 'critical linguistics' – generally speaking, a discipline which exploits linguistic techniques to uncover institutional and 'ideological' factors underlying the choice of linguistic forms. Michael Stubbs, for example, insists that linguistics is a social science, since 'social institutions and text-types are mutually defining' (1996: 12). It follows from this that 'textual analysis is a perspective from which to observe society: it makes ideological structures tangible' (p. 21). Stubbs's work is particularly interesting for the way his use of corpus data is informed by these principles. Amongst several practical case-studies contained in his book, for example, is a study of 'semantic engineering' in two speeches by Baden-Powell, one his final message to boy scouts, the other his final message to girl guides, illustrating how a relatively simple methodology can reveal the ideological nature of lexical and grammatical choices. Focusing on the occurrences in each text of the lexemes *happy* and *happiness*, Stubbs demonstrates what most modern readers of these speeches intuitively sense, namely that they enshrine linguistically a certain view of the sexes which now seems outdated or even offensive. He points out that Baden-Powell's use of these words is in itself entirely conventional. There are no unexpected collocations. But the pattern of use differs in the two speeches. For example, the collocation *make [someone] happy*, which occurs six times in the speech to girls (the direct object being *others or other people* on four occasions, *your husband* once, and *yourselves* once) is not found in the speech to the boys, in which the collocates of *happy* are *life*, *live*, *die*, and *be*. Only one collocation in the speech to boys (*give out happiness*) 'implies that other people are involved' (Stubbs 1996: 88). The differences in lexical patterning, easily identified from a concordance, are related to a larger, institutional and ideological discourse.

The concept of 'politicized lexicography' which follows from this 'institutional' approach to texts is framed by Stubbs with reference to Firth's notion of 'focal' or 'pivotal' words, and to Raymond Williams's (1976) notion of 'keywords' (Stubbs 1996: 165–72). These are eminent and eminently British patrons. Yet 'politicized lexicography' has if anything an even richer tradition in the German-speaking world – perhaps not surprisingly, given the German experience of fascism and cold war division in the twentieth century. One thinks of the tradition of political 'Sprachkritik' (language criticism) with such brilliant exponents as Karl Kraus, Bert Brecht, and Kurt Tucholsky. More recently, German linguistics has been attempting to accommodate social and political perspectives in the form of a 'scientifically grounded language criticism' ('wissenschaftlich begründete Sprachkritik', Wimmer 1982). Recent work in Germany includes a critical dictionary of 'contentious words' (*Brisante Wörter*, Strauß, Haß and Harras 1989) and a number of studies by Georg Stötzel and others on contested keywords (*Kontroverse Begriffe*, Stötzel and Wengeler 1995, cf. Böke et al. 1996). The authors of *Brisante Wörter*, which is based in part on IDS corpora,[19] point out that a serious gap in traditional lexicography is the failure to register the ideological nature of the way words are used in particular discourses (ibid., p. 9f.). The introduction to *Kontroverse Begriffe* (pp. 1–17) elaborates a similar project, which attempts to write a contemporary history of the German 'linguistic market' ('Sprachmarkt', p.11) through the history of certain contested concepts and terms in German public discourse since 1945. Stötzel's method is empirical, based on catalogued instances in the *Rheinische Post* in which the use of language is itself 'thematized' (p. 3) and implicitly or explicitly contested. The changeable and changing use of these vocabulary items, and indeed their power to constitute social reality and influence behaviour, Stötzel notes, proceeds from the arbitrariness of linguistic signs in the ideological marketplace. Only by situating the use of words within the particular historical discourse in which they are used is it possible to explain, for example, how a term such as *Bildungskatastrophe* can have semantically contrasting interpretations and partake in different discourses, signifying a shortage of teachers in 1964, and a surplus in 1982 (p. 12).

The use of electronic corpora, already evident in *Brisante Wörter*, has the potential to place the already well-established tradition of critical language studies in German (cf. also Good 1985, Townson 1992) on a new and more powerful footing. What corpus linguists like Stubbs have to offer here is an exemplary method and a series of case-studies demonstrating how even relatively simple techniques can produce impressive findings, and that ideological values are discernible not just in the more obviously 'contentious' words. Stubbs (1997: 157) insists that 'even the most frequent words, especially in their typical, central applications, express strong cultural connotations',[20] illustrating the point with a corpus-based study of English *care* and German *pflegen*. It may well be that German linguists have something to offer in return, for example the carefully elaborated method and the findings of Stötzel's lexically focused periodization of post-war German public discourse within a historically defined 'linguistic market'. The prospect of these two traditions coming together and collaborating is particularly exciting.

Literary studies

Strictly speaking, an electronic version of a literary text does not of itself constitute a corpus, but it would clearly be perverse to insist on this demarcation dogmatically, since there is obvious common ground and literary scholars were amongst the first to see the benefits of concordances and other forms of computerized text analysis, for example for authorship studies. Nevertheless, it seems to be the case that in 'language and literature' academic disciplines there is invariably a divide between those interested in language and those interested in literature. Communication, let alone cross-fertilization, between the 'two cultures' tends to be rare. In view of this, colleagues in literary studies may be unaware of, indifferent to, or indeed hostile to the application of corpus-based techniques within their specialism. The position will no doubt be exacerbated by the term 'corpus linguistics' to characterize the field as a whole, since this implies that literature is really a branch of linguistics. In important respects, of course, this is true – to the extent that literary scholars are interested in what Wolfgang Kayser famously termed 'the linguistic artefact' (*Das sprachliche Kunstwerk*). But literary scholars would be wrong to view 'literary linguistics' as a threat to their discipline, for example because some terms, such as 'genre', are reinterpreted within a broader linguistic typology. In reality, this poses no threat to literary studies. On the contrary, much is to be gained from work on text-types and discourse studies which can feed directly into literary criticism. An example which springs to mind is the increasing 'ideological' focus on the relationship between literary texts and particular dominant discourses of their time: recent work on Kafka, for example, has focused on how his texts reflect and refract the discourses of gender, ethnicity, and illness which significantly shaped the public discourse of his time.[21] Such studies have as much interest as those in critical linguistics in working out theoretical and methodological principles which can establish objectively how such discourses are created, maintained, and challenged by means of lexical and grammatical choices. Collocation and frequency are also likely to be instrumental in illuminating the particular literary qualities of texts (what Jakobson called *literaturnost*), by enhancing our understanding of the ways in which language is employed in literary texts – the patterns of repetition and variation, conformity to and deviation from norms of usage – as well as how these features compare with those found in other literary and non-literary texts. Such studies could help to illuminate the ways in which, for example, themes, motifs, and narrative voice are organized by an author.

The broader, linguistic view of the literary work implies, amongst other things, that the study of the linguistic aspect of canonical texts should be incorporated into 'literary linguistics' – or, conversely, that concepts such as 'genre' and 'stylistics' should be extended to the study of all text-types irrespective of their aesthetic or genre qualities.[22] This suggestion may not find favour amongst some literary scholars, but viewing literary texts as exemplars of particular discourse and text-types, alongside others, is simply an acknowledgment of a fundamental truth. The existence of literary texts in machine-readable form raises the prospect of a new, more intense collaboration between linguistics and literary studies. The corpora available in German are already large enough to allow scholars to begin comparative studies of literary and non-literary 'control' corpora.[23]

The impact of language corpora on our thinking about language

Typically, the initial focus of corpus analysis is the individual word or morpheme. In a computerized databank of language, the word (whatever its problematical status in linguistics) is a readily identifiable unit, being simply a string of characters bounded by spaces or followed by a punctuation mark. The implications of corpus studies, however, go far beyond the level of lexical description. It is not an overstatement to say that the advent of language corpora has begun to change our view of language quite dramatically, and particularly the way we approach grammar, lexicography, the study of texts, and the position of language in society. The leading practitioners have in fact made some important contributions to contemporary debates about the nature of language, with some large implications for all language-based disciplines. Probably the most frequent tenet found in the literature is the need for empiricism on the grounds that native speaker intuitions about one's language are generally a poor guide to linguistic reality (e.g. Sinclair 1991: 4; Sampson 1996). In other words: We cannot trust our private *Sprachgefühl*. My account in this section is particularly indebted to Sinclair, who has arguably developed the theoretical debate further than any other corpus linguist. Sinclair's dictum that 'usage cannot be invented, it can only be described' (Sinclair 1987: xv) informs the vast lexicographic and grammatical work on the Cobuild Bank of English, and throws down the gauntlet to traditional language description. An important statement of his position is to be found in Sinclair (1991), from which the following observations are taken: (i) distinctions in meaning are always accompanied by distinctions in formal patterning in the text (p. 6); (ii) meaning is contextual in the broadest sense, and the meaning of a word is the product of its context, not vice versa; (iii) the more common a particular word, the greater the number of senses it has (and the greater the number of patterns it enters into) (p. 101); (iv) our unreflecting familiarity with our language blinds us to the fact that 'most everyday words do not have an independent meaning' (p.108). From this it will be evident that close observation of the way words behave in context leads to some quite radical conclusions not just about the nature of words, but also the nature of texts, and of language itself.

Sinclair also throws into question traditional assumptions about the theoretical distinction between lexis and grammar/syntax. He finds that the physical evidence of 'collocational attractions' implies a widespread process of **lexical co-selection**: 'if words collocate significantly, then to the extent of that significance, their presence is the result of a single choice' (p.113).[24] Building on these observations, he argues that text is structured at any given point by one of two principles, the 'open-choice principle' and the 'idiomatic principle'. The former is a 'slot and filler' model which typically underlies traditional grammar. The latter has been neglected, but the investigation of corpus data shows it to be at least as significant. The idiomatic principle is the result of 'a large number of semi-preconstructed phrases that constitute a single choice, even though they might appear to be analysable into segments' (p. 110). Thus, instead of seeing grammatical frames into which lexical items are slotted according to their class membership, we are invited to see clusters of lexical items which, though they may not be physically adjacent, are dependent on a single choice for their particular occurrence in the text. The existence of multiple-word units, at a level between the word and the clause, and which frequently do not occur sequentially, will probably not come as a great surprise to experienced language teachers, who have always taught vocabulary as a branch of 'idiom' or 'phraseology'. The theoretical significance of Sinclair's argument, however, is far-reaching: traditional language description, he claims, has been guilty of unjustly 'decoupling' lexis and syntax (p. 104), thus obscuring the idiomatic principle and ignoring the syntactic constraints on much lexis, and the lexical nature of much syntax. It will be evident by now that having access to large language corpora does not mean that in describing the language we merely replace intuited examples of language in use with authentic ones, while everything else stays the same. The language, Sinclair remarks, 'looks rather different when you look at a lot of it at once' (p. 100).

Critique of Saussure and Chomsky

It may come as a suprise to some to learn that the standing of two of the twentieth century's most influential thinkers about language, Saussure and Chomsky, is rather low in corpus circles. This is partly explained by the fact that, as Stubbs (1996: 22–50) points out, the major intellectual tradition in which corpus linguistics has operated is the British empiricist tradition beginning with J. R. Firth and including the work of Michael Halliday, Randolf Quirk, Geoffrey Leech, and John Sinclair.[25] This tradition is contextual as well as empiricist: 'the complete meaning of a word is always contextual, and no study of meaning apart from a complete context can be taken seriously' (Firth 1935: 37). Its continuation in corpus linguistics has led to a substantial challenge to Saussurian and Chomskyan models of language. Chomsky's discounting of the empirical data of 'performance' in favour of a posited 'competence' located in a fictional 'idealized speaker-hearer', his focus on abstracted 'sentences of the language' rather than actual texts, makes him a marginal figure from the perspective of corpus studies. Stubbs (1997: 154) attacks Chomsky's lack of concern for a theory of 'performance': it is, he remarks, 'all that remains once we have explained competence. Even so, what remains is language use in its entirety'.[26] A particularly interesting account is given by Geoffrey Sampson of his conversion from Chomskyan to corpus linguistics under Geoffrey Leech ('the best career move I ever made').[27]

Saussure's major precepts are also being questioned as corpus-oriented theorists move 'beyond Saussurian dualisms' (Stubbs 1996: 44). Lexical co-selection undermines the strict opposition between Saussure's syntagmatic and paradigmatic axes. Perhaps the most far-reaching revision, however, relates to Saussure's fundamental distinction between 'langue' and 'parole'. In Saussurian terms, textual analysis of corpora stands open to the charge that it is merely concerned with 'parole', not engaging with the underlying rule-governed system of the 'langue'. Even if we accept Saussure's dualism and the the value-judgment inherent in it, this charge looks a lot less persuasive when hundreds of millions of words of 'parole' can be systematically interrogated. It may never be possible to cover 'the whole language' (if such a thing exists), but as corpora increase in size the likelihood diminishes of some significant feature, such as a structural pattern, remaining unattested. However, Sinclair and others reject the distinction between an 'abstract system' (Saussure's 'langue', Chomsky's 'competence') and particular 'instances' of the system (Saussure's 'parole', Chomsky's 'performance'), as an unnecessary abstraction which perpetuates a misconceived notion of language structure: 'the main simplification that is introduced by conventional grammar has nothing to do with the purity of abstraction as against the chaos of life. It is merely the decoupling of lexis and syntax' (Sinclair 1991: 104). By contrast, the task of corpus linguistics is to 'exemplify the dominant structural patterns of the language without recourse to abstraction, or indeed to generalization' (p. 103). In this respect, corpus linguistics is one of several recent developments in linguistics (one thinks, for example, of conversation analysis and other areas of pragmatics and critical discourse analysis) to concern themselves with what Saussurians would regard as 'only' parole, and to reject not just the value judgment inherent in the dichotomy but the dichotomy itself.

Somewhat paradoxically, whilst Saussure's insistence on descriptive rather than prescriptive linguistics is essentially empiricist in spirit, Sinclair stresses the need for evaluative selection of data, in which there is an element of subjective input by the researcher in attempting to bring out the typical features of the language from the mass of data. (Some corpus linguists, however, believe that at some point this process will become automated using statistical criteria.[28] It is a moot point whether this goal will be attained, or indeed is desirable.) Thus, Sinclair does not, surprisingly perhaps, regard prescriptive studies as taboo. They fall into disrepute 'only when they ignore or become detached from evidence' (Sinclair 1991: 61).

The essays in this book

The essays collected in this volume generally resist a neat compartmentalization: they illustrate the wide range of applications of corpus-based methods across the broad spectrum of the discipline.

The papers by Dodd, Gupta, and Witton exploit corpus data from Mannheim, in what might be termed corpus-based reassessments of earlier descriptive and theoretical work in the linguistics of contemporary German. Bill Dodd examines the ordering of expressions containing 'Ost' and 'West', as in *West-Ost-Gefälle* and *Verhandlungen zwischen Ost und West*, from three IDS corpora dating from before and during German unification. He finds that whilst the sequence *Ost* + *West* is consistently the 'norm', the frequency of the 'minority' sequence *West* + *Ost* increases noticeably in the data from 1989–90. In looking mainly at binomial expressions this study revisits a classic study on binomial reversibility by Yakov Malkiel (1959). Dodd also investigates possible semantic and pragmatic implications of the sequence when it is reversible, keeping in view the possibility that this political key term may also have a role in inscribing a larger, ideological discourse. Some at least of the more unusual examples from the time of the 'Wende' appear to come from the political leadership.

Piklu Gupta's paper uses corpus evidence to revisit and re-evaluate earlier studies of the syntactic and, especially, semantic valency characteristics of *be*-prefixed verbs in German. Pointing out that the verb alternations most frequently expressed by *be*-prefixation are realized differently in English, producing contrastively interesting variations in syntactic patterning between translation equivalents, he focuses particularly on the taxonomy proposed by Harmut Günther. Günther's distinctions and classifications, based largely on intuition and personal observation, hold up well in the face of corpus data. Endorsing Günther's comments on specialized use of verbs in particular registers, Gupta is led to argue for a greater use of specialized sub-corpora in this kind of investigation.

Nic Witton offers a corpus-based study of the relative occurrence of the periphrastic (analytic) second subjunctive form (e.g. 'würde kommen') and its equivalent synthetic form (e.g. 'käme') of eight common verbs in corpora of newspaper texts from the 1960s and the 1990s. His aim is to establish whether a case can be made for a change in usage in public written texts over this period. Focusing on these eight high-frequency verbs, and returning to seminal studies on this topic by Siegfried Jäger and Karl-Heinz Bausch, his purpose is twofold: to 'fill the information gap' left by these studies by investigating the evidence for a shift towards the analytic form in written standard German; and to investigate the various functions of the two forms. His initial hypothesis, that the analytic construction would have made inroads on the Subjuntive II forms in the intervening years, is not borne out by his findings. Indeed he finds a shift in the opposite direction, which he interprets as evidence of a continuing 'inherent conservatism in the print media'.

Jan Svartvik has remarked that 'conversation – the quintessence of spoken language – is either missing or seriously underrepresented in most existing corpora' ('Corpora are becoming mainstream', in Thomas and Short 1996: 10). This fundamental problem needs to be acknowledged, and addressed. The 600 000-word Brigham Young corpus of spoken German is thus a remarkable and valuable asset for examining features of the spoken language as used in conversation. The study by Randall Jones in this volume examines the way the set of 'dative/accusative' prepositions are used in this corpus, with some interesting findings – for example that their use in a spatial (locative or directional) sense is the exception rather than the rule. Generally, Jones observes, the distribution of case government is far from equal, even for a given preposition, and the 'classic' grammatical explanation of the case distinction ('wo/wohin?') is of limited use. The typology of prepositional usage offered in this study, using authentic data, provides some very useful material for language learners. It also provides a useful first step to a comparison of prepositional use in spoken and written German.

April Mackison's study is based on a corpus of some one million tokens constructed by her at the University of Birmingham, and consisting of whole texts taken over the same time span (1991–94) from two journals, *Wirtschaftswoche* and *technologie + management*. Her analysis of the frequency and distribution of the German equivalents of English 'manager' (*Manager, Leiter, Führer, Chef, Boß*) and 'management' (*Management, Leitung, Führung*), key lexical fields in management discourse, forms the basis of a contrastive study which reveals a 'mirror image' pattern of distribution in the two publications. She argues that these initial findings represent an important first step in a linguistic study of register variation which she also believes reveals important insights into the different assumptions each periodical makes about its readership.

The paper by Anne Wichmann and Jane Nielsen explores the linguistic means by which 'contractual modalities' are expressed in German legal contracts. This study exploits a specially tagged small corpus of selected legal documents, totalling some 25 000 tokens and constructed at the University of Central Lancashire. By tagging implicit as well as explicit expressions of modality, the authors are able to investigate the relative frequencies of the various means by which obligations and rights find expression in these texts. Their findings suggest that the use of modal verbs is actually one of the less frequent modes of such expression. Instead, lexical expressions and lexical verbs used in the present tense predominate, a finding which they argue is in keeping with the implicitly performative nature of this general text-type.

Wichmann and Nielsen's study has immediate applications for the training of specialist translators, and points up possibilities for future work in this and similar specialist registers. The tremendous potential of corpora for translation studies is also evident in Dorothy Kenny's paper, which is based on a specially constructed parallel corpus of modern German literary texts and their professional English translations. Collocational evidence drawn from control corpora for English (the British National Corpus) and German (the IDS public corpus) enables her to examine in detail the extent to which creative manipulations of semantic preferences and semantic prosodies by German authors are captured by their translators. Her paper demonstrates the inestimable value of such parallel and control corpora for the teaching and practice of translation.

Two essays are devoted to literary texts. Gordon Burgess's study of *Die Wahlverwandtschaften* uses concordance techniques to examine, for example, the use of particular verbs introducing indirect speech in the exchanges between Eduard and Charlotte, and the deployment of leitmotif. He also uses statistical data to compare the novella within the novel with the rest of the novel in general and with Ottilie's diary extracts, in what he terms 'an offshoot of authorship studies'. Computer-supported findings, he notes, are not necessarily revolutionary, and one of the interesting features of this essay is the way Burgess pursues the twin objectives of illuminating certain facets of the novel using the computer as an impartial research tool, while commenting on the potential strengths but also the shortcomings of such an approach, which, he notes, always needs supplementing by human intervention.

Ann Lawson's study exploits a machine-readable version of Thomas Mann's *Joseph und seine Brüder*. Coming to the corpus evidence with a close knowledge of this long text, she discovers that her memory is surprisingly corrected by the data, especially her perception of the phrase *schöne Geschichte* as a central and recurring motif. This leads her to look to corpus evidence to explore an intuitive insight about the way Mann manipulates patterns of language to 'weave a tapestry of image, irony, and "spielender Geist" ' in the novel. These patterns are explored both locally, within particular sections of the novel, and comparatively, with reference to Mann's contemporary speeches. She examines the collocational evidence for Mann's use of the polysemous key word *Geschichte* ('story/history') and relates her findings to Mann's linguistic strategies in the novel for subverting fascist discourse.

The potential of corpora as a tool to aid students' foreign-language learning is illustrated in Peter Roe's account of the Grammar in Context interactive program developed at Aston University as part of a collaborative venture with the University of Coventry. Based on a specially constructed corpus of about 100 000 tokens drawn from German language material for first-year undergraduates at British universities and, to a lesser extent, from A-level examination boards, this program enables students to explore typical lexical and grammatical patterns without resorting to cumbersome metalanguage. The pedagogic philosophy underpinning the design of this material views successful student-centred learning as a combination of meaningful input, focus on regularities rather than exceptions, and a judicious balance between explicit and implicit modes of developing grammatical competence. Roe also reports on a subsequent development of this model, Language inSight, which contains more sophisticated search tools.

Finally, an insight into the principles of corpus construction is offered by Jonathan West in his report on his work as one of a team of scholars working on the *Frühneuhochdeutsches Wörterbuch*. In addition to producing the first scholarly dictionary of Early New High German, the goal of this project is to construct a machine-readable corpus of some 500 ENHG texts, and a corpus of some 45 million words is in preparation at the University of Newcastle. His paper describes in detail the complexion of the corpora on which this work is based, their preparation and marking up, and their lexicographical exploitation. Some of the problems encountered, for example the at times uneven distribution of the textual evidence and the lack of a standardized orthography for the German-speaking areas, are also discussed. He points out that the creation of a reliable corpus is particularly necessary for work on a 'dead language', since scholars cannot rely on their subjective knowledge of the modern language.

The very diversity of these contributions is itself proof of the potential of corpus-based approaches to contribute to virtually every area of the discipline. It is always difficult, and probably foolish, to predict the future, but it seems likely that in the not-too-distant future the sheer availabilty of these tools and resources will attract more and more researchers and teachers to make use of them. Some will no doubt specialize in corpus methods as a discipline in its own right; most of us will probably be content to use corpora to support our work where it is convenient and useful to do so, though we will probably have to become more numerate and statistically aware if we want to make statements about 'typical', 'representative', or unusually 'significant' findings. So while it is true that the growth of corpus-based studies will of itself generate new areas of enquiry, it is probably the case that for most researchers and teachers corpora will be seen, in the words of one practitioner, 'as a complementary approach to more traditional approaches, rather than as the single correct approach. In fact, research questions for corpus-based studies often grow out of other kinds of investigations' (Biber 1998: 9–10). It is to be hoped that the work presented in this collection of essays will persuade more Germanists to consider what corpora can do for them, and prompt further work using this exciting resource.

Bill Dodd
Birmingham, 2000

Notes

1 For work on German see for example Teubert (1998, 1996); also Dodd (1997), Fernandez-Villanueva (1996), Jones (1997), Pemberger (1995), Wichmann (1995).

2 al-Wadi (1994).Website address: ,http://www.ids-mannheim.de.. For further information contact Dr Doris al-Wadi, <al-Wadi@ids-mannheim.de>. A useful list of currently available corpora of English and software tools can be found in Biber (1998: 281–7).

3 The acronym stands for 'Collins Birmingham University International Language Database'.

4 Further information can be obtained from Tim Johns' website: <http://web.bham.ac.uk/johnstf/l_text.html>.

5 Although use for academic purposes is normally envisaged, care should of course be taken in all cases to observe the terms of the licence.

6 In addition to the work of Sinclair and Stubbs, see for example: Aijmer and Altenberg (1991); Barnbrook (1996); McEnery and Wilson (1996); Thomas and Short (1996); Kennedy (1998); Biber et al. (1998).

7 Using Mike Scott's and Tim Johns', Microconcord, published by Oxford University Press in 1993 (now no longer available from OUP).

8 Mike Scott, Wordsmith, (Version 2), published by Oxford University Press in 1996. For further information see Mike Scott's homepage: <http://liv.ac.uk/~ms2928/wordsmith>.

9 A random collection of texts is sometimes referred to as a text archive.

10 The terms 'parallel corpus' and 'comparable corpus' are used differently by many scholars in translation studies. See the section on translation studies later in this Introduction.

11 For a summary of Biber's work on register see Kennedy (1998: 186). Several of the linguistic features used by Biber in his work on register variation in English clearly have no direct equivalents in German, and this raises the

question of the extent to which such a typology can readily be transferred from English to German.

12 Another source of data would be studies of German which identify this phenomenon, though they may not use the term semantic prosody. Examples can be found, for example, in Teubert's (1989: 62–3) corpus-based observations on the use of *Subvention* as a 'politisches Vexierwort', and in Kenny's (1998) study of semantic prosody as a problem in translation, which focuses on the negative collocational environments of (British) English *giro* and the consequent inadequacies of *Scheckheft* as a translation equivalent. See also note 21 below.

13 West (1992–95) is also based on consultation of a small corpus. West (1999) and Cornell and Roe (1999) report on forthcoming reference works which use corpus evidence.

14 For example, the publications issuing from the Institut für Deutsche Sprache, and, increasingly, the major publishing houses in Germany such as Duden and Langenscheidt, are now informed by corpus data. Collins in Glasgow currently have a German corpus of some 80 to 90 million words, shortly to rise to 150 million (personal communication from Horst Kopleck, Managing Editor for German).

15 Cf. Stubbs (1997: 161) for further comments on the collocational information contained in the *Stilwörterbuch*.

16 The *Stilwörterbuch* consulted contains no entry for *bewirken* and suggests an exclusively negative prosody for *hervorrufen*.

17 See for example Kjellmer (1994) on English.

18 See for example the Cobuild series, including Sinclair (1987, 1990), and the *Bridge-Bilingual English–Portuguese Dictionary* (Sinclair 1995). There is currently no German–English bridge-bilingual dictionary.

19 *Brisante Wörter* is based in part on evidence from the IDS 'Handbuchkorpora' of 1986 and 1987.

20 '[weil]... sogar die häufigsten Wörter, insbesondere in ihren typischen, zentralen Verwendungen, starke kulturelle Konnotationen ausdrücken'.

21 See for example Anderson (1992), Boa (1996), Gilman (1995).

22 The use of these terms also varies amongst linguists. Stubbs (1996) uses the terms 'genre' and 'text-type' synonymously, but Biber sees an important distinction, genre denoting 'categorizations assigned on the basis of external criteria', and text-type 'groupings of texts that are similar with respect to their linguistic form, irrespective of genre categories' (Biber 1988: 70). See also Aijmer and Altenberg (1991: 204–20).

23 There are corpora at the IDS in Mannheim devoted to the works of Goethe (1.4 million words), the Grimm brothers (0.5 million), and Marx and Engels (2.5 million). In addition, the Mannheimer Korpus I (MK1) includes the following works: Heinrich Böll: *Ansichten eines Clowns*; Werner Bergengruen: *Das Tempelchen*; Max Frisch: *Homo faber*; Günter Grass: *Die Blech-*

trommel; Uwe Johnson: *Das dritte Buch über Achim*; Thomas Mann: *Die Betrogene*; Erwin Strittmatter: *Ole Bienkopp*. Website information can be found at <http://www.ids-mannheim.de/kt/corpora-ges.html>.

24 What constitutes significant collocation, however, can only be answered statistically. Raw frequencies of lexical items will not do, since not all items in the lexicon have an equal statistical likelihood of occurring in a given text (see Barnbrook 1996: 87–106). Hence the need to consider the relative frequencies of two collocates, and the concept of 'upward collocation' (in which the node word has a lower absolute frequency in a given text or corpus than its collocate, e.g. 'went back', where we are looking at the collocates of 'back'), and 'downward collocation', in which the situation is the reverse (e.g 'arrived back') (Sinclair 1991: 116).

25 For a review of the Lancaster tradition of corpus linguistics and Leech's contribution, see Jan Svartvik, 'Corpora are becoming mainstream', in Thomas and Short (1996: 3–13).

26 'Perfomanz ist alles, was übrig bleibt, wenn wir Kompetenz erklärt haben. Allerdings ist alles, was übrig bleibt, der ganze Sprachgebrauch.'

27 See Sampson (1996).

28 See for example Cyril Belica's account of a strategy to automate the detection of neologisms in a time-phased corpus, the IDS 'Wendekorpus': 'Statistische Analyse von Zeitstrukturen in Korpora' (Teubert 1998: 31–42).

References

Aijmer, Karin and Bengt Altenberg (1991), *English Corpus Linguistics. Studies in honour of Jan Svartvik*. Longman: New York and London.

al-Wadi, Doris (1994), *COSMAS Benutzerhandbuch*, Version R.1.3-1. Institut für Deutsche Sprache: Mannheim.

Anderson, Mark (1992), *Kafka's Clothes. Ornament and aestheticism in the Habsburg fin de siècle*. Clarendon: Oxford.

Baker, Mona (1995), 'Corpora in translation studies: an overview and some suggestions for future research', *Target* 7(2): 223–43.

Baker, Mona (1998), 'Investigating the language of translation: a corpus-based approach' in Laviosa (ed.), *The Corpus-Based Approach: a new paradigm in translation studies* (special edition of *Meta*): 480–5.

Baker, Mona (ed.) (1998a), *Routledge Encyclopaedia of Translation Studies*. Routledge: London.

Barnbrook, Geoff (1996), *Language and Computers. A practical intro-*

duction to the computer analysis of language (Edinburgh Textbooks in Empirical Linguistics). Edinburgh University Press: Edinburgh.

Biber, Douglas (1988), *Variation across Speech and Writing*. Cambridge University Press: Cambridge.

Biber, Douglas, Susan Conrad and Randi Reppen (1998), *Corpus Linguistics. Investigating language structure and use*. Cambridge University Press: Cambridge.

Boa, Elizabeth (1996), *Kafka. Gender, class and race in the letters and fictions*. Clarendon: Oxford.

Böke, Karin, Matthias Jung and Martin Wengeler (eds) (1996), *Öffentlicher Sprachgebrauch. Praktische, theoretische und historische Perspektiven. Georg Stötzel zum 60. Geburtstag gewidmet.* Westdeutscher Verlag: Opladen.

Botley, Simon, Julia Glass, Tony McEnery and Andrew Wilson (eds) (1996), *Proceedings of Teaching and Language Corpora 1996* (UCREL Technical Papers, Vol. 9), Lancaster.

Cornell, Alan and Ian Roe, 'A valency dictionary for English-speaking learners of German', in Steve Giles and Peter Graves (eds), *From Classical Shades to Vickers Victorious: Shifting Perspectives in British German Studies*, Peter Lang: Bern/Berlin, pp. 153–70.

Dodd, Bill (1997), 'Exploiting a corpus of written German for advanced language learning' in A. Wichmann, S. Fligelstone, T. McEnery and G. Knowles (eds), *Teaching and Language Corpora*. Longman: London, pp. 131–45.

Drosdowski, Günther (1970), *Stilwörterbuch der deutschen Sprache*, sechste Anflage, Bibliographies Institute AG: Mannheim.

Durrell, Martin (1996), *Hammer's German Grammar and Usage. Third Edition*. Edward Arnold: London.

Farrington, Brian (1996) 'Data-driven learning: a new horizon for CALL' in R. Adamson et al. (eds), *Ça m'inspire. Mélanges en l'honneur du Professor S.S.B. Taylor* (New Directions in French Language Studies). University of Dundee: Dundee, pp. 177–92.

Fernandez-Villanueva, Marta (1996), 'Research into the functions of German modal particles in a corpus' in Botley et al.(eds), *Proceedings of Teaching and Language Corpora* (UCREL Technical Papers, Vol. 9). Lancaster, pp. 83–93.

Firth, J. R. (1935), 'The technique of semantics', *Transactions of the Philological Society*: 36–72.

Gilman, Sander (1995), *Franz Kafka, the Jewish Patient*. Routledge: New York and London.

Goethe, Johann Wolfgang von (1995), *Die Leiden des jungen Werther*, Philipp Reclam jnr: Stuttgart, Silver Spring, Berlin.

Good, Colin (1985), 'Aspektkatalog zur Texterschließung' in Good, *Presse und soziale Wirklichkeit. Ein Beitrag zur 'kritischen Sprachwissenschaft'* Schwann: Düsseldorf, pp. 19–46.

Große Konkordanz zur Luther Bibel (1979), Calwer; Christliches Verlagshaus: Stuttgart.

Jappy, Tony (1996), 'Investigating grounding across narrative and oral discourse' in Botley et al. (eds), *Proceedings of Teaching and Language Corpora 1996* (UCREL Technical Papers, Vol. 9), Lancaster, pp. x-xx.

Johns, Tim (1991), 'Should you be persuaded – two samples of data-driven learning materials' in Tim Johns and Philip King (eds) (1991), pp.1–13.

Johns, Tim (1993), 'Data-driven learning: an update', *TELL&CALL* (1993/2): 4–10.

Johns, Tim (1997), '*Contexts*: the background, development and trialling of a concordance-based CALL program' in A. Wichmann, S. Fligelstone, T. McEnery and G. Knowles (eds), *Teaching and Language Corpora*. Longman: London, pp. 100–15.

Johns, Tim (forthcoming), 'Reciprocal learning: a practical application of parallel concordancing'.

Johns, Tim and Philip King (eds) (1991) '*Classroom concordancing*', *Birmingham University English Language Research Journal* 4: 27–45.

Jones, Randall (1997), 'Creating and using a corpus of spoken German', in A. Wichmann, S. Fligelstone, T. McEnery and G. Knowles (eds), *Teaching and Language Corpora*. Longman: London, pp. 146–56.

Kafka, Franz (1997), *Die Verwandlung*. Philipp Reclam jnr: Stuttgart, Silver Spring, Berlin.

Kennedy, Graeme (1998), *An Introduction to Corpus Linguistics*. Longman: London and New York.

Kenny, Dorothy (1998), 'Creatures of habit? What translators usually do with words', in Laviosa (ed.), *The Corpus-Based Approach: a new paradigm in translation studies* (special edition of *Meta*): 515–23.

Kjellmer, Göran (1994), *A Dictionary of English Collocations: based on the Brown corpus*. Clarendon Press: Oxford.

Laviosa S. (ed.) (1998), *The Corpus-Based Approach: a new paradigm in translation studies* (special edition of *Meta*).

Leisi, Ernst (1975), *Der Wortinhalt. Seine Struktur im Deutschen und Englischen* (fifth edition). Quelle and Meyer: Tübingen.

Lewis, D. R. (1998) 'Accessing multilingual texts: evaluating a literary translation using computer-based text-alignment techniques' in *Maschinelle Verarbeitung altdeutscher Texte. Internationales Colloquium 1997*. Niemeyer: Tübingen.

Louw, Bill (1993) 'Irony in the text or insincerity in the writer? The diagnostic potential of semantic prosodies' in Mona Baker, Gill Francis, and Elena Tognini-Bonelli (eds), *Text and Technology: in honour of John Sinclair*. John Benjamins: Amsterdam and Philadelphia, pp. 157–76.

Malkiel, Yakov (1959), 'Studies in irreversible binomials', *Lingua* 8: 113–60.

McEnery, Tony and Andrew Wilson (1996), *Corpus Linguistics* (Edinburgh Textbooks in Empirical Linguistics). Edinburgh University Press: Edinburgh.

McKinnon, Alastair (1972), *Ausgewählte Konkordanz zu Wittgensteins Philosophischen Untersuchungen*. Blackwell: Oxford.

Pemberger, Marianne (1995), 'Konkordanzen bei der mündlichen Reifeprüfung', *TELL&CALL* (1995/1): 26–8.

Pusch, Luise (1984) 'Sie sah zu ihm auf wie zu einem Gott. Das Duden-Bedeutungswörterbuch als Trivialroman', in Pusch, *Das Deutsche als Männersprache*. Suhrkamp: Frankurt/Main, pp. 135–44.

Sampson, Geoffrey (1996), 'From central embedding to corpus linguistics', in Jenny Thomas and Mick Short (eds), *Using Corpora for Language Research*. Longman: London and New York, pp.14–26.

Scott, Mike (1996), *Wordsmith* (Version 2). Oxford University Press: Oxford.

Scott, Mike and Tim Johns (1993), *Microconcord*. Oxford University

Press: Oxford.

Sinclair, John (ed.) (1987), *Collins Cobuild English Language Dictionary*. HarperCollins: London and Glasgow.

Sinclair, John (ed.) (1990), *Collins Cobuild English Grammar*. HarperCollins: London and Glasgow.

Sinclair, John (1991), *Corpus, Concordance, Collocation*. Oxford University Press: Oxford.

Sinclair, John, et al. (1995), *Collins Cobuild Bridge-Bilingual English–Portuguese Dictionary*. HarperCollins: London and Glasgow.

Speidel, W. (1978), *A Complete Contextual Concordance to Franz Kafka, 'Der Prozeß'*. W.S. Maney and Son: Leeds.

Stötzel, Georg and Martin Wengeler (1995), *Kontroverse Begriffe. Geschichte des öffentlichen Sprachgebrauchs in der Bundesrepublik Deutschland*, Walter de Gruyter: Berlin/New York.

Strauß, G., U. Haß and G. Harras (1989), *Brisante Wörter von Agitation bis Zeitgeist*, de Gruyter: Berlin/New York.

Stubbs, Michael (1996), *Text and Corpus Analysis. Computer-assisted studies of language and culture*. Blackwell: Oxford.

Stubbs, Michael (1997), ' "Eine Sprache idiomatisch sprechen": Computer, Korpora, kommunikative Kompetenz und Kultur' in K. J. Mattheier (ed.), *Norm und Variation*, Peter Lang: Frankfurt/Main, pp. 151–67.

Svartvik, Jan (1996), 'Corpora are becoming mainstream' in Jenny Thomas and Mick Short (eds), *Using Corpora for Language Research*. Longman: London and New York, pp. 3–13.

Teubert, Wolfgang (1989), 'Politische Vexierwörter' in J. Klein (ed.), *Politische Semantik*. Westdeutscher Verlag: Opladen, pp. 51–68.

Teubert, Wolfgang (1996), 'Comparable or parallel corpora?', *International Journal of Lexicography* 9(3): 38–64.

Teubert, Wolfgang (ed.) (1998), *Neologie und Korpus*, (Forschungen des Instituts für Deutsche Sprache, Band 11). Gunter Narr: Tübingen.

Townson, Michael (1992), *Mother-Tongue and Fatherland. Language and politics in German*. Manchester University Press: Manchester and New York.

Thomas, Jenny and Mick Short (eds) (1996), *Using Corpora for Language Research*. Longman: London and New York.

West, Jonathan (1992–94), *Progressive Grammar of German*. Authentik: Dublin.

West, Johnathan (1999), 'A functional-notional grammar of modern German', in Steve Giles and Peter Graves (eds), *From Classical Shades to Vickers Victorious: Shifting Perspectives in British German Studies*, Peter Lang: Bern/Berlin, pp. 139–52.

Wetzel, Heinz (ed.) (1971), *Konkordanz zu den Dichtungen Georg Trakls*. Otto Müller: Salzburg.

Wichmann, Anne (1995), 'Using concordances for the teaching of modern languages in higher education', *Language Learning Journal* 11: 61–3.

Williams, Raymond (1976), *Keywords*, Fontana: London.

Wimmer, Rainer (1982), 'Überlegungen zu einer linguistisch begründeten Sprachkritik' in H.-J. Heringer (ed.), *Holzfeuer im hölzernen Ofen. Aufsätze zur politischen Sprachkritik*. Gunter Narr: Tübingen, pp. 290–313.

Wisbey, Roy (1968), *A Complete Concordance to the Vorau and the Strassburg Alexander*. Edward Maney: Leeds.

Wisbey, Roy (ed.) (1971), *The Computer in Literary and Linguistic Research*. Cambridge University Press: Cambridge.

Corpus analysis in the service of literary criticism: Goethe's *Die Wahlverwandtschaften* as a model case

Gordon J. A. Burgess

Introduction: convincing the sceptics

Using a computer in the service of literary criticism is viewed with scepticism in some quarters. Two views seem to have common currency. The first is that the computer is something of a blunt instrument for an activity requiring such sensitivity: 'A collection of wires, magnets, and transistors lacks even the most elementary *Sprachgefühl*' (Wachal 1966: 16). The second is that a computer-aided analysis of a literary text is simply a matter of 'running the text through a computer',[1] with little or no human intervention. As we shall see, the two views are, in fact, linked: and the second is wrong because the first is right.

The computer is not so much a blunt instrument as an imperfect and inadequate tool.[2] The main family of software for use in literary analysis is the concordance. It was once suggested that the minimum length of a text suitable for a computer-aided analysis of authorship distinction is 1000 words.[3] This figure was suggested in 1962: nowadays, most corpora analysts would put the minimum figure ten or a hundred times higher. The following comments are based on a computer-assisted analysis of a single novel: Goethe's *Die Wahlverwandtschaften*; for reasons detailed below, the amount of textual material did not lend itself to a detailed statistical analysis, and, accordingly, this aspect of computer-aided literary criticism will not be covered in the following pages.[4] Instead, I will be concentrating on the use and limitations of a concordance-based approach.

Concordances have a long and respectable history in the field of literary criticism. They were first produced to facilitate biblical exegesis, later as aids to the examination of literary texts. It might be that part of the respectability of concordance work originally stemmed from the scholarly and secretarial labour which it once took to produce a concordance manually, with the aid of a hand-written or typed card index, rather than the use to which the results were sometimes put. Moreover, pre-computer concordances had obvious drawbacks: they took an inordinately long time to produce – years, perhaps – and required what would nowadays be an unacceptable amount of man- or woman-power. The resultant concordance was static: if the cards or slips had been arranged in ascending alphabetical order (A > Z, i.e. the most obvious arrangement), all the cards and slips had to be reshuffled by hand if a list was required in a different order. And, finally, a concordance could (then as now) be very large in comparison with the original text: printed concordances may consume huge amounts of paper. But then this was transformed by the advent of computer programs to do the job: the production of indexes and concordances was the first application of computers to literary research.[5]

Not only did computer programs eradicate the problems outlined above, they also introduced new facilities – unknown in the days of the card index – for the researcher. This is not the place to go into the history of computer-generated concordances, but even a glance at specimens generated as late as the 1980s will show the advances made in the 1990s in areas such as upper- and lower-case letters, non-American character sets, and presentation of output.[6] Vinton A. Dearing puts it somewhat more bluntly: 'Many of the first concordances made with the help of computers were ugly and some were downright crude.'[7] This is not, however, to detract from their scholarly rigour or their usefulness.

The final great hurdle as regards the production of computer-generated concordances has also been overcome: that of text entry. We have moved a long way from the early typing-in of text, via the use of optical character recognition (OCR) machines from the 1980s onwards, to the present availability of texts in electronic form on CD-ROMs or from any number of online archives available via the World Wide Web.[8] The resultant texts can be checked with the electronic spelling checkers available for many languages or, indeed, with an index or concordance.

In its simplest form, a concordance is a list of some or all the words in a piece of text.[9] This may not sound very impressive. However, the power of the computer-generated concordance as a tool for literary or linguistic analysis lies in the facility it offers the researcher to group words together according to various specifications, to sort and arrange words, parts of words, or phrases by various criteria, and to point to the location of the sorted results within the original text – and to do this reliably, repeatedly and, for all intents and purposes, immediately.

The use of concordances, moreover, may not only highlight linguistic patterns in a text that might otherwise be difficult or impossible to detect, but may also impart a degree of scholarly discipline on the researcher and the results. As Roy Wisbey put it in 1971:

> the presence of a textual illustration facilitates the recognition and separation of homographs, the detection of formulaic elements and, to a limited extent, the study of syntactic patterns. With the aid of a concordance the scholar can quickly trace all the passages where a philosopher employs a specific concept or a poet a particular image. Merely to group such elements in a concordance is a creative act which renders inescapable certain insights into the linguistic preferences of an author. At the same time it adds enforced rigour to critical decisions by ensuring that inconvenient evidence is not simply overlooked, one of the most frequent means of scholarly self-deception. (1971: 25)

And Wisbey adds: 'The concordance, as this implies, is not an end in itself'.[10]

Wisbey's warning still holds true. Whilst a computer analysis of a text can provide the building blocks of evidence which may lead the researcher to certain conclusions, what it cannot do is interpret that evidence. Susan Hockey's dictum, 'Using a computer does not remove the need for human thought and judgement' (1980: 14), cannot be writ large enough in the armoury of the literary researcher who ventures into the field of computer-assisted textual analysis. Too much is going on in any literary text to be 'scientifically' analysable – and not only within the text itself but outside it too: the historical and cultural context in which it was written, the registers of the language, usage and allusions, the whole complex of internal and external elements which make up the common currency of writer and reader. Literature is an expression of the world of the imagination: 'What if ...?'; it opens up possibilities. Computers, on the other hand (still) work best in a well-defined environment. An exclusively computer-aided analysis is minimalist in nature, concentrating on specifics: repetition of words or related words or phrases, collocations, and statistics.

Recognizing the limitations of the computer-aided corpus linguistics approach, though, can help us to decide what can best be left to the computer and what needs to be done by the human researcher. The purpose of the following pages is not primarily to offer a new interpretation of Goethe's novel, but rather to use the work to illustrate the potential and the shortcomings of a computer-based analysis of a literary text.[11]

Selecting terms for investigation: direct speech as an example

Why *Die Wahlverwandtschaften*? In short, because it is recognized as being self-referential to an extreme degree. Its narrative economy goes hand-in-hand with a densely patterned intratexture of leitmotifs, situations, aspirations and events, imagery and symbolism, and ironic prefigurations and mirrorings. There is nothing in the novel which does not, in some way, relate to the narrative as a whole. As such, it is ideally suited to a computer-assisted corpus-based analysis, which can lead to critical insights unobtainable with any other method.

With such richness of the material to be examined, one of the initial problems facing a concordance-based analysis is how to determine the yardsticks of the examination. Producing a single KWIC concordance, for example, is going to be so unwieldy as to be unusable. Selections have to be made, terms have to be chosen for more detailed analysis, and this clearly cannot be left to serendipity – or to the computer. Human intervention, as mentioned above, is the only sensible way forward.

In the present case, an initial index was made of all words in the novel, excluding specified terms such as the articles, conjunctions, and prepositions. This index was then sorted twice, once alphabetically and then, separately, by frequency, and the resultant lists were examined to see whether any patterns emerged which seemed worthy of further investigation. One word-field which yielded unexpected results – unexpected because of the lack of commentary on this in the critical literature on the novel hitherto – was the wide variety of terms used to introduce direct and reported speech (see list below). For the purpose of illustration here, I will consider briefly the variety of terms used in connection with direct speech, and then limit myself further to the ways in which direct speech is introduced in the opening chapter of the novel.

The accepted critical view of the opening conversation is that the narrator is absent. Martin Swales, for example, states: 'Chapter I consists almost entirely of dialogue. It is an opening which is, therefore, virtually devoid of narrative commentary or assessment' (Swales 1979–80: 88). Harriet Murphy concurs: 'The narrator does not exercise any of his own analytical skills or express any personal preference in the form of evaluative interpretation or commentary' (Murphy 1990: 18).[12] We will see how the seemingly impartial presentation of this conversation is, in fact, being subtly manipulated through the terms used to convey each direct speech utterance.

Much of *Die Wahlverwandtschaften* is devoted to reporting conversations or discussions between two or more characters, in the form of direct or indirect speech. Speech, of course, is the stuff of drama, and it is not without significance that contemporary critics of the novel highlighted its 'dramatic' qualities.[13] Immermann later went so far as to claim that *Die Wahlverwandtschaften* and *Hermann und Dorothea* were 'dramatischer' than any of Goethe's actual plays.[14]

Table 1 gives a breakdown of the terms used to introduce direct speech in *Die Wahlverwandtschaften*. As well as figures and percentages, the table also gives, for the sake of comparison, figures for these terms when introducing indirect speech and when used to introduce speech acts which cannot be classified as either direct or indirect speech, e.g. 'Sie bat um Aufschub',[15] or 'Sie sagte das in der besten Gesellschaft, doch niemand nahm es ihr übel' (236). However, this also illustrates the fact that a merely 'mechanical' listing of terms can be misleading. The following terms do not always introduce a speech act, and such occurrences have not been counted in the following table. Examples include:

'Der Hauptmann bemerkte die dazu getroffenen Vorrichtungen nicht mit Vergnügen' (157), or 'Für sie sprach ohnehin seit einiger Zeit eine stille freundliche Neigung in seinem Herzen (78).

Table 1 Words introducing direct speech in *Die Wahlverwandtschaften*

Word	Direct speech		Indirect speech		Other		Total	
antwortete	8	2%	2	9%	0	0%	10	2%
bat	0	0%	2	9%	3	11%	5	1%
befahl	1	0%	1	5%	1	4%	3	1%
begann	2	0%	0	0%	1	4%	3	1%
bemerkte	1	0%	0	0%	0	0%	1	0%
entgegnete	7	2%	0	0%	0	0%	7	2%
erwiderte	11	3%	0	0%	0	0%	11	2%
fiel...ein	6	1%	0	0%	1	4%	7	2%
fing...an	2	0%	0	0%	0	0%	2	0%
fragte	12	3%	3	14%	3	11%	18	4%
fügte...hinzu	3	1%	1	5%	0	0%	4	1%
fuhr...fort	22	5%	0	0%	0	0%	22	5%
richtete (ihre Frage)	1	0%	0	0%	0	0%	1	0%
rief	45	11%	0	0%	0	0%	45	10%
ruft/rief...aus	32	8%	0	0%	0	0%	32	7%
sagt (sich)	2	0%	0	0%	0	0%	2	0%
sagte	127	31%	4	18%	0	0%	131	29%
setzte...hinzu	3	1%	1	5%	0	0%	4	1%
sprach	2	0%	8	36%	18	67%	28	6%
versetzte	123	30%	0	0%	0	0%	123	27%
Totals:	410	100%	22	100%	27	100%	459	100%

It can be seen from Table 1 that *sagte* and *versetzte* account for almost two-thirds of all words introducing direct speech. Perhaps surprisingly, for a society that apparently prides itself on the studied decorum of its behaviour,[16] *rief, rief ... aus* and *ausrief* amount to almost a fifth of such terms (18 per cent). On the other hand, *schrie* does not occur, except once, and then it does not introduce either direct or indirect speech. It describes Luciane's reaction when Charlotte offers to provide her with a whole volume of 'der wunderlichsten Affenbilder': 'Luciane schrie vor Freuden laut auf' (236).

The differentiated use of *sagen* and *versetzen* is admirably illustrated in the first conversation between Eduard and Charlotte. They are sitting in the moss-covered hut, and Charlotte has been careful to place Eduard so that he can enjoy the view. Her deliberateness and her consideration for her partner are both echoed in the carefully engineered discussion that ensues.[17] We are not privy to the beginning of the conversation ('setzte er hinzu'), but Eduard has the first word we are allowed to hear (or read), and it is a negative statement in contrast to Charlotte's careful planning:

> Nur Eines habe ich zu erinnern, setzte er hinzu: die Hütte scheint mir etwas zu eng.
>
> Für uns beide doch geräumig genug, versetzte Charlotte.
>
> Nun freilich, sagte Eduard, für einen Dritten ist auch wohl noch Platz.
>
> Warum nicht? versetzte Charlotte, und auch für ein Viertes. Für größere Gesellschaft wollen wir schon andere Stellen bereiten. (5)

Charlotte's reaction allows Eduard to embark on outlining his plan to invite the Hauptmann. The conversation at this point enters a new stage, and the term used in association with Eduard here is 'sagte', not 'versetzte':

> Da wir denn ungestört hier allein sind, sagte Eduard, und ganz ruhigen heiteren Sinnes; so muß ich dir gestehen, daß ich schon einige Zeit etwas auf dem Herzen habe, was ich dir vertrauen muß und möchte, und nicht dazu kommen kann. (5)

He is evidently, even now, having some difficulty in opening his heart to Charlotte (although he is only wanting to invite a friend to stay with them). Charlotte's reply, introduced by 'versetzte', encourages Eduard to continue. The following concordance of words introducing their speeches indicates the to-and-fro of this initial conversation between them (5–13):

5	wir denn ungestört hier allein sind,	**sagte** Eduard, und ganz ruhigen heiteren
5	Ich habe dir so etwas angemerkt,	**versetzte** Charlotte. § Und ich will nur
5	...lotte. § Und ich will nur gestehen,	**fuhr** Eduard fort, wenn mich der Postbote
5	geschwiegen. § Was ist es denn?	**fragte** Charlotte freundlich entgegen...

5	unsern Freund, den Hauptmann,	**antwortete** Eduard. Du kennst die
6	bin ich bereit dir mitzutheilen,	**entgegnete** ihr Eduard. In seinem letzten
6	...keit empfindet. § Ich dachte doch,	**sagte** Charlotte, ihm wären von ver...
7	nicht ohne Wirkung. § Ganz recht,	**versetzte** Eduard; aber selbst diese
7	schön und liebenswürdig von dir,	**versetzte** Charlotte, daß du des Freundes
7	gedenken. § Das habe ich gethan,	**entgegnete** ihr Eduard. Wir können von
8	nicht unterbrechen. § Recht gut,	**versetzte** Charlotte: so will ich gleich mit
10	du sagst, eigentlich euer Element ist,	**versetzte** Eduard: so muß man euch
10	Einsiedler gethan sein? § Recht gut!	**versetzte** Charlotte, recht wohl! Nur daß
11	dachte. § Wenn mir nur nicht,	**versetzte** Eduard indem er sich die Stirne
12	mich denn dir aufrichtig gestehen,	**entgegnete** Charlotte mit einiger Unge...
12	... ihr Frauen wohl unüberwindlich,	**versetzte** Eduard: erst verständig, daß man
12	...rikt. § Ich bin nicht abergläubisch,	**versetzte** Charlotte, und gebe nichts auf
12	wurde. § Das kann wohl geschehen,	**versetzte** Eduard, bei Menschen, die nur
12	Das Bewußtsein, mein Liebster,	**entgegnete** Charlotte, ist keine
13	...eide nicht! § Wie die Sache steht,	**erwiderte** Eduard, werden wir uns auch
13	ihn dem Loos anheim. § Ich weiß,	**versetzte** Charlotte, daß du in
13	aber dem Hauptmann schreiben?	**rief** Eduard aus: denn ich muß mich gleich
13	vernünftigen, tröstlichen Brief,	**sagte** Charlotte. § Daß heißt so viel wie
13	Daß heißt so viel wie keinen,	**versetzte** Eduard. § Und doch ist es in
13	doch ist es in manchen Fällen,	**versetzte** Charlotte, nothwendig und

In the conversation as a whole, there are thirty separate utterances, of which no fewer than seventeen are introduced by 'versetzte': eleven by Charlotte, and six by Eduard. Charlotte acts as she does throughout the novel: overridingly self-restrained, unwilling to take any action which will cause disruption to her carefully ordered life, seeking to avoid anything which will upset her or others. The narrator's use of the term 'versetzte', here as elsewhere, underlines the non-inflammatory nature and tone of her replies. She is conciliatory – 'freundlich entgegenkommend' – where Eduard is confrontational. Eduard's utterances are twice rendered with 'entgegnete' to Charlotte's once (although the term 'entgegnete' is not as confrontational as might at first be thought), and his frustrated exclamation has no counterpart in Charlotte's speeches here.

The main part of the discussion is carried on in measured terms, and the lengthy speeches by both partners are introduced by 'versetzte'. Of all words used to introduce direct speech, it is this which seems to be the most neutral, almost 'flat' in tone.[18] But even this is dependent upon the context. Charlotte here has the last word of the conversation and the chapter. As they reach the end of their discussion, their statements have become shorter, potentially more heated: Eduard's growing impatience at not getting his own way ('Sich etwas zu versagen, war Eduard nicht gewohnt', 14) is shown by his calling out; Charlotte's quiet firmness is underlined by the use of 'sagte', and the discussion ends on an apparently conciliatory, if negative, note: both statements are introduced by 'versetzte'. Calm consideration has prevailed, at least on the surface.

This initial discussion is placed in context by the ensuing conversation between the couple, when the roles are more or less reversed, and it is Charlotte who is endeavouring to persuade Eduard to let her have what she wants, i.e. to invite Ottilie. In a sense, Charlotte is 'not herself' during this conversation. Eduard has put her 'in die heiterste Laune', and she is 'ganz aus der Fassung', so that she – uncharacteristically – calls out to him: 'so daß sie zuletzt ausrief: Du willst gewiß, daß ich das, was ich dem Ehemann versagte, dem Liebhaber zugestehen soll' (16). The ensuing dialogue runs as follows:

16	aus der Fassung, so daß sie zuletzt	**ausrief**: Du willst gewiß, daß ich das, was
16	Wenigstens, mein Lieber,	**fuhr** sie fort, sollst du gewahr werden,
16	selbst zumuthe. § Das hör' ich gern,	**sagte** Eduard; ich merke wohl, im
17	Nun sollst du also erfahren,	**sagte** Charlotte, daß es mir mit Ottilien
19	Wir sind wunderliche Menschen,	**sagte** Eduard lächelnd. Wenn wir nur
19	Betrachten wir es genauer,	**fuhr** er fort, so handeln wir beide thöricht
19	§ Es möchte noch zu wagen sein,	**sagte** Charlotte bedenklich, wenn die
20	Ich weiß doch auch nicht,	**versetzte** Eduard, wie du Ottilien so hoch
20	hätte. § Das ist löblich an dir,	**sagte** Charlotte, denn ich war ja

Throughout this conversation, Charlotte is much more pro-active than she had been previously, reflected in the use of 'sagte', as opposed to 'versetzte', to introduce her speeches. The only occurrence of 'versetzte' is in connection not with her but with Eduard, and he is reacting to her praising Ottilie's beauty and her warning that she could prove to be too attractive to the Hauptmann who is, after all, like Eduard himself, just at what a later generation might have called a dangerous age: 'Hübsch ist sie, besonders hat sie schöne Augen; aber ich wüßte doch nicht, daß sie den mindesten Eindruck auf mich gemacht hätte' (19–20).

A close analysis of the terms which introduce the speech acts here and elsewhere shows a consistency of usage of 'versetzte' versus 'sagte' throughout the novel, which disproves the accepted wisdom that the narrator is absent from the presentation of this first conversation. Although the narrator ostensibly takes a back seat, as it were, his manipulative presence is still effective, and the reader's attitudes towards the two characters are already being formed at an almost subliminal level. The question, of course, arises as to whether this use of 'versetzen' is restricted to this one novel or Goethe's own usage, or whether it was common currency at the time Goethe was writing *Die Wahlverwandtschaften*: in other words, would contemporary readers of the novel have intuitively understood the implications of the differentiated usage of, in the present case, *versetzen* and *sagen*? This type of question is continually thrown up by a stylistic examination of *Die Wahlverwandtschaften*, where the force of the evidence is unequivocal and overwhelming. This question cannot be answered here: it can only be answered by a large-scale examination of contemporary writings, based on a variety of extensive and wide-ranging corpora.

Symbols and leitmotifs

An obvious use of concordances is to pick out the recurrence of individual images, and see whether, and if so, how, they interact with one another. Of the leitmotifs present in this novel, three have most often been selected for analysis in the secondary literature: the plane trees, the moss hut, and Eduard's glass.[19] Although none of the leitmotifs and theme- and symbol-clusters stands in isolation, that of Eduard's glass can be conveniently singled out as an illustration of the power of the concordance in analysing a recurrent symbol of this kind.

A search of the text of *Die Wahlverwandtschaften* for the terms 'Kelch' and words beginning with 'Glas-' or 'Gläs-' yields the following result:

82	...d dieses Metall, dieses	**Glas** macht mir tausend Ängste, wenn Sie
101	er ein wohlgeschliffenes	**Kelchglas** auf Einen Zug aus und warf es
101	...nete es sich anders: das	**Glas** kam nicht wieder auf den Boden,
101	...n. Dort hinauf flog das	**Glas** und wurde von einem aufgefangen
101	...hnitten: es war eins der	**Gläser**, die für Eduarden in seiner Jugend
191	gehen. Sehen Sie dieses	**Glas**! Unsere Namenszüge sind darein
255	...rgen, indem sie in ein	**Glas** Wein blickt, das sie eben auszuschlürfen
256	aus dem durchsichtigen	**Glase**, worin sich, ob sie gleich zu trinken
344	könne die Meine werden. Ein	**Glas** mit unserm Namenszug bezeichnet
345	will ich an die Stelle des	**Glases** zum Zeichen machen, ob unsre
408	allenfalls nur mit einem	**Glasdeckel** zugedeckt und eine immer
411	... sollte, der unter seiner	**Glasdecke** gar liebenswürdig dalag. Aber
414	...ung scheint er aus dem	**Glase** zu schlürfen, das ihm freilich kein

Here, as elsewhere, the textual control is amazing, and the results of the KWIC search are unequivocal. The two examples on pages 255 and 256 refer to the glass from which the 'mother' is drinking in the *tableau vivant* of 'die sogenannte väterliche Ermahnung von Terburg' (254). All other references to a glass in the novel refer to one or other of Eduard's glasses, and allude to his relationship with Ottilie. But even the references to the glass in the picture provide a link with Eduard. For one thing, the verb 'schlürfen' is used only twice in the novel, here in the form 'auszuschlürfen' – somewhat strangely, surely, for a supposedly respectable middle-aged lady! – and later with regard to Eduard (see the above KWIC list, p. 414). In contrast to Eduard's own immoderate drinking habits, here the wine does not diminish in her glass, however long the 'mother' seems to be drinking: 'die Mutter brachte Nase und Augen nicht aus dem durchsichtigen Glase, worin sich, ob sie gleich zu trinken schien, der Wein nicht verminderte' (256).

Apart from the above, all the references to a glass in the novel refer to *the* glass which was thrown up into the air at the combined celebration of the foundation stone laying and Ottilie's birthday party. This glass initially seems to betoken good fortune: it is 'von einem aufgefangen, der diesen Zufall als ein glückliches Zeichen für sich ansah' (101) – and by Eduard himself. He tells Mittler: 'ich trinke nun täglich daraus, um mich täglich zu überzeugen: daß alle Verhältnisse unzerstörlich sind, die das Schicksal beschlossen hat' (191–2). And when this glass, that has survived so much and so long – it is one that had been made for Eduard 'in seiner Jugend' (101) – really is broken, and another is substituted, it does not bring Eduard happiness. On the contrary, he sees it as a symbol that his fate is sealed: 'Eduard kann nicht zürnen, sein Schicksal ist ausgesprochen durch die That: wie soll ihn das Gleichniß rühren?' (415).

The advantage of a KWIC listing such as the above is that it not only provides evidence for what is to be found in the text, it also, conversely, proves that other uses of the term(s) are not to be found. It is what we might call this negative result that makes the positive evidence (here and elsewhere in the text) so compelling. Since all the mentions of a glass in some way refer to Eduard, and all mentions of *the* glass refer to his relationship with Ottilie, we are surely entitled to adduce the two other occurrences of the term. The first is when Eduard asks Ottilie to give him the miniature of her father that she wears, as he has noticed and tells her, 'unter Ihrem Gewand, auf Ihrer Brust' (82). It is the metal and the 'glass' which makes him so worried. She gives it to him to keep, and he is tempted, but does not dare, to press it to his lips. The second is after Ottilie's death: she is placed in an open coffin, sealed with a glass lid. And even this, we may note, is at Eduard's insistence:

> Es fiel schwer seine Einwilligung zu erhalten, und nur unter der Bedingung, daß sie im offenen Sarge hinausgetragen, und in dem Gewölbe allenfalls nur mit einem Glasdeckel zugedeckt und eine immer brennende Lampe gestiftet werden sollte, ließ er sich's zuletzt gefallen und schien sich in alles ergeben zu haben. (408)

Thus, the leitmotif of the glass, and glass, links Eduard and Ottilie from beginning to end. As with other leitmotifs in the novel – the plane trees and the moss hut, for example – the events associated with the image progress gradually, but unequivocally and ineluctably, from positive to negative. And, ironically, in the image of the glass coffin-lid, it is precisely this leitmotif which has attained the cruellest and bleakest significance of all.

Authorship investigations

Die Wahlverwandtschaften begins by placing the narrator in the forefront of the reader's attention. The fourth word of the text is the narratorial 'wir', in an intrusive aside: 'Eduard – so nennen wir einen reichen Baron im besten Mannesalter –' (3). On a number of occasions in *Die Wahlverwandtschaften*, however, the narrator explicitly 'disowns' parts of the text, disclaiming responsibility, as it were, for specific passages, including a delegation of the narratorial voice to one or other of the figures of the novel. There are apparently authentic letters written by various figures with which the narrative is interspersed and which are clearly separated from the mainstream narrative: from the Vorsteherin, the Gehülfe, from Eduard to Charlotte and Ottilie, and from Ottilie to her 'friends'.

The interspersion of 'authentic' material happens most consistently, and repeatedly, in the case of the extracts from Ottilie's diary – but the intrusive narrator is evident even here, for it is he who has selected the extracts – he refers to 'jede einzelne von uns ausgewählte und mitgetheilte Stelle' (212) – and he expressly casts doubt on the authenticity, or at least the originality, of some of the diary entries.[20]

The narrator's 'disowning' of text also happens, however, in the Novelle 'Die wunderlichen Nachbarskinder'. This, we are told, is just one of 'den vielen angenehmen und bedeutenden Anekdoten und Geschichten' (322) with which the Lord's Companion has been enriched ('bereichert') during their travels together. Although most critics nowadays regard the Novelle as being more or less integrated into the novel as a whole and reflecting on the events of the main narrative,[21] the question arises as to whether – and, if so, in how far – the style of the Novelle is differentiated from that of the narrative proper of the novel.

We are, of course, on tricky ground here. It could be argued that *all* of *Die Wahlverwandtschaften* is the supposed product of the one fictional narrator, and that passages presented by him as having been authored by various figments of his imagination should be regarded on a fictional par with the remaining narrative text. Such an argument, however, fails to appreciate the various levels of fictiveness in the text. Paradoxically, the events of the central narrative are presented *as* fiction from the opening 'so nennen wir einen reichen Baron' to the closing fairytale-like words 'und welch ein freundlicher Augenblick wird es sein, wenn sie dereinst wieder zusammen erwachen'. The narrator's reporting the words or thoughts of the various characters in direct or indirect speech, or *erlebte Rede*, is part of this fiction.[22] As such, we may distinguish them from the passages in which the characters express themselves without narratorial intervention or interpretation.

For the sake of brevity and clarity in what follows, I will assign the term 'narrative passages' to those parts of the text apparently related by the narrator, and 'non-narrative passages' to those which purport to be 'authentic'. In particular, I will concern myself with the Novelle, drawing comparisons between it and Ottilie's diary extracts. The Novelle is the most sustained passage of 'authentic' prose in the novel, even though it is apparently incomplete. The narrator equivocates as to whether the tale is finished or not, suggesting first one thing and then the opposite: 'Der Erzählende machte eine Pause, oder hatte vielmehr schon geendigt' (336).

Is there, for example, any stylistically measurable distinction between the language of the narrator and that of the English Lord's Companion? On the one hand, the episodes of the Companion's story do have their (near) parallels with those in the main plot of the novel,[23] so we are, from the standpoint of content and theme, comparing like with like. But there are imponderables. Is it valid to distinguish between an oral narration tailored by a non-native German speaker for two German ladies of the landed gentry, and the mainstream narration – of which, of course, we do not know whether this is meant to be written/read or spoken/heard? And, moreover, the sheer discrepancy in length between the two passages could invalidate any statistical stylistic comparison.

'Style' is, perhaps, the least easily defined element of language and that which lends itself least readily to non-subjective statistical analysis – it is, in Roy Wisbey's words, 'that most elusive of all entities' (Wisbey 1971a: 25). The study of 'style' however, is linked with the other aspects of this investigation of *Die Wahlverwandtschaften* in that it is similarly concerned with linguistic patterns. For Sally and Walter Sedelow,

> Stylistic analysis, which focuses upon certain distributional properties of linguistic units within and among natural-language strings, is the study of patterns formed in the process of the linguistic coding of information. Such patterns serve to distinguish one language-user from another. ... An intense, quantitatively rigorous study of pattern, or style, in natural language we may call 'computational stylistics'. (Sedelow and Sedelow 1966: 1–2)

In effect, what we are attempting to do here is decide whether the narrator is, in fact, measurably *not* the 'author' of the Novelle. To this extent, the following remarks may be regarded as being an offshoot of authorship studies.[24] The basic theoretical assumption of any authorship analysis is that any given author will have a specific 'stylistic profile' or 'fingerprint', measurable by analytical and/or statistical means: 'that a writer's practices contain certain stable and distinctive elements which he cannot disguise and which others cannot simulate' (Rudall and Corns 1987: 103).

Authorship studies have had a mixed reception. In some cases, their results have rightly been regarded with some scepticism, particularly where they have been based on only a limited amount of the data available for investigation. This is not necessarily to invalidate the method, however, particularly where a delimitable corpus of data is available and can be analysed in its entirety. One pre-computer authorship study, for example, by T. C. Mendenhall and published at the turn of the century, compared the word lengths in known plays by Shakespeare with texts by Marlowe, Bacon and Jonson, and discovered that Shakespeare and Marlowe were distinguished by their high use of four-letter words in contrast to the texts of other writers which peaked at three-letter words.[25] An early computer-aided authorship study which has been widely accepted and is still often held up as a model for such analyses is that by Frederick Mosteller and David L. Wallace on the disputed authorship of twelve of the *Federalist Papers*.[26]

It has to be recognized that, clearly, computational stylistics can only be concerned with certain, limited, linguistic features of a text. In particular, the following account ignores such features as linguistic register, common or uncommon usage, metaphor and imagery, and denotative and connotative use of language. As mentioned in the introduction to this chapter, computers deal best with closed worlds, and natural language is anything but a neatly delimitable entity. We are also not examining here the sounds of the words and sentences, or their appearance on the page. Nevertheless, as long as limitations such as these are borne in mind, computational linguistics may still have a role to play in the analysis of a literary text.[27]

Following the established practice of conventional authorship studies, I will concentrate on the following linguistic features: word counts, word length, relative word frequencies, sentence count, sentence length, paragraph count, and paragraph length. On the face of it, counting things seems to be the least problematic: after all, computers should be good at computing arithmetical sums. It was assumed that average word length could be obtained by dividing the number of characters by the number of words, and the average number of sentences per paragraph by dividing the number of sentences by the number of paragraphs. However, whilst this may seem simple in theory, in practice a number of problems arose. Some of the problems and solutions are generic to corpus analysis rather than specific to the text under examination, and may be summarized as follows.

First: for the character count the text had to be stripped of all characters not properly parts of words: paragraph marks, page references, all punctuation, spaces, and so on, so that what was left was only the alphabetic characters that make up the text of the novel. If anyone ever needed to be persuaded of the value of such non-textual markers to aid our understanding of a piece of writing, the following sample of the result, taken at random, must surely be convincing!

> etenwardaßOttiliedenKofferzumerstenmalausgepacktunddarausVer
> schiedenesgewähltundabgeschnittenhattewaszueinemeinzigenaber
> ganzenundvollenAnzughinreichteAlssiedasÜbrigemitBeihülfeNann
> yswiedereinpackenwolltekonntesiekaumdamitzuStandekommender
> RaumwarübervollobgleichschneinTheilherausgenommenwarDasjun
> gehabgierigeMädchenkonntesichnichtsattsehenbes

(For the purposes of comparison, this text occurs on p. 400.)

Second: the word count raised the question of what is a word in the text. As a first step, words extraneous to the text proper were removed. Thus, 'genuine' words such as chapter headings were excluded, and a decision was taken also to exclude the sub-headings of the non-narrative passages ('Aus Ottiliens Tagebuch' etc.). Secondly, there was the problem of hyphenated words or groups of words (genuine hyphenations, not hyphenations generated because of typesetting), e.g. 'Secunden-Uhr' 'Guts-Karte'. Moreover, there is the phenomenon of a series of compound nouns in which two or more initial elements are linked by a hyphen to the final element (or vice versa), as in: 'Pferde-Kaufen, -Tauschen, -Bereiten und -Einfahren' (36)', or: 'Schweizer-Bauart, sondern zur Schweizer-Ordnung und -Sauberkeit' (71). Here, it was decided to count each compound as one word and each additional separate prefix or suffix as an additional word: thus the last-cited example of Swiss orderliness counts as six words, including 'sondern', 'zur' and 'und'. The only way in which an accurate list of such compound terms could be obtained was to search through the text manually, making a list of such words in each chapter – and whether they occurred in a narrative or non-narrative passage – and make adjustments to the total counted by the word count function appropriately in each case. In the end, accurate results were obtained on short pieces of text which were checked manually, and this led to the assumption that the methodology would be accurate for the text as a whole.

Third: although paragraph markers had already been inserted in the basic scanned-in text, no sentence markers had been inserted. A survey of the text led to the formulation that sentences were delineated by a full stop, a question mark or an exclamation mark followed by a space or paragraph mark and then a capital letter. This led, for example, to exclamations such as 'Alles vergebens!' and 'Vergebens!'being regarded as sentences. The number of occurrences of this kind of sentence not containing a finite verb is extremely low, however. More contentious, perhaps, was the decision to regard any string of words as a sentence, even if it contained one of the three punctuation marks listed above, as long as the subsequent phrase did not begin with a capital letter (subsequent phrases beginning with a noun were judged on their individual merit in the light of the following syntax). Although this may sound tortuous, it proved a reliable rule-of-thumb in practice. Thus, the following thought of Charlotte, with its various questions, is treated as one sentence for the purpose of this analysis: 'Sagt er das mit Vorsatz? dachte sie bei sich selbst: Weiß er schon davon? vermuthet er's? oder sagt er es zufällig, so daß er mir bewußtlos mein Schicksal vorausverkündigt?' (138); as is the following statement containing the narrator's feigned inability to characterize Ottilie's reaction to the re-appearance of the Architect who then ignores her: 'Ottilie ward einen Augenblick – wie soll man's nennen? – verdrießlich, ungehalten, betroffen; sie hatte ein gutes Wort an ihn gewendet, sie gönnte dem Bräutigam eine vergnügte Stunde nach seinem Sinne, der bei seiner unendlichen Liebe für Lucianen doch von ihrem Betragen zu leiden schien' (237). Such sentences, however, are fortunately the rare exception rather than the rule in the novel.

Table 2 gives the word counts for the narrative sections of the novel, the Novelle and the extracts from Ottilie's diary.

Table 2 Word count for narrative sections

		Word count	
Narrative passages Part I		35615	
Narrative passages Part II		37587	
	Total narrative		*73202*
Ottilie's diary		2934	
Novelle		2525	

Ottilie's diary is included here and elsewhere in the following discussion for the purposes of comparison with the Novelle. The two sets of texts are roughly comparable in length, and this may serve to contextualize the results of our comparative analysis of the Novelle *vis-à-vis* the narrative passages as a whole.

A breakdown of the average word lengths for the passages under examination yields the results shown in Table 3.

Table 3 Breakdown of average word lengths in narrative sections

		Average word length	
Narrative passages Part I		5.27	
Narrative passages Part II		5.36	
	Total narrative passages		*5.31*
Ottilie's diary		5.22	
Novelle		5.30	

We must bear in mind that a precise statistical analysis based on such very limited material may well be misleading. However, the average word length of the Novelle is comparable with that of the narrative passages proper. The picture looks somewhat different, however, if we examine the *distribution* of words of various lengths in the narrative and non-narrative passages. The overall curve of the narrative passages alone amalgamated for Parts 1 and 2 is as shown in Figure 1.

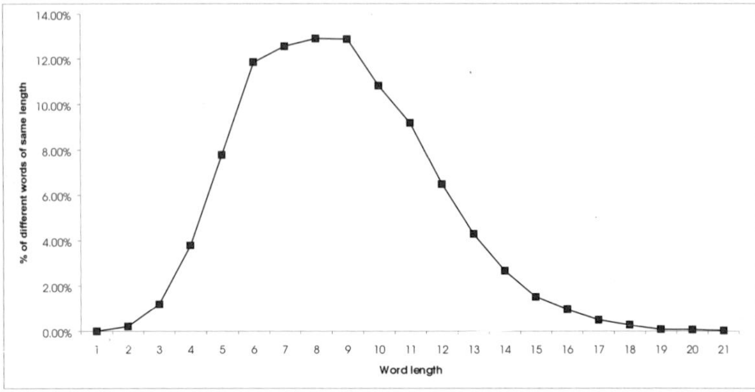

Figure 1 Distribution of word length in narrative passages

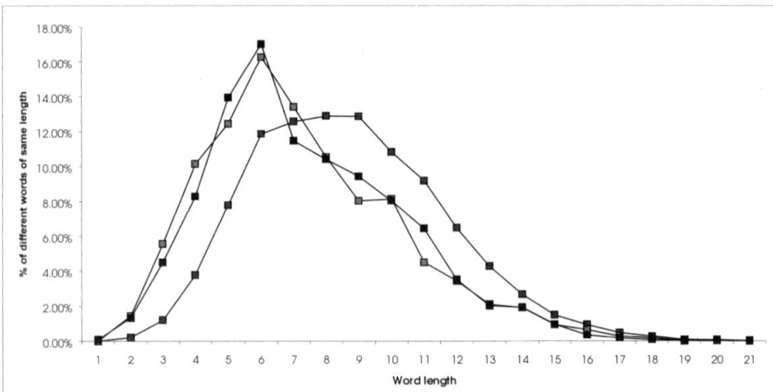

Figure 2 Word length: comparison of narrative passages with Ottilie's diary and the Novelle

Figure 1 and Figure 2 represent the word-length distribution, expressed as a percentage of the total words for each set of passages within the novel. Figure 1 shows the percentage of individual words of each length occurring only in the narrative elements of the novel. The word length is indicated by the horizontal axis, the percentage of different words of that length by the vertical axis. It should be stressed that Figure 1 and Figure 2 do not represent the raw word counts as such but their relation to each other. If we superimpose the pattern of word lengths in the Novelle on that for Ottilie's diary, we see that the two results are so close as to be sometimes difficult to distinguish from each other. In Figure 2, the black squares represent Ottilie's diary, the light-grey squares represent the Novelle. They are placed against the above curve (grey squares) of the narrative passages for comparison. The word-length peak occurs at five, six, and seven letters (here 12.44 per cent, 16.27 per cent, and 13.40 per cent respectively); and again the curve later imitates that of the narrative passages, although – again – shifted to the left. And the 'tail' at the long-word end of the curve is similar in both the diary extracts and the Novelle (numbers of actual words in brackets) (see Table 4).

Table 4 Word-length distribution: longest words

	14 letters	15 letters	16 letters	17 letters	18 letters
Ottilie's diary	1.94% (22)	0.97% (11)	0.35% (4)	0.18% (2)	0.09% (1)
Novelle	1.91% (20)	0.96% (10)	0.67% (7)	0.29% (3)	0.19% (2)

Let us recall that the total word count of Ottilie's diary extracts is 2934, that of the Novelle is 2525. Given that the nature and content of the two non-narrative elements is so disparate, we may suspect that the parallel pattern of word lengths in each may be more due to the amount of textual data on which the analysis has been based than on any intended stylistic distinction. At this point, let us turn to an analysis of sentence and paragraph lengths in the various elements of the novel, and see whether these can shed any further light on this problem.

For the novel as a whole, the average number of words per sentence is 22.43, the average number of sentences per paragraph 3.57.

For Part I the figures are 21.62 and 3.46, for Part II 23.20 and 3.68 respectively. To this extent, then, the novel is characterized by a stylistic 'sameness': a measured pace which does not appear to quicken, for example, as the events and disasters and deaths gather pace towards the end. We might even go so far as to say that the measured sameness of the style is at variance with the events being recounted, dampens down both them and their significance with a sort of subdued and subduing narrative overlay. Critics have highlighted the apparent discrepancy between stylistic tone and content: 'Es hat seinen Reiz, in einem so kühlen Medium die heiklen und unheimlichen Geschehnisse des Romans dargestellt zu sehen' (Stöcklein 1960: 15);[28] 'Der Sprachstil selbst verrät das Gewalttätige und Tragische der Handlung kaum' (Reiss 1963: 151).

Table 5 Word, sentence and paragraph count

	Words	Sentences	Paragraphs	Av. words/ sent.	Av. sent/§	Av. words/ §
Total narrative Part I	35609	1646	487	21.63	3.38	131.47
Total narrative Part II	35728	1490	373	23.98	3.99	95.79
Total narrative	71337	3136	860	22.75	3.65	82.95
Ottilie's diary	2934	166	86	17.67	1.93	34.12
Novelle	2525	106	21	23.82	5.05	120.24

Table 5 gives the word, sentence and paragraph count for the various narrative and non-narrative passages of the novel under examination, together with calculations for the average words per sentence and average sentences per paragraph. Although no clear overall pattern emerges from these figures, certain trends can be detected. In the orally narrated 'Die wunderlichen Nachbarskinder' the average number of words per sentence is comparable to that of the narrative proper, but the average number of words and sentences per paragraph (as represented on the page) is higher – not what we would necessarily expect of oral narration, perhaps.

Within the context of the Novelle *vis-à-vis* the narrative passages in the novel, the results are, at best, inconclusive. This mimics 'real-life' authorship studies. To quote Susan Hockey once again: 'The computer will not provide an absolute solution to an authorship study. ... and in many cases this may only be a negative conclusion' (Hockey 1980: 141) Measured by the – admittedly limited – yardsticks of conventional computational stylistics, there is no stylistic distinction between 'Die wunderlichen Nachbarskinder', narrated orally and by an Englishman, and the narrative proper as such. Thus, the present study has been able neither to prove nor to disprove views on the 'authorship style' of the Novelle such as that propounded (without, it must be said, a shred of textual evidence) by Paul Stöcklein: that this 'Meisterstück' of a Novelle is one in which the narrator 'seine Erzählweise eigenartig verdichten und sozusagen in die zweite Potenz setzen muß, da er ja jetzt "doppelt" erzählt. Seine Laune schafft so ein wunderlich verdichtetes Kunstwerk' (Stöcklein 1960: 14).

In these respects, then, the conclusions may seem rather unsatisfactory. However, even negative results may shed light on the work under examination. Writing in 1962 without a computer program at his disposal, Hans Reiss concluded that the novel is characterized by a stylistic sameness throughout (Reiss 1963: 144),[29] and this certainly seems to be borne out by the limited investigation outlined above.

Conclusion: pointers for the future

We have largely been concerned with interpreting the results of a computer-aided analysis of one novel. An equally interesting question would be to explore how far the conclusions we have reached on *Die Wahlverwandtschaften* reflect Goethe's own usage in his other prose writings; or, wider still, whether there are discernible, measurable parallels or contrasts between Goethe's own literary-linguistic practice and that of his contemporaries. Roy Wisbey articulated the scope and problems of just such an investigation in 1971. His specific example was Kafka:

> Franz Kafka's novels, we may observe, depend for their effect not least on the impressive austerity of the language he employs. How-

> ever, before we speak of conscious artistry it would be as well for us to compare our findings with those for Kafka's letters and diaries. Above all, we must use our computer techniques to analyse the language of other German-speaking novelists who spent their formative years in Czech Prague and who were active there during the first quarter of the twentieth century, in case they also show signs of a linguistic impoverishment which is not unusual when an enclave is cut off from the main stream of a language. In turn, these latter results cannot be seen in perspective without comparative material for the contemporary German novel at large. (Wisbey 1971a: 26)

With the speed of advances in electronic corpora collection and availability, and with the rapidly increasing processing power and storage capacity of modern computer hardware, the sort of project envisaged by Wisbey is already becoming feasible. Limited-corpora analysis yields results which in turn open up questions which can only be answered by the analysis of larger and more wide-ranging corpora. For the first time in the history of computer-aided textual analysis, however, we have reached a point where the methodology is beginning to lag behind the technology. There is no established theory or accepted practice for the computer-based analysis of literary texts. In view of this, it is hoped that the techniques outlined in this chapter will, at the very least, have provided pointers to the way forward in the future.

Notes

1 On the subject of authorship studies, Rudall and Corns wrote in 1987: 'Armchair experts still muse that this or that ancient question of authorship may be resolved by "running it through a computer". The procedures involved are, of course, much more demanding than that facile phrase would indicate' (1987: 102).

2 Here and elsewhere I am using the term 'the computer' in accordance with popular usage, when I am really referring to the software.

3 O'Donnell (1966: 114) highlights the problem of comparing short passages with each other: 'Mosteller, Yule, and Ellegard all consciously attempt to avoid predicting small texts. Ellegard goes further in saying that 1000 words is the minimum text size on which accurate prediction can be made.' The reference to Ellegard is to Alvar Ellegard's *A Statistical Method for Deter-*

mining Authorship: the Junius letters, 1769–1772 (1962).

4 For an introduction to the use of statistics for literary analysis and/or authorship studies, the reader is referred *inter alia* to the following: Hays (1967); Hockey (1980); Kenny (1982); and Landow and Delany (1993).

5 Hockey (1980: 41). This view is echoed by Oakman (1984: 69), who then goes on to discuss the pros and cons of using concordances for a variety of literature-based work, illustrated by several useful examples (69–87).

6 See, for example, the part concordances reproduced in Hockey (1980: 50–61). A further discussion of concordances, with examples, is given in Rudall and Corns (1987: 59–78). But even here the concordance examples are still entirely in upper-case. Concordance programs and their output can be found in Abercrombie (1984: 70–84). An illuminating discussion of the problems faced in producing early concordances of Middle High German texts can be found in Murdoch (1971: 35–44).

7 Dearing continues, however, 'but the best concordances of today are as well designed as and better executed than the best concordances of the past' (Dearing 1986: 28–9).

8 In respect of German literary texts, the Gutenberg Project available at the University of Hamburg (currently <http://gutenberg.informatik.uni-hamburg.de/gutenb/>) is particularly useful and wide-ranging, although the texts are not always as reliable as they might be. A landmark in CD-ROM provision has been the publication of the Weimar Edition of Goethe's works by Chadwyck-Healey. However, whilst the texts themselves are reliable, the software supplied with the CD-ROM is limited, as are the text downloading facilities for use by other applications (a concordancing program, for example).

9 Here, as in the rest of this chapter, we are concerned with single-language and single-text concordances. For an account of so-called parallel concordancing of a single text in two languages, see, for example, Burgess and Kohn (1996).

10 Wisbey's comment is echoed by Rudall and Corns (1987: 59): 'A concordance is a research implement, not an end in itself.'

11 For a fuller analysis of the novel than is possible in this chapter, using the techniques outlined here, see Burgess (1999).

12 Murphy adds of the narrator here: 'His presence is restricted to the use of verbs such as "versetzen", "sagen", "fragen", "antworten", "entgegnen", "erwidern", "ausrufen", to make continuous in other words, the verbal exchanges between Charlotte and Eduard.' Murphy is right, however, in noting that the conversation 'is carefully contained by the rituals of decorum to which both Charlotte and Eduard subscribe' (1990: 16, n. 22), even going so far as to consider that in the novel as a whole 'dialogue was something of a charade, either in terms of the absence of consensus ... or in terms of the absence of mutuality' (1990: 176).

13 See Kolbe (1968: 22): 'schon die zeitgenössische Kritik hat den *Wahlverwandtschaften* eine eigentümliche Nähe zum Wesen des Dramas bescheinigt, welche Verbindung zweifellos Entscheidendes zur "Legitimation der Romanform" beigetragen hat.' Solger, for example, writing in 1809 or 1810, states categorically: 'Alle heutige Kunst beruht auf dem Roman, selbst das Drama [...]. Und das ist der Gipfel der heutigen Kunst, der tragische Roman. [...] Die Größe des Gegenstandes und die reine Ansicht desselben [in *Die Wahlverwandtschaften*] hat eine solche Einfachheit der äußeren Hilfsmittel der Darstellung hervorgebracht, daß sich auch hierin das Werk der alten Tragödie sehr nähert [...]'. Quoted from Härtl (1983: 200-1). Conz expresses himself similarly in his anonymous review (Härtl 1983: 93).

14 Quoted in Kolbe (1968: 101). More recently, Harriet Murphy has investigated what she sees as the role of the 'dramatic monologue' in the novel (1990: 75–110; 139–154, passim).

15 *Die Wahlverwandtschaften*, Weimar Edition on CD-ROM, Section 1, vol. 20, p. 27. Further page references to this edition in the text.

16 Riemer quotes Goethe as having stated to him that the figures of the novel 'betragen sich wie vornehme Leute, die bei allem inneren Zwiespalt doch das äußere *Decorum* behaupten'. The novel had been criticized in certain 'Philister-Critiken' because 'man keinen Kampf des Sittlichen mit der Neigung sehe'. Goethe's retort was that this struggle had taken place 'behind the scenes': 'G. bemerkte dabei gegen mich: "dieser Kampf ist aber hinter die Scene verlegt, und man sieht, daß er vorgegangen seyn müsse".' *Mitteilungen über Goethe* (1809/10), quoted in Härtl (1983: 211).

17 Isabella Kuhn (1990: 24-5) interprets the content of this opening discussion, and the underlying attitudes of the partners, in a negative light: 'Dieser an den Anfang der "Wahlverwandtschaften" gesetzte förmliche Kriegsrat der Gatten'; 'Weder zarte Gattenrücksicht noch Verantwortungsgefühl für Ottilie kommt in Frage. Charlottens einzige Sorge ist offenbar die Sicherung ihres eigenen und eigensüchtigen Lebensplanes.' Kuhn's interpretation is difficult to sustain in the light of the conciliatory terms used to guide the reader's interpretation of the ebb and flow of the discussion between Eduard and Charlotte here.

18 Graham (1982: 45-6) diagnoses the tenor of (not only) this conversation as one of 'Künstlichkeit', and adds: 'Seit jeher hat mich das "Du" zwischen Eduard und seiner Frau eigenartig berührt. Der Verkehr zwischen den beiden Gatten verläuft so reibungslos glatt und formvollendet, daß ein "Sie" genau so gut am Platz schiene.' Ehrke-Rotermund (1981: 155) similarly refers to 'diese künstliche Atmosphäre' of this conversation: 'so fällt die merkwürdig indirekte, vorsichtige Art auf, in der das Ehepaar miteinander umgeht'. Notably, however, not a single contemporary reader represented in Härtl's (1983) comprehensive collection of material draws attention to this, which suggests that we should be circumspect about drawing any such

conclusions about the tone of this conversation.

19 For a concise treatment of a number of the leitmotifs in the novel, see Dickson (1965).

20 For example, 'Weil aber die meisten derselben wohl nicht durch ihre eigene Reflexion entstanden sein können, so ist es wahrscheinlich, daß man ihr irgend ein Heft mitgetheilt, aus dem sie sich, was ihr gemüthlich war, ausgeschrieben' (238). We may note, however, that the narrator does not go so far as to claim that he has *changed* what Ottilie has actually written.

21 Benjamin's view may, *mutatis mutandis*, be taken as representative: 'Mit alledem darf als unumstößlich gewiß betrachtet werden, daß im Bau der "Wahlverwandtschaften" dieser Novelle eine beherrschende Bedeutung zukommt. Wennauch erst in dem vollen Licht der Haupterzählung all ihre Einzelheiten sich erschließen, bekunden die genannten unverkennbar: den mythischen Motiven des Romans entsprechen jene der Novelle als Motive der Erlösung' (Benjamin 1967: 216).

22 On the complex issue of 'erlebte Rede' in the novel, see especially Ludwig Kahn (1974).

23 On the relationship of the theme of the Novelle to the main plot of *Die Wahlverwandtschaften*, see, *inter alia*, Jacobs (1979). However, Jacobs does not consider the relative styles of the Novelle/novel.

24 See, for example, Sedelow and Sedelow (1966: 4): 'Aspects of form and texture can provide clues as to authorship. ... Patterns of word association, integral to texture, are valuable stylistic discriminators. ... [T]he importance of the detection of verbal patterns should be clear.'

25 See Hockey (1980: 122–3).

26 Mosteller and Wallace (1964). The findings are discussed at some length by, *inter alia*, Francis (1966). See also Hockey (1980: 134–6). A list of 'some of the more influential classical essays in author identification' is given in Rudall and Corns (1987: 108–9).

27 For an analysis of the aesthetic qualities of the 'style' in *Die Wahlverwandtschaften*, see Stephenson (1994: 404), and his more recent article in which he states: 'Aesthetic relations … exploit equally *both* meaning *and* the look and shape of words, phrases, sentences and even paragraphs … . This aesthetic exploitation of language may … be labelled (expressive) "style"' (1996: 34, Stephenson's italics).

28 See also Stöcklein (1960: 13): 'Im demonstrierenden Tonfall eines Anatomen zeigt er [= the Narrator] uns Schritt für Schritt die Wachstumsstufen einer Wucherung'.

29 'In den *Wahlverwandtschaften* herrscht derselbe Sprachstil, derjenige des Erzählers, den ganzen Roman hindurch.' See also Reiss 1963 (150): 'Es ist Prosa, die einen ausgeglichenen Geist verrät. Wessen Worte wir auch vorfinden, die des Erzählers oder der Personen des Romans, *eine* Konsequenz der Auffassung beherrscht die ganze Erzählung.'

References

Abercrombie, John R. (1984), *Computer Programs for Literary Analysis*. University of Pennsylvania Press: Philadelphia.

Benjamin, W. (1967), 'Goethes Wahlverwandtschaften' in Hans Mayer (ed.), *Goethe im XX. Jahrhundert: Spiegelungen und Deutungen*. Wegner: Hamburg, pp. 179–240.

Burgess, G. (1999), *A Computer-Assisted Analysis of Goethe's 'Die Wahlverwandtschaften': the enigma of elective affinities*. Edwin Mellen Press: Lampeter.

Burgess G. and J. Kohn (1996), 'The use of parallel concordancing for literary and linguistic text analysis' in A. Gimeno (ed.), *Technology Enhanced Language Learning: focus on integration. Eurocall 1995 Conference Proceedings*. Universidad Politécnica de Valencia: Valencia, pp. 61–72.

Dearing, Vinton A. (1986), 'Personal computers and literary research' in William C. Creasy and Vinton A. Dearing (eds), *Microcomputers and Literary Scholarship*. University of California/William Andrews Clark Memorial Library: Los Angeles.

Dickson, Keith (1965), 'Spatial concentration and themes in *Die Wahlverwandtschaften*', *Forum for Modern Language Studies* 1: 159–74.

Ehrke-Rotermund, Heidrun (1981), 'Gesellschaft ohne Wirklichkeit', *Jahrbuch des freien deutschen Hochstifts*, 44: 131–188.

Ellegard, Alvar (1962), *A Statistical Method for Determining Authorship: the Junius letters, 1769–1772*. Elander: Stockholm.

Francis, I. S. (1966) 'An exposition of a statistical approach to the *Federalist* dispute' in J. Leed (ed.), *The Computer and Literary Style*. Kent State University Press: Kent, pp. 38–78.

Graham, Ilse (1982), 'Wintermärchen: Goethes Roman *Die Wahlverwandtschaften*', *Goethe Jahrbuch*, 99: 41–75.

Härtl, Heinz (ed.) (1983), *Die Wahlverwandtschaften. Eine Dokumentation der Wirkung von Goethes Roman 1808–1832*. Akademie Verlag: Berlin.

Hays, D. G. (1967), *Introduction to Computational Linguistics*. Macdonald: London.

Hockey, S. (1980), *A Guide to Computer Applications in the Humanities*. Duckworth: London.

Jacobs, Jürgen (1979), 'Glück und Entsagung: Zur Bedeutung der Novelle von den "Wunderlichen Nachbarskindern" in Goethes *Wahlverwandtschaften*', *Jahrbuch des freien deutschen Hochstifts* 42: 153–69.

Kahn, Ludwig (1974), 'Erlebte Rede in Goethes *Wahlverwandtschaften*', *Publications of the Modern Language Association of America* 89: 268–77.

Kenny, A. (1982), *The Computation of Style: an introduction to statistics for students of literature and humanities*. Pergamon: Oxford.

Kolbe, Jürgen (1968), *Goethes 'Wahlverwandtschaften' und der Roman des 19. Jahrhunderts*. Kohlhammer: Stuttgart.

Kuhn, Isabella (1990), *Goethes Wahlverwandtschaften oder das sogenannte Böse. Im besonderen Hinblick auf Walter Benjamin*. Lang: Frankfurt am Main.

Landow, G. P. and P. Delany (eds.) (1993), *The Digital Word: text-based computing in the humanities*. MIT Press: Cambridge, Mass.

Mosteller, F. and D. L. Wallace (1964), *Inference and Disputed Authorship: The Federalist*. Addison Wesley: Reading, Mass.

Murdoch, Brian O. (1971), 'Concordances from early medieval German manuscripts' in Roy Wisbey (ed.), *The Computer in Literary and Linguistic Research*. Cambridge University Press: Cambridge, pp. 35–44.

Murphy, Harriet (1990), *The Rhetoric of the Spoken Word in 'Die Wahlverwandtschaften': communication and personality in the novel*. Lang: Frankfurt am Main.

O'Donnell, Bernard (1966), 'Stephen Crane's *The O'Ruddy*: A problem in authorship discrimination' in J. Leed, (ed.), *The Computer and Literary Style*. Kent State University Press: Kent, pp. 107–15.

Oakman, Robert L. (1980, ²1984), *Computer Methods for Literary Research*. University of Georgia Press: Athens/Georgia.

Reiss, Hans (1963), *Goethes Romane*. Francke: Berne/Munich.

Rudall B. H. and T. N. Corns (1987), *Computers and Literature: a practical guide*. Abacus: Tunbridge Wells.

Sedelow, S. and W. Sedelow (1966), 'A preface to computational stylistics', in J. Leed (ed.), *The Computer and Literary Style*. Kent State University Press: Kent, pp. 1–13.

Stephenson, Roger (1994), ' "Man nimmt in der Welt jeden, wofür er sich gibt": the presentation of Self in Goethe's *Die Wahlverwandtschaften*', *German Life and Letters*, NS 47: 400–6.

Stephenson, Roger (1996), 'Goethe's prose style: making sense of sense', *Publications of the English Goethe Society*, NS 66: 33–41.

Stöcklein, Paul (1960, second edition), *Wege zum späten Goethe*. Schröder: Hamburg.

Swales, Martin (1979–80), 'Consciousness and sexuality. Reflections on *Die Wahlverwandtschaften*', *Publications of the English Goethe Society*, NS 50: 79–117.

Wachal, Robert S. (1966), 'On using a computer' in J. Leed (ed.), *The Computer and Literary Style*. Kent State University Press: Kent, pp. 14–37.

Wisbey, Roy (1971), 'Publications from an archive of computer-readable literary texts', in Roy Wisbey (ed.), *The Computer in Literary and Linguistic Research*. Cambridge University Press: Cambridge, pp. 19–34.

Wisbey, Roy (1971a), 'The computer and literary studies' in R. Reed (ed.), *Symposium on Printing*. Leeds Philosophical Society: Leeds, pp. 9–26.

When *Ost* meets *West*: a corpus-based study of binomial and other expressions before and during German unification

Bill Dodd

1 The corpora

This corpus-based study examines the distribution of the terms *Ost* and *West* in three corpora of German held at the Institut für Deutsche Sprache in Mannheim, totalling almost ten million words:[1]

1 the Bonner Zeitungskorpus (BZK), with 3 148 628 tokens;
2 the Handbuchkorpus 1986 (HK86), with 3 150 970 tokens;
3 the Wendekorpus (WK), with 3 266 516 tokens.

All three corpora are roughly the same size. The BZK and the WK are both composed of 'East German' and 'West German' texts in roughly equal measure. The texts in the BZK date from between 1949 and 1974, while those in the WK date from 1989 and 1990. Unfortunately, there is no comparable corpus of East-West texts for the period between 1974 and 1989, so it was decided to include the HK86 because, although composed exclusively of West German texts, it was a 'pre-Wende' sample which otherwise was broadly comparable to the other two corpora in size and text-type (i.e. journalistic texts). A copy of the BZK was generously donated by the Institut to the Department of German Studies at Birmingham for teaching and research purposes, and initial research on this corpus was done in Birmingham, using Johns and Scott's Microconcord, on a 'clean' version of the corpus, stripped of all marking up (Johns and Scott: 1987). However, all three corpora reported on in this study have been investigated using the IDS COSMAS software, so as to guarantee the statistical comparisons between the corpora.

(Microconcord and COSMAS calculate word counts on a different basis, for example.)

2 *'Ost + West'* as a reversible binomial

One of the aims of this study is to contribute further to the investigation of the particular characteristics of public discourse in Germany at the time of unification, as these are captured in the WK (cf. Herberg 1998a, 1998b, 1996, 1993; Herberg and Steffens 1997; Hellmann 1996). The main focus is the distribution of *Ost* and *West* in binomial expressions as identified by Malkiel (1959). In his study of irreversible binomials, Malkiel defines a binomial as consisting of 'two words pertaining to the same form class, placed on an identical level of syntactic hierarchy, and ordinarily connected by some kind of lexical link' (113), adding that the sequence A + link + B is 'occasionally reducible to AB, a plain juxtaposition' (134).[2] Thus structures such as *(in) Ost und West*, *im Westen wie (im) Osten*, *Ost-West-Verhandlungen*, and *west-östlich* are binomials in Malkiel's sense, though, crucially, as Malkiel himself observes, this particular binomial behaves differently in German and English. Indeed, Malkiel seems to regard *West + Ost* as the normal (irreversible) German sequence, citing structures such as *West und Ost*, *westöstlicher (Divan)* (132), and stating that English *east and west* 'contradicts' German *West(en) und Ost(en)* (143, 121). Malkiel also sees the importance of statistical evidence in future studies, given the degrees of reversibility for many binomial expressions. He notes that reversibility correlates with 'semantic nuance' and that reversible expressions 'are best attacked from a position other than linguistics', taking into account social and pragmatic perspectives such as the margin of age between A and B, their order of appearance, or their closeness to the narrator. He concludes his survey with a tentative list of overlapping 'discrete forces' which may influence the precedence of A over B (143ff.). Amongst these he includes chronological – and, by extension, geographical – proximity (or 'priority'), as in *here and there*; social hierarchy, as in *Mr and Mrs*; and the 'precedence of the stronger of two polarized traits', as in *heaven and hell.*

In looking at the statistical evidence drawn from corpora of German, the present study focuses on semantic and pragmatic factors which may correlate with the choice of sequence, leaving aside issues of prosodic phonology, which Malkiel also includes in his list of forces. The main semantic feature used in this study is directionality. It is important to distinguish between unidirectional and bidirectional uses of this binomial, in both languages. Even in English, where irreversibility is firmly established, there are occasions when the sequence *west* + *east* is encountered. In such cases we are typically dealing with marked expressions indicating a unidirectional movement *from* west *to* east. A search in the COBUILD Bank of English for the sequences *[Ee]ast-[Ww]est* and *[Ww]est-[Ee]ast* produced 1025 occurrences of the former and only 22 occurrences of the latter in some 329 million words. This clearly indicates the strength of irreversibility in English, with *east-west* accounting for some 98 per cent of all occurrences. Most of the *west-east* sequences found here are clearly unidirectional, as in '*the main west-east air route from Manchester to Europe*'. The remainder constitute a tiny residue.[3]

Unidirectionality may of course be explicitly indicated in the co-text (e.g. *exporting from the West to the East*) or there may be no explicit indicators of directionality in the co-text (e.g. *West-East trade*). A structure such as the latter is marked as unidirectional in English because of the strength of the norm of irreversibility in the English binomial, so that while *West-East trade* is understood to refer to movement in one direction only, *East-West trade* refers in principle (without contextual evidence to counter the assumption) to trade back and forth, in both directions. Turning to German, where the determining constraints of irreversibility are not so clearly evident, we find that while it is of course possible to express unidirectionality with the aid of the lexical context (e.g. *in Richtung West-Ost*; *in Richtung Ost-West*), problems of interpretation might be predicted when such explicit markers of unidirectionality are suppressed. For example, if both *Ost-West-Handel* and *West-Ost-Handel* are found, how does one determine whether the sense is unidirectional or bidirectional, and indeed whether there is a difference in sense – in denotation and/or connotation – between the two sequences? A number of questions might follow, for example: Do we find instances of both sequences being used by the same author?/ in the same text? Is (or was) there a difference in usage between East German texts and West German texts? In the compound noun of the type A+B+HEAD NOUN (e.g. *Ost-West-Konflikt*), do certain head nouns collocate with one sequence rather than the other, and do the semantics of the head noun influence the interpretation of directionality? This last question implies that the ordering of the binomial may correlate to some degree at least with the existence of 'semantic prosodies'.[4]

As a first step to resolving these questions, a purely quantitative statement of the relative frequency of the two types in German (*Ost* + *West*; *West* + *Ost*) ought to shed light on the notion of 'reversibility'. Strictly, reversibility as a concept implies that the distribution of the two sequences will be more or less equal, an assumption which a corpus linguist is likely to regard with scepticism. The expectation underlying this purely quantitative search is thus that the two patterns are unlikely to be represented in equal strength in a corpus of German, and that one will be found to be dominant. A subsequent, interpretive, and rather more difficult step is to investigate the collocational evidence in the light of the relative frequency of the two sequences, and to look for significant patterns of correspondence. The study was carried out in these two stages.

3 *Ost* + *West* as norm? Distribution of the two sequences

The findings show a very strong preference in all the corpora for the sequence *Ost* + *West*, though this preference is not as absolute as it is in English. The *Ost* + *West* sequence constitutes eighty per cent or more of all occurrences of the binomial in the three corpora. One question which follows from this is whether the *Ost* + *West* ordering can be regarded as a 'norm', an unmarked sequence, in the same way English *east* + *west* clearly can – and, conversely, whether the *West* + *Ost* ordering can be regarded as a 'marked' sequence on the basis of these statistics. As Stubbs (1997: 157) argues, the concept of a linguistic norm needs to be seen statistically, in terms of probabilities, expectations, and quantitative distributions. The German binomial is clearly reversible to a degree, and there are variations between the corpora, the most interesting of these suggesting a considerable increase in the frequency of *West* + *Ost* in the WK. Table 1 shows the distribution of the binomial across various grammatical categories (explained below), together with aggregate, 'global' scores for the different corpora and, finally, an adjusted average score per million words for each corpus.

Table 1 Distribution of the binomial by construction

prep/conj+A+(prep/ conj+)B	**Ost-West**	**West-Ost**	**Binomial**	**Ost-West%**
BZK	66	9	75	88.00%
HK86	67	15	82	1.71%
WK	352	82	434	81.11%
Total	485	106	591	82.06%
A(+)B	**Ost-West**	**West-Ost**	**Binomial**	**Ost-West%**
BZK	15	5	20	75.00%
HK86	13	4	17	76.47%
WK	48	21	69	69.57%
Total	76	30	106	71.70%
A+B+Head (tokens)	**Ost-West**	**West-Ost**	**Binomial**	**Ost-West%**
BZK	54	4	58	93.10%
HK86	58	3	61	95.08%
WK	91	34	125	72.80%
TOTAL	203	41	244	83.20%
'Global' scores (raw)	**Ost-West**	**West-Ost**	**Binomial**	**Ost-West%**
BZK	135	18	153	88.24%
HK86	138	22	160	86.25%
WK	491	137	628	78.18%
AVERAGE	254.67	59.00	313.67	81.19%
'Global', per 1 000 000 words	**Ost-West**	**West-Ost**	**Binomial**	**Ost-West%**
BZK	42.88	5.72	48.60	88.24%
HK86	43.73	6.97	50.70	86.25%
WK	150.34	41.95	192.28	78.18%
AVERAGE	78.98	18.21	97.19	81.26%

Where automated routines were not available, these figures were obtained manually by scrutinizing KWIC concordances and allocating examples to one of the following three grammatical categories (all examples are taken from the WK):

i) PREPOSITION+A+(PREPOSITION+)LINK+B (e.g. *zwischen West und Ost, aus dem Osten wie (aus) dem Westen*). This captures all occurrences of the binomial in prepositional phrases. The criterion was that a preposition occurred one or two words to the left of the word containing one of the binomial pair.

ii) A(+)B (e.g. *Ost-West, Ost und West, weder Ost noch West*). This category captures nominal groups which typically function as the subject or object of a verb, as in *darin gleichen sich Ost und West*, and *ein Europa, das Ost und West vereint*. Occasionally, examples of adverbials are captured here which could be interpreted as reduced prepositional phrases. Other examples included under this heading include *West-Professoren und Ost-Professoren, Reclam-Ost und Reclam-West, Polizei-West und VoPo-Ost, zwischen den Historikerschaften West und Ost*, and *als West-Konsument des Ost-TV*.

iii) A+B+HEAD NOUN (e.g. *Ost-West-Beziehungen, West-Ost-Beziehungen*). This category contains all occurrences of the binomial as the pre-head qualifier in compound nouns. For this category, separate counts were made of types and tokens.

Table 1 gives only the scores for tokens in the category A+B+HEAD NOUN. The scores for types are shown in Table 2.

Table 2 Distribution of types in the construction A+B+Head

A+B+Head (types)	Ost-West	West-Ost	Binomial	Ost-West%
BZK	26	2	28	92.86%
HK86	24	3	27	88.89%
WK	56	20	76	73.68%
TOTAL	106	25	131	80.92%

A simple statistical test suggests that these findings are statistically significant when comparison is with the WK.[5] It will be seen from Table 1 that the most numerous category is the prepositional phrase, which accounts for over half of all examples. As with all the other constructions, the WK shows a substantial increase in the incidence of the binomial as such. Both sequences are about five times more frequent in prepositional phrases in the WK than in the HK86. However, this is the only one of the three categories investigated in which the WK is not out of line with the other two corpora as far as the ratio of *Ost* + *West* to *West* + *Ost* sequences is concerned. Both the WK and the HK86 show a higher proportion of *West* + *Ost* prepositional sequences than the BZK. Looking more closely at two constructions, *von A nach B* and *zwischen A und B*, produces the following figures:

Table 3 Comparison of selected prepositional phrases

	von Ost nach West	*von West nach Ost*	Ost-West %
BZK	1	1	50%
HK86	3	1	75%
WK	21	27	43.75%
	zwischen Ost und West	*zwischen West und Ost*	Ost-West %
BZK	31	5	86.11%
HK86	21	3	87.50%
WK	76	20	79.17%

From this we can see that *von A nach B*, the only prepositional phrase which is explicitly unidirectional, is barely documented in the BZK and the HK86 but is much more common in the WK, where it is the only such structure in which *West* + *Ost* is the more common sequence. We can also see that *zwischen West und Ost* is both much more numerous and has a greater relative frequency in the WK.

Turning to the category A(+)B, we find the WK out of line with the HK86 and the BZK, not only in terms of absolute frequency but also in the distribution of the two sequences. In the WK, the *West* + *Ost* sequence has increased its share of the binomial from about twenty-five per cent to about thirty per cent. A similar, though more striking, pattern emerges for the binomial as modifier in compound nouns. There are almost twice as many tokens with the *Ost-West-* order in the WK than in the BZK or the HK86; and the *West-Ost-* order is eight to ten times more frequent. The compound nouns, discussed in more detail in the following section, show a marked shift in the relative distribution of the two sequences, from a figure for the BZK and the HK86 which is close to 'English' proportions, to a position where the *West-Ost-* sequence accounts for more than one in every four occurrences in the WK.

To sum up, the evidence shows a clear preference for the sequence *Ost* + *West*, which is found in about four-fifths of all instances of the binomial. On the other hand, there is also a substantial increase in the relative frequency of the ordering *West* + *Ost* in the WK, particularly in the categories A(+)B and A+B+HEAD NOUN. The global figures for the BZK and the WK are 88.24% and 78.18% (*Ost* + *West*) respectively. It is perhaps not difficult to think of an explanation for these findings, since the WK reflects a period in which one might predict that there would be talk of moving things from the West to the East, especially in a German context. Equally, the virtual absence of *von Ost nach West* and *von West nach Ost* in the BZK (just one instance of each in over three million words) might be taken as evidence of the scarcity of exchanges between East and West in a period of 'cold war' spanning the years in which the BZK was constructed (1949–74).

4 *Ost-West-Konflikt/ West-Ost-Gefälle*: Collocation in the type A+B+HEAD NOUN

I would like to focus in this section on collocational evidence for compound nouns beginning with *Ost-West-* and *West-Ost-*, and particularly on the 'exotic' examples with *West-Ost* as qualifier. There are only two examples of this type found in the BZK: one token of *-Akkreditive* and three tokens of *-Handel(s)*:

```
1  Ende Februar) enthalten. Die schwebenden West-Ost-Akkreditive betrugen 6,3 (8,3) Mill. VE
2 ungsverschiedenheiten auf dem Gebiete des West-Ost-Handels ergeben. Die britische Regierun
3 llem Handelskrieg - den größten Anteil am West-Ost-Handel in seine Hände gebracht. Also ri
4 aaten die Bewegung für die Entfaltung des West-Ost-Handels. Kürzlich betonte sogar der Lei
```

All four instances come from *Neues Deutschland*,[6] and the context in each case reveals that the semantics of the compound are unidirectional. In the case of *-Akkreditive*, the larger context also captures the same headword with the reverse order, also used unidirectionally:

> Im Interzonenzahlungsverkehr ergab sich am 31. März ein Debetsaldo zu Lasten der Sowjetzone von 25,3 Mill. Verrechnungseinheiten (VE) gegenüber 17,9 Mill. VE am 27. Februar. Darin waren *Ost-West-Akkredi-*

> *tive* von knapp 4 Mill. VE (3,7 Mill. VE Ende Februar) enthalten. Die schwebenden *West-Ost-Akkreditive* betrugen 6,3 (8,3) Mill. VE.

Thus, the *Akkreditive* in the arrangements for inter-German trade flowed from West to East and from East to West. *West-Ost-Handel* (which is also found only in the *Neues Deutschland* sub-corpus, together with two tokens of *Ost-West-Handel*) is also clearly unidirectional:

> Wie aus Pressemeldungen hervorgeht, wächst auch in den Vereinigten Staaten die Bewegung für die Entfaltung des *West-Ost-Handels*. Kürzlich betonte sogar der Leiter des US-Amtes für Auslandstätigkeit, Harold Stassen, in einer Rundfunkansprache die Notwendigkeit der Wiederherstellung normaler Handelsbeziehungen zwischen *West und Ost* im Interesse der krisenbedrohten amerikanischen Wirtschaft.

and appears to be equivalent to *West-Ost-Export*. The proximity of words such as *Meinungsverschiedenheiten*, *Handelskrieg*, *britisch*, and *USA-Amt* in the KWIC lines reveals that the term features in reports of the Western allies falling out amongst themselves over attempted trade and credit embargoes against the GDR:

> Zwischen den westdeutschen Ultras und der englischen Regierung haben sich ernsthafte Meinungsverschiedenheiten auf dem Gebiete des *West-Ost-Handels* ergeben. Die britische Regierung hatte sich bekanntlich auf der letzten NATO-Ratstagung geweigert, dem Drängen der westdeutschen Ultras nachzugeben, etwaige Kredite an Länder des sozialistischen Lagers auf eine Laufzeit von höchstens fünf Jahren zu begrenzen.

In the East German sub-corpus of the BZK, however, the *Ost + West* sequence, at ninety-three per cent, constitutes a significant norm, even for negative sequences like *Ost-West-Konflikt*. The two examples of *Ost-West-Handel* found in the *Neues Deutschland* part of the corpus seem, in context, to be semantically bidirectional, as the following example, from 1949, suggests:

> Aus dem Bezirk Wedding erfahren wir, daß sich dort eine größere Anzahl von währungsgeschädigten Handwerkern zu einer Produktivgenossenschaft zusammengeschlossen haben. Die Gründung erfolgte auf Initiative des 'Komitees für Währungsgeschädigte'. Die Genossenschaft will auf der nächsten Leipziger Frühjahrsmesse mit einer eigenen Ausstellung in Erscheinung treten. Hier zeigen die Handwerker eindeutig ihr Interesse an einem stärkeren *Ost-West-Handel.*

The full list of types (and tokens) in the 'BZK-East' with the *Ost-West-* sequence is as follows: *Ost-West-Akkreditive* (1), *Ost-West-Ausscheidungen* (1), *Ost-West-Begegnung* (2), *Ost-West-Beziehungen* (1), *Ost-West-Entspannung* (1), *Ost-West-Fahrbahn* (1), *Ost-West-Gespräch/e* (5), *Ost-West-Gipfelkonferenz* (2), *Ost-West-Gipfeltreffen* (1), *Ost-West-Handel* (2), *Ost-West-Kampfes* (1), *Ost-West-Konferenz* (4), *Ost-West-Konflikts* (4), *Ost-West-Lage* (1), *Ost-West-Politik* (1), *Ost-West-Probleme* (1), *Ost-West-Redaktion* (1), *Ost-West-Spannung* (1), *Ost-West-Spiel* (1), *Ost-West-Straße* (1), *Ost-West-Verhältnis/ses* (2), *Ost-West-Verhandlungen* (4), *Ost-West-Verkehr* (1).

In HK86 (a West German corpus), too, the *West-Ost-* type is very rare, with only three tokens:

```
jetischen Verhältnisses für das gesamte West-Ost-Verhältnis unterstrichen und di
öglichkeiten für eine neue Phase in den West-Ost-Beziehungen nicht versäumt werd
   tsche Küste Interesse haben muß: Die West-Ostströmung befördert die Schadstof
```

Of these, *West-Ostströmung* is clearly unidirectional. However, this cannot be said of either *West-Ost-Verhältnis* or *West-Ost-Beziehungen* (found twelve and six times respectively in the same corpus with the *Ost-West-* ordering. Of the twenty-four tokens in HK86 beginning with *Ost-West-*, the most frequent are *Ost-West-Verhältnis* (12), *Ost-West-Beziehungen* (6), *Ost-West-Dialog* (5), and *Ost-West-Politik* (4)). For the first time in this study, the rationale behind choosing the less common *West + Ost* sequence is not immediately explicable in terms of directionality. The problem posed by these two examples is one which also presents itself in the WK, where the *West-Ost* sequence is significantly more productive, and worthy of closer scrutiny. From a semantic point of view, several 'anomalous' examples can be found amongst the thirty-four tokens and twenty different types of compound in the WK beginning with *West-Ost-* (the figures in brackets show the number of tokens):

West-Ost-Annäherung (1)
West-Ost-Beziehungen (9)
West-Ost-Dialogs (1)
West-Ost-Export (1)
West-Ost-Gefälle (3)
West-Ost-Geschenkdienst (1)
West-Ost-Gesellschaften (1)
West-Ost-Kämpfer (1)
West-Ost-Konflikt (1)
West-Ost Kulturpolitik (1)
West-Ost-Kulturwerks (1)
West-Ost-Planungsgesellschaft (1)
West-Ost-Realität (1)
West-Ost-Stadtbahnverbindung (1)
West-Ost-Transfer (5)
West-Ost-Verbindung (1)
West-Ost-Verhältnis (1)
West-Ost-Verhältnisses (1)
West-Ost-Wirtschaftszusammenarbeit (1)
West-Ost-Verbindungen (1)

The most frequent compounds in the WK beginning with *West-Ost-* are thus *Beziehungen* (9), *Transfer* (5), and *Gefälle* (3). The most frequent types in the same corpus beginning with *Ost-West-* are *Handel* (10), *Konflikt* (8), *Beziehungen* (6), *Verhältnis* (5), *Dialog* (5), and *Kooperation* (4). (*West-Ost-Handel* is not found at all in WK.) It is immediately apparent that there is some overlap between the two lists, though generally there seems to be a tendency for some words to occur with one sequence rather than the other. Table 4 tabulates the number of tokens for each sequence for a given head noun. I have grouped the words into discrete categories, admittedly on an impressionistic basis, according to what seem to me to be the main semantic areas: trade relations; difference and conflict; (bilateral) relationship; dialogue and rapprochement. The figures in brackets after the category show the ratio of *West-Ost* to *Ost-West* tokens. These seem to be more revealing than the figures in brackets in the list, which show the number of occurrences of a given type found in the WK-West (W) and the WK-East (E). This information, relating to the provenance of the texts, does not seem to point to a significant difference in usage between 'East' and 'West'. The only figures which really stand out are that all instances of *AB-Transfer* are *West-Ost-Transfer* and are all found in the WK-West, and that all instances of *AB-Verbindungen* are found in the WK-East. There is a roughly equal distribution between WK-East and WK-West of *AB-Beziehungen*, *AB-*

Table 4 Binomial sequence in compound nouns, by semantic category (five instances in each sub-corpus, with the single example of *West-Ost-Konflikt* in the Western sub-corpus)

West-Ost-		*Ost-West-*
Trade relations (9:15)		
5 (W5, E0)	Transfer	0
0	Vermittlungsgeschäft	1 (W0, E1)
0	Wirtschaftsbeziehungen	1 (W1, E0)
0	Geschäft/e	2 (W1, E1)
0	Handel	10 (W8, E2)
3 (W1, E2)	Gefälle	1 (W0, E1)
1 (W1, E0)	Export	0
Difference/ Conflict (1:18)		
0	Konfrontation	3 (W1, E2)
0	Divergenz	1 (W0, E1)
1 (W1, E0)	Konflikt	9 (W4, E5)
0	Gegensatz	2 (W2, E0)
0	Differenz/en	3 (W1, E2)
(Bilateral) relationship (13:13)		
2 (W2, E0)	Verhältnis	5 (W3, E2)
9 (W3, E6)	Beziehungen	6 (W4, E2)
2 (W0, E2)	Verbindungen	2 (W0, E2)
Dialogue/ rapprochement (2:11)		
1 (W1, E0)	Dialog	5 (W2, E3)
1 (W1, E0)	Annäherung	0
0	Kooperation	4 (W2, E2)
0	Versöhnung	1 (W0, E1)
0	Debatte	1 (W0, E1)

Dialog (with the single example of *West-Ost-Dialog*, also in the Western sub-corpus), *AB-Kooperation*, and *AB-Konflikt*.

In the group relating to trade relations, *Handel*, *Geschäfte*, and *Wirtschaftsbeziehungen* occur only with the sequence *Ost-West*, whereas

Export and *Transfer* occur only with *West-Ost*. This seems to confirm the nouns used with *Ost-West* as superordinate terms for 'trade', with reciprocity or at least bidirectionality as a strong semantic feature. In contrast, the unidirectional semantics of *West-Ost-Export* and *West-Ost-Transfer* seem to derive from the 'marked' binomial sequence. The preference for *West-Ost-Gefälle* over *Ost-West-Gefälle* is clearly a related phenomenon, which could be interpreted in terms of Malkiel's factors either as proximity *(here and there)* or, more plausibly, as 'the precedence of the stronger of two polarized traits' (*rich and poor*).

Turning to the grouping which I have glossed as 'difference/ conflict', it is noticeable that these terms show a very marked tendency to occur with the ordering *Ost-West*, with eighteen instances (half of them provided by *Ost-West-Konflikt*) against only one prefaced with *West-Ost-*. It is tempting to read into this a semantic motivation which is closely related to unidirectionality, namely that this sequence implies the semantic structure AGENT: GOAL AFFECTED, in other words that the *Konflikt* originates in the *Ost* and is directed towards the *West*. However, such an interpretation fails to account for the fact that *Ost-West-Konflikt* appears to be the established concept in the East as well as the West, not only at the time of unification but, more significantly, during the period of the cold war, as the evidence from the BZK-East suggests. The single occurrence of *West-Ost-Konflikt* comes from a West German newspaper article from 1990, which reports the views of the Head of the Political Science section at the Friedrich Engels Military Academy in Dresden, Colonel Erich Hocke:

> WKB/RM2.20576, Rheinischer Merkur (1. Hj. 1990), Eine Armee macht Feierabend, 90.05.25, S. 6
> Hocke sieht für eine nicht näher definierte 'begrenzte Zeit' NVA-Truppen auf dem Gebiet der DDR, die 'nicht NATO-Streitkräfte und auch nicht NATO-assigniert sind'. Alles weitere stehe in den Sternen eines 'europäischen Sicherheitssystems'. Dieses vielbenutzte Zauberwort für eine neue Ordnung nach dem *West-Ost-Konflikt* muß in den nächsten Monaten allerdings erst noch strategisch austariert werden. Vor derlei strategischen Gedankenspielen sind die Rekruten in Lehnitz Lichtjahre entfernt.

In context, one possible explanation for the use of this 'reversed' sequence is as an actual or imagined piece of indirect speech adopting the perspective of the NVA colonel. However, this assumes that the semantics of the term are shaped by directionality, and the evidence for this is, to say the least, problematical. A further complicating factor is that the sequence *Ost-West-Konflikt* may have had a strong unidirectional sense in the West but a generic, 'bidirectional' interpretation in the East. This too, however, seems an unsatisfactory explanation in the light of the evidence from the '(bilateral) relationship' category, where further examples of the *West-Ost-* ordering are found in West German texts. The words in this latter category show the greatest fluidity in their choice of sequence, with no strong preference emerging for either. *Verbindung*, *Verhältnis*, and *Beziehungen* are fairly neutral terms which simply express the existence of a relationship between two things. The term most strongly represented, *West-Ost-Beziehungen*, owes its prominence in the corpus to Helmut Kohl's use of it in the period of negotiations preceding and accompanying formal unification of the two states:

WKD/bhk.03023, Bundeskanzler Helmut Kohl. Reden und Erklärungen zur Deutschlandpolitik/90.02.00/s:112-125, Zehn-Punkte-Programm zur Überwindung der eilung Deutschlands und Europas, S. 115

- Eine bedeutende Rolle hat nicht zuletzt der KSZE-Prozeß gespielt, in dem wir gemeinsam mit unseren Partnern auf einen Abbau von Spannungsursachen, auf Dialog und Zusammenarbeit und vor allem auf die Achtung der Menschenrechte gedrängt haben.
- Ein neues Vertrauen in den *West-Ost-Beziehungen* konnte auch Dank der kontinuierlichen Gipfeldiplomatie der Großmächte und der zahlreichen Begegnungen wachsen, die in diesem Zusammenhang möglich waren – Begegnungen zwischen Staatschefs und Regierungschefs *aus West und Ost*. Der historische Durchbruch bei der Abrüstung und Rüstungskontrolle ist ein sichtbarer Ausdruck dieses Vertrauens.

The above example suggests that Kohl was prone generally to favour the sequence *West* + *Ost* in his public pronouncements in this period.

One of the questions raised by this study is whether a privileged group of speakers, namely politicians (who feature prominently in the WK) adopted the 'marked' sequence as a deliberate stratagem, for reasons which can only be speculated on – perhaps to invest the *Ost-West-Frage* with new vitality, or perhaps to introduce a new semantics in which the West enjoyed the privileges, such as 'priority', which Malkiel believes attach to the first-mentioned term.

The words which I have grouped under the heading 'dialogue' tend to focus on cooperation and rapprochement, thus contrasting with the 'problem' group, which focuses on difference, conflict and confrontation (though difference and conflict are clearly a prerequisite for rapprochement). Here, once again, the *Ost-West* sequence is clearly the norm, though there is the occasional example of the reverse ordering. All of these words would seem to be semantically reciprocal. A *Dialog* must, after all, be a two-way exchange (though it does not have to be balanced). This word is found five times with *Ost-West* and once with *West-Ost*, the 'rogue' example once again originating with Helmut Kohl:

> WKB/BT1.50014, Bundestagsprotokolle (2. Hj. 1989), Sitzung Nr. 173, Bd. 151, S. 13010-13059, 89.11.08, S. 13036
> Eines der zentralen Themen muß dabei die Entwicklung in der DDR sein.
> Der KSZE-Prozeß hat Menschenrecht und Bürgerrecht zu einem legitimen Thema des *West-Ost-Dialogs* gemacht, das nicht mehr unter Berufung auf das Nichteinmischungsprinzip vom Tisch gewischt werden kann. Mit der Verabschiedung des Abschlußdokuments des Wiener Folgetreffens haben alle Partnerstaaten weiteren Fortschritten im Bereich der Menschenrechte und der zwischenmenschlichen Kontakte in ihren Ländern zugestimmt.

In context, it is difficult to resist the implication that the *West-Ost-Dialog* to which Kohl refers is something rather different to, and more semantically specific than an *Ost-West-Dialog*. The reference to the Western allies and the CSCE Helsinki process gives this statement a partial, Western perspective. Kohl is careful to include mention of the Federal Republic's Western partners and to acknowledge their shared interests, and also, perhaps, to connote the dominant negotiating position of the West.[7]

If this case is problematic, then the semantics of the single example of *West-Ost-Annäherung*, which also originates with Kohl, are even more intriguing:

> WKB/BT1.50014, Bundestagsprotokolle (2. Hj. 1989), Sitzung Nr. 173, Bd. 151, S. 13010-13059, 89.11.08, S. 13050
> Anlaß zur Sorge wäre ein nationaler Alleingang. Er wäre nicht nur Anlaß zur Sorge für unsere Nachbarn, es wäre auch Anlaß zur Sorge für uns selbst. (Frau Schulte < Hameln > < SPD > :Das ist wohl wahr!). Neutralistische Alleingänge wären ein Rückfall in die Vergangenheit. Sie würden neue Instabilitäten in Europa schaffen. Sie würden den Prozeß der *West-Ost-Annäherung* ernsthaft gefährden. Sie würden damit auch den nationalen Interessen der Deutschen, die heute mit den europäischen Interessen identisch sind, schaden.

Logically, it is of course possible for *Annäherung* to take place unilaterally, when one party moves towards the position of the other, but Kohl surely does not mean to imply that the West is moving towards a position held by the East. If there is a semantic rationale to this choice of sequence, then it would seem to be that the West is the major player in this process – it is *Annäherung* on the West's terms. Thus, the transitivity relation of influence runs from West to East. Curiously, this would mean that beneath or behind the 'surface' sequence *West-Ost* there is an underlying *Ost + West* directionality, as in *die Annäherung des Ostens an den Westen*.

These reflections on the data show how difficult it is to discern a semantic rationale underlying the choice of sequence in some contexts. Perhaps it is better in such cases not to try. After all, speakers do not always deliberate on the precise semantic nuances of their lexical and syntactic choices, and there may be purely phonological factors influencing the choice of sequence (though I cannot imagine what they might be in this case). 'Anomalous' examples such as those cited above could merely be the result of a rhetorical concern for stylistic variety. Alternatively, the unexpected ('marked') ordering could be the result of a semantically or pragmatically motivated choice, and whilst I cannot hope to adjudicate on this question here, it is conceivable that corpus techniques will one day furnish us with evidence to prove or disprove the hypothesis that a certain group of speakers is consistently making statistically unusual linguistic choices. In the absence of such conclusive evidence, we can perhaps only note a case such as *West-Ost-Annäherung* against the background of a (conscious or unconscious) trend evidenced around the time of unification – possibly amongst a small but influential group of speakers – to use the *West* + *Ost* sequence in new and semantically complex ways. Tempting as it may be to attribute this usage to a politically conservative rhetoric characteristic of the CDU/CSU, an acquaintance with the speeches of Helmut Schmidt (not captured in our corpora) soon reveals that the *West* + *Ost* sequence was also a feature of public discourse in the Federal Republic before 1982 (Dodd 1988: 308–9). Evidence gathered from the publicly available texts on the Federal Government's website seems to confirm the use of *West-Ost-* in such compounds; although interestingly a search of Kohl's speeches leading up to the election in September 1998 found only *Ost-West-*, in combination with *-Konflikt* and *-Gegensatz*.[8] I also know of at least one occasion on which an indirect report of a speech by Kohl reversed the original *West-Ost-Verhältnis* to produce the statistically more 'normal' *Ost-West-Verhältnis*.[9]

To sum up: what strikes one about the list of *West-Ost-* compounds in the WK is that while some of them fairly clearly invite a unidirectional interpretation, several could just as well be reversed (and are indeed also found with the *Ost-West-* order). The kind of semantic problems described above with *West-Ost-Dialog* and *West-Ost-Annäherung* demonstrate the limits of a purely semantic approach and the importance of a cultural competence for the construction of nuance and connotation, in particular. It is difficult to see how an automated routine could make such culturally vital nuances explicit.[10] My own feeling after looking at this evidence is that unidirectionality is *always* implied when the *West* + *Ost* sequence is found, though the precise semantic and pragmatic value which attaches to it may be extremely subtle. Terms beginning with *West-Ost* also tend to belong to a discourse of economic and trade relations. Terms beginning with *Ost-West* tend to be harder to interpret unidirectionally and are more difficult to characterize by field. In this sense, they seem more semantically opaque than the reversed sequence.[11] One hypothesis which I would put forward, however, is that one can make a fairly confident prediction that there will be a transitivity relation from West to East in economic contexts, whilst in political contexts the distribution is less predictable, though the *Ost* + *West* sequence predominates. The following example seems to encapsulate the point:

> WKD/hfs.11008, Handzettel/90.03.00/s:1-2, S. 2
> Der alte Traum von einem vereinigten Europa kann und muß heute verwirklicht werden, wenn der bisherige ideologische und militaristische *Ost-West-Konflikt* nicht durch ein ebenso gefährliches *West-Ost-Gefälle* auf sozialem, wirtschaftlichem und technologischem Gebiet ersetzt werden soll. Wir wollen einen selbständigen Beitrag der DDR für die Gestaltung des europäischen Hauses und eine neue Qualität des KSZE-Prozesses.

The transitivity relations recoverable from the juxtaposition of the two binomials here seem to suggest that international conflict ran from East to West (AGENT: GOAL AFFECTED), but that economic relations, especially in post-unification Germany, flow from West to East (HIGH: LOW, compare *Nord-Süd-Gefälle* when discussing the world economy, but *Süd-Nord-Gefälle* when discussing the distribution of wealth within the Federal Republic).

5 *Ost-Kinder überhören West-Autos*: Transitivity relations at clause level

The concept of a transitivity relation can also be applied to larger structures. In addition to looking at the three major categories of binomial described in section 3, the KWIC concordances for all corpora were also examined for instances where *Ost* and *West* co-occurred outside nominal groups. This category (termed 'other structures') captures some interesting examples of *Ost* and *West* being used as opposing or complementary terms at a higher level of organization, i.e. at clause or sentence level. The criteria for capturing these examples were that *Ost* and *West* must appear in the KWIC line and must occur within the same sentence. This captured syntactic phenomena such as the following:

```
WKB im Frühjahr , als es für eine D-Mark-West sieben Ost-Mark gab , hatten
WKB n , die es je gab : . die Deutschen Ost stürmten Deutschland West .
WKD nach der Fusionierung der Grünen ( Ost ) mit den Grünen ( West ) wird es nu
WKB ie Vereinigung von 25 Gramm Würmern Ost mit 25 Gramm Würmern West vollzogen
WKB alle Partner trefflich leben : . an Ost-Autoren verdienten Deutsche ( West )
WKD á viele DDR-Bürger die spektakuläre Ost-Kandidatur des West-Wirtschaftlers a
WKB u+ Ost-Kinder überhören West-Autos +u .
WKB en dürfen . sie kaufen billig gegen Ost-Mark auf , um später gegen West-Mark
WKB Solidarausgleich der Beitragszahler West mit den Versicherten Ost nach dem F
WKB üssen der Rentenversicherungsträger West an die Kollegen Ost zurückzuüberwei
WKD arktes folgend - das Wohnungproblem West zu Lasten von Ost zumindest gelinde
```

The number of instances in which *Ost* precedes *West*, and vice versa, was also recorded for this category but the statistics were not included when calculating the 'global' scores, because it was thought that at sentence and clause level there were many more factors influencing the choice of sequence than at word and phrase level. In fact the distribution is roughly equal in both the HK86 and WK, whilst in the BZK the sequence *Ost* + *West* is found in about two thirds of such contexts (see Table 5).

Table 5 Distribution of the binomial in other structures

Other structures	Ost-West	West-Ost	Binomial	Ost-West%
BZK	11	6	17	64.71
HK86	15	17	32	46.88
WK	23	27	50	46.00
TOTAL	49	50	99	49.49

It is perhaps not surprising that at clause and sentence level the distribution of the two sequences is much more equal. Here, merely noting the order in which A and B occur is not always a reliable indicator of the direction in which this transitivity relation flows: each context must be considered individually, since the order of elements does not necessarily dictate the direction of the transitivity relation (passive constructions, for example, introduce a different syntactic ordering of agent and goal from that found in active sentences). Two examples must suffice here to illustrate the point. The first is the headline '*Ost-Kinder überhören West-Autos*', in which the surface syntax order gives us a human agent, a mental process (perception), and a category of objects as the goal of the mental process. In fact, although *Ost-Kinder* is the topic of the sentence, it performs, potentially at least, the semantic role of GOAL AFFECTED, and the subtext is the superior economic and technological level of the Western society. The second example is a caption to a photograph:

> WKB/RM2.20613, Rheinischer Merkur (1.Hj. 1990), Patienten ohne Lobby, 90.06.08, S. 9
> x+ Foto +x.
> Der Kranke in der DDR: seine Interessen drohen zwischen Ärzteängsten Ost und Kassenstreit West unterzugehen.

The topic of this text is the medical patient in the East, whose interests are in danger of being forgotten 'between doctors' anxieties (in the) East and the insurance dispute (in the) West'. This might be explained in terms of the proximity to the East German patient, who is the topic of this sentence: from his perspective, the ordering places what is adjacent ('Ärzteängste') before what is distant ('Kassenstreit West'), as in *here and there*. But the underlying (active) sentential structure here is 'Streit-West verursacht Ängste-Ost drohen Interessen des Patienten' ('insurance dispute in the West causes doctors' anxieties in the East [which] threatens patient's interests'), and is thus a variant of the structure AGENT (West) – GOAL AFFECTED (East), and indeed of the West-East directionality typically found in economic contexts. Hence the surface structure, in which *Ost* precedes *West* in the binomial, can be seen as a transform of an underlying semantic structure which is essentially the same as that for *West-Ost-Gefälle* or *West-Ost-Geschenkdienst*.

6 *Ostblock/ Westmächte*: *Ost-* and *West-* in 'ideological' compounds

We have seen occasional evidence suggesting that the provenance of the text as an East German or West German text correlates with the choice of ordering; for example in the use of *West-Ost-Handel* in the BZK. But on the whole it cannot be said that provenance is a strong predictor of the order in which the binomial occurs: even in *Neues Deutschland* in the period of the cold war, we find *Ost-West-Konflikt*, not *West-Ost-Konflikt*, and the only examples of *West-Ost-Konflikt* found in the three corpora is from a West German text. The situation is thus clearly far from straightforward. A search of prepositional phrases in the BZK, for example, reveals a roughly proportionate crop of *Ost + West* structures from *Neues Deutschland*, even where negative concepts are in play (e.g. *Spannung zwischen Ost und West*). Of twenty-eight occurrences in *Neues Deutschland*, only five have the order *West + Ost*.

On the other hand, there is a quite striking asymmetry, both between Eastern and Western usage and between the two 'East-West' corpora, about the way *Ost** and *West** are used as qualifiers in compounds, particularly with *Deutschland* and *Deutsche* as the head. Table 6 shows some interesting divergences here between East German and West German usage, and between the two East-West corpora (figures show the number of tokens).

Table 6 *Ost** and *West** in selected compound nouns in the BZK and WK

	BZK-West	BZK-East	WK-West	WK-East
Ostblock*	90	0	78	9
Westblock*	0	5	0	0
Ostmächte*	0	0	0	0
Westmächte*	93	157	0	0
Ostdeutschland*	8	23	100	30
Westdeutschland*	165	990	105	4
Ostdeutsche*	2	1	63	22
Westdeutsche*	88	33	118	2

In the BZK, *Ostblock* and *Westmächte* are firmly entrenched concepts and even seem to operate as a conceptual pair in the West. *Ostmächte* is not found at all, and *Westblock* only five times – all in East German texts. The importance of *Ostblock** as an ideological concept in the West is clear from the fact that all ninety examples of it are found in West German texts – the most frequent compound types being *Ostblockland* and *Ostblockstaaten* (twenty-one tokens each). *Block* in this usage appears to be applied only to the other side in the military-ideological confrontation, which suggests that it has negative semantic prosody, at least in pre-*Wende* political contexts. It is also interesting to find that *Westdeutschland* greatly outnumbers *Ostdeutschland* in both East and West German texts, with by far the highest number of tokens being registered for *Westdeutschland* in East German texts. (The relatively low score for *Ostdeutschland* in East German texts is presumably accounted for by the rigorously observed use of the formal designation *DDR/ Deutsche Demokratische Republik*; whilst in West German texts the relative scarcity of *Ostdeutschland* presumably has a similar explanation – e.g. the deliberate use of terms such as *SBZ*, *'DDR'*, *drüben* or even *Mitteldeutschland*). There seems to be evidence, too, of *Westdeutsch** being more firmly established than *Ostdeutsch** in both the East and the West.

Turning from the BZK to the WK, one is struck by the continuing currency of *Ostblock*, which even appears nine times in the East German sub-corpus (a sign indeed of changed times and the effect on usage in the former GDR[12]), whilst *Westblock*, already marginal in the BZK-East, is not attested at all. Even more striking is the complete absence of *Westmächte* from both Eastern and Western texts in the WK. Both *Ostdeutschland* and *Westdeutschland* are quite common in the WK-West, but much less frequent in the WK-East, with *Westdeutschland* barely attested at all. The reasons for this particular asymmetry are not immediately apparent. Perhaps GDR journalists may have been reluctant to think of their territory as *Ostdeutschland*, while referring to West Germany consistently by its more formal title *Bundesrepublik (Deutschland)*. Finally, the WK also documents the appearance of *Ossi* and *Wessi*, though here too a certain asymmetry is noticeable, the form *Ossi** being found thirty-four times in the WK-West but only fourteen times in the WK-East. This pattern is repeated for *Wessi**, found forty-six times in the West but only thirteen times in the East.

7 Just a turn of phrase? Conclusions and desiderata

The findings of this study are not straightforward, and further investigations are needed to determine whether the reversibility of this binomial is anything more than just a semantically insignificant 'turn of phrase'. Future investigations need ideally to be conducted on larger, historically and geographically discrete corpora, with a particular focus on political registers, political groupings, and personalities. For the present, I would offer the following observations:

i) This binomial shows a degree of 'reversibility' not found in its English counterpart.
ii) The sequence *Ost* + *West* accounts for approximately eighty per cent of all instances in the corpora investigated. The values for all three categories of the binomial investigated here are significantly higher in the WK, where *West* + *Ost* accounts for up to thirty per cent of all occurrences in some categories.
iii) Given this distribution of the two sequences, the question arises whether the sequence *Ost* + *West* constitutes a significant norm. Perhaps more pertinent is the converse question: whether *West* + *Ost* should be regarded as a marked sequence.
iv) The semantics of the *West* + *Ost* sequence are typically, and perhaps invariably, unidirectional. The semantics of the *Ost* + *West* sequence are typically relational or 'bidirectional'.
v) In the discourse of international politics, *Ost* + *West* is the preferred sequence. In economic contexts relating to international or German–German trade, *West* + *Ost* is the more common sequence.
vi) Provenance (whether the source is 'West German' or 'East German') is generally not a strong predictor of which ordering is encountered. However, a small number of compound nouns are found in West German texts with the *West-Ost-* sequence when the semantics of the head noun are not obviously unidirectional. The earliest examples in the corpora investigated here date from 1986, but even earlier examples are attested.
vii) The same author may use both sequences, with different expressions, in the same text. Evidence was not found of an author chang-

ing back and forth between the two sequences for the same expression in the same text, but this is not a finding likely to be made in this study since whole texts were not examined. Evidence is noted of a newspaper report reverting to the *Ost* + *West* sequence when the original text used the *West* + *Ost* sequence.

viii) Unidirectionality strongly implies a transitivity relationship, but 'surface' ordering does not always reflect the underlying relationship of, for example, semantic agent to semantic goal. This is true of nominal groups and of clauses.

ix) The *Ost* + *West* sequence may be interpreted as relational or as unidirectional, and so it is theoretically possible that a term such as *Ost-West-Konflikt* will be given different interpretations by different writers and readers. Against this, the inroads made by the *West* + *Ost* sequence, especially in the WK-West, may suggest that this sequence is losing its 'marked' status, so that, in theory at least, a term such as *West-Ost-Konflikt* may be interpreted generically and not unidirectionally.

x) In focusing on pragmatic and semantic factors it should be remembered that phonological factors may impose purely formal constraints on sequence in the binomial.

xi) *Ost** and *West** show an asymmetrical distribution in certain key terms of the (now historical) ideological discourse of difference and conflict. The evidence here is much more straightforward than for binomials, and provenance is very significant.

Notes

1 I wish to thank the staff of the Institut für Deutsche Sprache in Mannheim for making it possible for me to work on these corpora during several study visits. I am particularly indebted to Professor Gerhard Stickel, the Director, to Eva Teubert, the Institute's librarian, and to Dr Irmtraud Jüttner for her instruction in the use of the COSMAS software. I would also like to thank Dr Manfred Hellmann for his always helpful consultations. Thanks are also due to Ramesh Krishnamurthy, who commented on an earlier draft, and Oliver Mason for advice on chi square (see note 6).

2 I will follow Malkiel's notation, in which A stands for the first and B for the second member of the pair. See also Cruse (1986: 47).

3 I am grateful to Ramesh Krishnamurthy for this information. Examples not

obviously explainable in terms of unidirectionality include: *West-East discourse*, *West-East disputes*, and the curious pair *most west-east diplomacy is conducted bilaterally*, and *a west-east rail link from Hull to Liverpool.* Looking at authorship suggests that some of these examples may be attributed to authors whose first language is not English. There is also the example of *West-East arms cuts*, which I think can be viewed in terms of unidirectionality.

4 See for example Louw (1993), and the Introduction to the present volume.

5 A chi square calculation across all three corpora, based on the raw scores per three million words, produces the following result:

	BZK	HK86	WK	Total
Ost-West	128.6	131.2	451	710.8
West-Ost	17.16	20.9	125.9	163.96
Total	145.76	152.1	576.9	874.76

Degrees of freedom: 2/Chi-square = 10.743/p is less than or equal to 0.01. / The distribution is significant.

A pair-wise comparison of individual corpora reveals the relationship between them and in particular the extent to which the WK is ‘out of line’:

BZK: HK86	$p > 1.0$ (the distribution is not significant)
HK86: WK	$p > 0.05$ (the distribution is significant)
BZK: WK	$p > 0.01$ (the distribution is significant).

I am indebted to Jeff Connor- Linton for this introduction to chi square (at <http://www.georgetown.edu/cball/weebtools/web_chi_tut.htm>)

6 Although the BZK, unlike the WK, is not explicitly divided into ‘Western’ and ‘Eastern’ subcorpora, it is possible to ‘separate’ the files according to provenance. See al-Wadi (1994: 134, section 12.2.3).

7 An example brought to my attention by April Mackison is that of the *West-Ost-Autobahn, die Frankfurt mit Dresden verbindet*. In the corpus constructed by her (see elsewhere in this volume) there are only three types with the *West-Ost* ordering, each represented by a single token:

```
esländern vervielfacht, insbesondere in der West-Ost-Richtung. Bei den Verarbeiteten Industriewaren
optimal angebunden - auf halber Strecke der West-Ost-Autobahn, die Frankfurt mit Dresden verbindet.
ußfinanzierung der ostdeutschen Wirtschaft (West-Ost-Transfer) verdeutlicht er in einer eindrucksvol
```

The case of *West-Ost-Autobahn* is of particular interest, since a motorway running west-east presumably also runs east-west. However, the effect of the ‘marked’ order for the binomial here is to radically alter the ‘two-way’ semantics of *Ost-West-Autobahn*, so as to signal that the motorway ‘belongs to’ the West in some significant sense, being initiated and paid for by the West German state – in effect a form of *West-Ost-Transfer*.

8 A 154 000-word corpus of Helmut Kohl’s speeches for the period July–September 1998 was made using the texts published in the Federal Govern-

ment's Bulletin (website <http//:www.bundesregierung.de>). These contained five instances of the binomial in compound nouns, all of them having the sequence *Ost-West* and a semantically negative headword:

```
1 unismus ist zusammengebrochen, der Ost-West-Konflikt gehört der Vergangenheit an. Für die
2 1.  Jahrhundert. Nach dem Ende des Ost-West-Konfliktes ist in Europa und im Nahen Osten da
3 amen und Herren, nach dem Ende des Ost-West-Konfliktes haben wirtschaftliche Fragen noch m
4 opas in den langen Jahrzehnten des Ost-West-Gegensatzes dauerhaft zu überwinden. Wir müsse
5 en kein Zurück in diese Zeiten des Ost-West-Gegensatzes. Wir wollen Frieden schaffen mit w
```

9 Helmut Kohl's New Year's address on New Year's Eve 1988 contained the sentence: 'Die Fortschritte im West-Ost-Verhältnis zeigen, dass vieles in Bewegung geraten ist' (*Bulletin der Bundesregierung*, 1/1989, p. 2). The indirect report of this speech in the *Süddeutsche Zeitung* runs: 'Im Ost-West-Verhältnis habe es Fortschritte gegeben' (31.12.88). It would appear that the newspaper report has the effect of 'unmarking' Kohl's original wording, found elsewhere in the speech in the phrase *West-Ost-Dialog*.

10 A similar set of examples occur in the corpus constructed by April Mackison (see elsewhere in this volume), in which *Ost-West-Reisen*, *Ost-West-Transit*, and *Ost-West-Wanderung* are found. It is debatable whether an automated routine would differentiate between, on the one hand, the bidirectional *Ost-West-Reisen* and *Ost-West-Transit*, and, on the other, the unidirectional *Ost-West-Wanderung*, the interpretation of which is culturally and historically determined.

11 Cruse (1986: 47) observes further that 'usually one ordering is more common than the other', adding that 'the most common ordering is usually semantically opaque'.

12 Cf. Dieter Herberg, who comments that the 'Wende' of 1989/90 was 'eine Phase, die – vor allem, was ihre sprachliche Spezifik betrifft – im wesentlichen nur einen Teil Deutschlands, die DDR, berührt hat' (Herberg 1998b: 330).

References

al-Wadi, Doris (1994), *COSMAS Benutzerhandbuch* Version R.1.3-1. Institut für Deutsche Sprache: Mannheim.

Cruse, Alan (1986), *Lexical Semantics*, Cambridge University Press: Cambridge.

Dodd, W. J. (1988), 'The changing rhetoric of 'Deutschlandpolitik', *German Life and Letters* 41(3): 293–311.

Hellmann, Manfred (1996), 'Lexikographische Erschließung des Wendekorpus. Werkstattbericht' in N. Weber (ed.), *Semantik, Lexikographie und Computeranwendungen* (= Sprache und Information 23), Tübingen, pp. 195–216.

Herberg, Dieter (1998a), 'Neues im Wortgebrauch der Wendezeit. Zur Arbeit mit dem IDS-Wendekorpus' in Wolfgang Teubert (ed.), *Neologie und Korpus*. Gunter Narr: Tübingen, pp. 43–61.

Herberg, Dieter (1998b), 'Schlüsselwörter – Schlüssel der Wendezeit', in Heidrun Kämper and Hartmut Schmidt (eds), *Das 20. Jahrhundert. Sprachgeschichte – Zeitgeschichte* (= Institut für Deutsche Sprache Jahrbuch, 1997). de Gruyter: Berlin & New York, pp. 330–44.

Herberg, Dieter (1996), 'Schlüsselwörter der Wendezeit. Ein lexikologisch-lexikographisches Projekt zur Auswertung des IDS-Wendekorpus' in Arne Zettersten and Viggo Hjørnager Pedersen (eds) *Symposium on Lexicography VII* (= Reihe Lexicographica, Series Maior 76). Gunter Narr: Tübingen, pp. 119–26.

Herberg, Dieter (1993) 'Die Sprache der Wendezeit als Forschungsgegenstand. Untersuchungen zur Sprachentwicklung 1989/90 am IDS', *Muttersprache* 103: 264–6.

Herberg, Dieter, Doris Steffens and Elke Tellenbach (1997), *Schlüsselwörter der Wendezeit. Wörter-Buch zum öffentlichen Sprachgebrauch 1989/90*. de Gruyter: Berlin/New York.

Johns, Tim and Mike Scott (1987), *Microconcord*. Oxford University Press: Oxford.

Louw, Bill (1993) 'Irony in the text or insincerity in the writer? The diagnostic potential of semantic prosodies' in Mona Baker, Gill Francis, and Elena Tognini-Bonelli (eds), *Text and Technology: in honour of John Sinclair*. John Benjamins: Amsterdam and Philadelphia, pp. 157–76.

Malkiel, Yakov (1959), 'Studies in irreversible binomials', *Lingua* 8: 113–60.

Stubbs, Michael (1997), '"Eine Sprache idiomatisch sprechen": Computer, Korpora, kommunikative Kompetenz und Kultur' in K. J. Mattheier (ed.), *Norm und Variation*, Peter Lang: Frankfurt/Main, pp. 151–67.

German *be-* verbs revisited: using corpus evidence to investigate valency

Piklu Gupta[1]

1 Introduction

German prefix verbs have been a subject of interest for linguists since the time of Grimm and have provided material for a number of monographs since at least the 1960s. The set of verbs chosen for this investigation consists of a subset of the so-called *be-* verbs. In examining the valency of these verbs I am interested in the semantic status of their complements (mainly their subjects and accusative objects), rather than merely looking at valency in syntactic terms, since the syntactic status of most *be-* verbs is fairly predictable. The most exhaustive treatment in the field is Hartmut Günther's *Das System der Verben mit BE-in der deutschen Sprache der Gegenwart* (1974). A substantial part of Günther's monograph consists of his taxonomy of *be-* verbs and it is this taxonomy that will be focused on here with particular reference to validating and re-examining his hypotheses in the light of corpus evidence. Günther devotes a section to debating the usefulness of a corpus as a source of data and makes a number of comments on the problems of corpus selection and coverage. He also alludes to the need for large amounts of data and adequate computational resources to process them, which were not at his disposal in the early 1970s but are obviously now far easier to gain access to. The present investigation explores not only the use of corpora as a source of linguistic examples with measures of their raw frequencies but as a sound basis for the discussion of (statistically) significant collocations of *be-* verbs which in turn often provide information on their semantic valency patterns.

2 *Be*- verbs

There are a number of reasons why *be*- verbs are of particular interest. First of all, *be*-prefixing is still a highly productive form of affixation in modern German and is therefore easily attestable. Secondly, for purposes of contrastive analysis, the verb alternations most often expressed by *be*-prefixing are also present in English, although they are, of course, realized differently (mainly by zero derivation). Thirdly, the relationship between a *be*- verb and its corresponding simplex verb is often of interest in syntactic terms. Indeed, Eroms (1980), unlike Günther, bases his taxonomy on such factors rather than on membership of a semantic field. If we look at research on *be*- verbs since the early 1970s we see that areas of emphasis range from a case grammar analysis (Becker 1971) and treatment of the holistic-partitive distinction (Pusch 1972) through the lexicalist work of Günther (1986) and Eroms's word syntactic treatment. Later research includes that of Wunderlich (1987), who claims prepositional status for *be*- on the basis of diachronic evidence and Olsen (1995), who argues that *be*- is the result of the lexical incorporation of a prepositional relation. Note that little or no use is made of corpus data in the literature referred to above.

3 Prefix verbs vs. particle verbs

Reference grammars intended for an English-speaking readership such as Durrell (1996) employ the terms separable and inseparable verbal prefixes. I propose to use instead the terms 'prefix verbs' and 'particle verbs' and differentiate between them as follows: prefix verbs are distinguished from particle verbs by the morphemic status of the prefix or particle. Prefix verbs consist of a bound morpheme plus verbal stem, whereas particle verbs comprise a particle and verbal stem – the particle can either occur post-verbally in V2 clauses or is integrated with the verb in verb-final clauses as illustrated by the following:

(1) a. Ich rufe an
b. . . weil ich anrufe

Prefixes include *ver-*, *ent-* and *be-*, whilst particles are homonymous with prepositions such as *an* or *ab*. Durrell does point out that some 'prefixes' can be either separable or inseparable (e.g. *durch, um, über*) as shown by the following examples

(2) a. Peter **umfuhr** das Verkehrsschild
Peter around-drove the traffic sign
'Peter drove around the traffic sign'
'*Peter knocked down the traffic sign'
b. Peter **fuhr** das Verkehrsschild **um**
Peter drove the traffic-sign around
'*Peter drove around the traffic sign'
'Peter knocked down the traffic sign'

Note also that the stress pattern is different for both variants – the prefix variant being *'umfahren* and the particle variant *um'fahren*.

4 Systematic study of *be*- verbs

Before looking at the taxonomy in Günther (1974), I will first deal with a salient area for the study of *be*- verbs – that of so-called ornatives and their treatment by Günther and Eroms (1980).

4.1 Ornatives

Since I shall be adopting the term ornative, which seldom appears in English (an exception being Pounder (1997)), it is appropriate to outline what is meant by this term and to investigate critically its treatment in the literature. In semantic terms ornatives express a situation in which an item (usually denoted by a concrete noun) is provided with another item, or enhanced by one. Perhaps the most useful explanation of ornatives in syntactic terms is that they display what is referred to in the contemporary English literature as the locative alternation, in which a prepositional phrase (expressed by *with*) alternates with an accusative object. A well known example of this alternation in English is the *spray/load* alternation. Levin (1993: 118) has an analogous form in German, the salient difference being that German generally expresses the accusative alternation by addition of the *be*-prefix, for example:

(3) a. Er lud Heu auf den Wagen
b. Er belud den Wagen mit Heu

Günther posits an ORN (ornative) case role in addition to using 'ornative' to refer to a type of verb. He argues that too little attention has been paid to the distinction between INSTR (instrumental) in traditional case grammar and ORN in his notation and cites (Günther 1974: 69) an example from Grimm in which the prepositional phrase with *mit* is treated as an instrumental in both cases, which Günther feels is erroneous:

(4) a. Er begießt die Blumen mit Wasser.
b. Er begießt die Blumen mit der Gießkanne.

This judgement can be supported by the following in which coordination is impossible in the case of 5b:

(5) a. Er begießt die Blumen mit Wasser mit der Gießkanne
b. * Er begießt die Blumen mit Wasser und der Gießkanne

Günther (1974: 69–71) explains the ornative case role in detail, including examples of when the subject of a sentence can be assigned the ORN case role, for example:

(6) Die Schutzplane bedeckt den Rasen

He posits the rule relating to subject position which states that ORN is the subject in sentences lacking AG (agent) and INSTR. Eroms (1980: 32) is, however, not convinced by such an interpretation and argues that to assign the subject the case role OBJECTIVE is more appropriate, illustrated by the structurally identical sentence

(7) Ein Tuch bedeckt den Käfig

and he contends that we are dealing with a causative/recessive relation rather than an ornative in such an agentless sentence. Günther certainly sees ornatives and the ORN case role as not simply a phenomenon which can be explained in terms of a syntactic alternation.

Eroms's discussion of ornatives focuses on the locative alternation rather than on expressing their function in terms of case roles. He also provides a critique of Pusch's (1972) claims for a purely holistic interpretation of *be-* verbs when compared to the base simplex verb. Eroms agrees with the holistic interpretation of most of Pusch's examples, but gives the following example from his small corpus as a counter-example of Pusch's assertion:

(8) ....die Zeit wird kommen, da sie dich einreißen oder dich mit ihren habgierigen Firmenschildern bekleben (Eroms 1980: 21)

arguing that it is not necessarily the case that the whole wall will be covered in signs.

4.2 Günther's *Das System der Verben mit BE-in der deutschen Sprache der Gegenwart*

Günther initially provides the reader with an historical overview of the *be-* prefix from Jacob Grimm onwards. Since diachronic analysis is not our concern, we will not discuss this issue here.

Günther (1974: 65) uses a set of case roles based on Fillmore (1968) but omits some while adding others of his own (e.g. ORN to mark ornatives) which are relevant to his treatment of *be-* verbs. The AFF (affective) category replaces Fillmore's GOAL, OBJECT and to a certain extent INSTR. Günther (p. 67) points out what he considers to be the flaw in Fillmore's assertion that all sentences with an agent can also have an instrumental using the example

(9) Hans belauscht die Männer

and maintains that it is doubtful that a phrase representing INSTR can be added at will (e.g. *mit den Ohren*), claiming that the motivation for such phrases is purely extralinguistic.

4.2.1 Classification of be- *verbs*

The most substantial part of Günther's 1974 monograph consists of his taxonomy of *be-* verbs. He posits eight categories and labels the first six of them with an arbitrarily chosen infinitive from the set of verbs, which does not serve as a representative superordinate, but nevertheless is said to loosely represent the typical members of its set. The seventh group is composed of those verbs he considers to be idiosyncratic and therefore impossible to assign to one of the other categories, and the eighth group is made up of lexicalized *be-* verbs. Around sixty-five per cent of the non-lexicalized *be-* verbs belong to groups I to VI. These types are further subdivided into semantically organized subgroups. The following subsection describes the main characteristics of groups I to VI. Note that Günther's notation for semantic features is the same as that found in Helbig and Schenkel (1969) and case roles are expressed in capital letters. All example sentences are taken from the monograph.

4.2.2 Be- *verb categories*

Type I – BEDECKEN This group is the largest described by Günther and therefore provides a fundamental pattern for *be-* verbs. Type I verbs are almost exclusively deverbal, the root always denoting a concrete activity. The common syntactic characteristic of members of this group is the relationship between the simplex and the *be-* verb – that is the replacement of the locative prepositional phrase required by the simplex with an accusative object complement for the corresponding *be-* verb. Example sentence:

(10) Hans bedeckt den Käfig mit einem Tuch

Type II – BEFLAGGEN Type II verbs are largely derived from denominal simplex verbs. This is another highly productive type of word formation, especially in the technical domain. Type II verbs are not usually ornative. Example sentence:

(11) Sie beflaggen den Mast

Type III – BEARBEITEN Typically these are activity verbs. The base simplex verbs are generally denominal zero derivations (e.g. *feilen*) and are regarded by Günther (p. 138) as being genuine prefix constructions ('echte Präfixbildungen') which simply means that the activity denoted by the prefix verb is subsumed by the simplex verb, for example *befeilen* is a particular instance of *feilen*. They are never ornatives. There appear to be a number of sublanguage uses, for example *beackern* verbs which are encountered in the agricultural domain. The *beforsten* verbs are deemed to be 'pseudo-prefix' constructions with the structural meaning 'A uses B to X', where X is the root of the verb (p. 140). Example sentence:

(12) Der Handwerker bearbeitet das Werkstück

Type IV – BESCHAUEN Type IV verbs can be semantically grouped together in terms of perception by the senses. They rarely have an instrumental PP (prepositional phrase complement), since this would lead to tautologous constructions, such as

(13) Er beschaut ihn mit den Augen (p.149)

(but the addition of such a PP is arguably possible with a modifier or synonym that adds meaning). As a further consequence, the subject of such sentences is only exceptionally an INSTR.

Type V – BESPRECHEN The verbs in this section all denote expression of, for example, opinion or judgement in terms of thought or speech. Günther discusses the problematic nature of defining the distributional characteristics of the accusative object, since it should always have the semantic feature [-Konkr]

(14) a. Er beklagt den Verlust
b. * Er beklagt das Auto

but nevertheless often admits [+Hum], demonstrated by his example:

(15) Er beklagt den Toten (p. 158)

Type VI – BEEINFLUSSEN Verbs grouped in the *beeinflussen* category are the so-called 'psych' verbs which express psychological states. In

English they are typically found in passive constructions with a following preposition other than *by* such as *be surprised at*. Günther takes issue with the usefulness of Fillmore's case role of Experiencer and contends that AFF is sufficient for the case representation of the accusative object, and he states that certain syntactic features of these verbs have nothing to do with their respective case frames (p. 171). Verbs such as *beängstigen* can have either an AG or INSTR as their subject and some of the other verbs in this category can only have INSTR. Example sentence:

(16) Die Stille beängstigt mich

5 Corpus analysis and *be-* verbs

Günther (1974: 84) voices a number of misgivings concerning the use of corpus data in developing a taxonomy of *be-* verbs. Apart from the practicalities of gaining access to appropriate computing facilities at the time of writing in the early 1970s, his major objection relates to the coverage of corpora. He correctly points out that no corpus can be expected to contain all possible instances of *be-* verbs. He also maintains that a corpus cannot be expected to differentiate between novel and established usage, since the *be-* prefix remains productive in modern German, which therefore means that novel usage would be present in a representative corpus. He further states that inclusion of literary usage can skew the analysis, giving the example of Goethe's usage of *bespiegeln* in *Auen, die den Fluß bespiegeln...* (which, incidentally, is to be found in the Mannheim corpora) since creative usage in literature often deviates from the norm. Even in view of the fact that introspection is unavoidable when analysing *be-* verb complements, some of Günther's objections to the use of corpus data are open to question.

In a sense these objections appear to mirror those which first emerged in the early days of generative linguistics, which rejected the empiricism of corpus-based studies in favour of establishing the primacy of native speaker introspection as the source of data for the explanation of linguistic competence. Indeed, Chomsky regarded linguistic judgements based solely on corpus data as observation of performance rather than competence. Since one of the goals of generative linguistics is the modelling of competence, it is hardly surprising that performance was regarded as being of only secondary importance. The shift from empiricism (i.e. use of corpus evidence) to rationalism is discussed extensively by McEnery and Wilson (1996: 2–11), who trace the development of corpus-based methodology from its rejection in the 1950s through to its 'rehabilitation' in the early 1980s. It becomes clear from their exposition that modern corpus linguistics does not regard the corpus as sole explicandum of language and that introspection and empirical observation are not seen as mutually exclusive. In fairness to Günther, he does not voice 'ideological' objections to using corpora, which is unsurprising in the light of the use of corpus evidence in non-generative German linguistics and valency lexicography in the 1970s. In particular, he notes that frequency measurements offer a practical basis for investigation and in support he cites the work of Lipka (1972) who made extensive use of the Survey of English Usage corpus in his study of English particle verbs. Interestingly, many of Günther's comments on the shortcomings of acceptability judgements by native speakers seem unwittingly to present a case in favour of using corpus evidence. For example, he contends that his own *Sprachgefühl* may have been 'corrupted' by prolonged exposure to *be-* verbs thus allowing him to accept constructions that other speakers would deem unacceptable. Use of corpus data would certainly obviate this problem.

5.1 Corpus selection and practical application

The main corpus used in this study is the 62.9 million word 'public' corpus, held at the Institut für Deutsche Sprache (IDS), Mannheim. This is a composite of all the written language corpora held there. Content includes popular science texts from the 1960s, literature (including Goethe), 1980s newspaper and magazine articles and a newspaper monitor corpus. Literary usage was not excluded; it emerged that it represented only a small percentage of the successful searches for *be-* verbs in the written corpora, as can be seen from the sources of examples in section 5.3.2. This may be due to the fact that there is a large amount of newspaper and magazine text in some of the corpora and the presence of a newspaper monitor corpus also means that newspaper journalism is, to an extent, over-represented in the 'public' corpus. COSMAS, the standard IDS client software (see al-Wadi 1994), allows the user to select individual corpora (including the two spoken language corpora) and perform searches using a number of standard operators. In the case of the character-based software (available via telnet access) the user can export the KWIC (key word in context) displays and their contexts and optionally export statistical information relevant to the searches. Unlike, for example, the British National Corpus, the Mannheim corpora were at the time of data collection not part-of-speech (POS) tagged, so it was not possible to search for complements on the basis of POS tags. (However, the 'public' corpus has since been morphosyntactically annotated.)

5.2 Collocations

In using corpus data to validate a taxonomy of *be-* verbs, it was not sufficient to confine the analysis to measuring raw frequency of occurrences of their nominal complements, since a frequency measurement on its own reveals little or nothing about the relationship between a verb and its arguments. Raw frequency data do not tell us enough about the strength of the link between verb complements and the verbs which select them. Instead I looked wherever possible at collocations. By collocation I mean the characteristic co-occurrence patterns of certain words. There is considerable literature in the field of lexical semantics on collocation, since these patterns are invaluable for the identification and disambiguation of word senses. Contextual information provided by collocation analysis is therefore also of use to lexicographers, natural language processing systems, and those preparing language-teaching materials. It is, however, important to be able to distinguish between random co-occurrences and those collocations which are said to be statistically significant and therefore unlikely to be attributable to chance. There are a number of methods commonly used to measure the statistical significance of collocations, and detailed explanations (for the mathematically inclined reader!) of these methods with comments on their suitability for work with corpora are to be found in Manning and Schütze (1999). Useful starting points for discussion of collocations and statistical significance are McEnery and Wilson (1996) and Barnbrook (1996).

5.3 COSMAS statistical functions

The collocation analysis function which can be invoked in COSMAS[2] allows the user to analyse the statistical significance of collocations in terms of log likelihood ratio, also known in the literature as G score (referred to in COSMAS as *G-Wert*) or G square, first introduced by Dunning (1993). Extensive discussion of its usefulness and applications can be found in both Oakes (1998) and in Manning and Schütze (1999). Manning and Schütze state that 'It is simply a number that tells us how much more likely one hypothesis is than another' (p. 172). There is no absolute scale, since the value is calculated according to frequency of co-occurrence of the search term and its collocates and in relation to other words it co-occurs with; therefore knowledge of frequency is important when using such a measure; for instance the relative significance of two different collocates found in different searches cannot be compared simply by looking at the G scores. In this study statistical evidence was used to aid the interpretation of the author's findings and, although important, were not the sole guiding factor.

The numerical value given by G square (and other statistical measures) represents the degree of lexical cohesion between the search term and its collocates. The higher the value, the 'stickier' the 'glue' between words. To cite an obvious example, the values given for collocates of *Salz* in the public corpus range from 507 (41 hits from a total of 571) for *Pfeffer* and 44 for *Essig* (1 hit). These values show that the first collocation is more cohesive than the second.

5.3.1 Search strategy

Using the '& base form' operator, infinitive forms of the relevant verbs were entered (e.g. *&bedecken*) as an initial search term. The & operator generates all inflected forms of the search term, including present participles. These forms are displayed and constitute a new set of search terms. Unambiguously non-finite forms of the verbs (e.g. *bedeckend*) were then excluded from the search terms and KWIC displays were then generated. Where sufficient 'hits' were registered, a collocation analysis was invoked. G scores are not always generated; sometimes there are no results deemed by the software to be of statistical significance, in which case a value of zero is returned. Some of the searches which are outlined below were carried out on the 'public' corpus and on the newspaper corpus subset on its own for reasons of comparability.

5.3.2 Search results

Using the search strategy outlined above, infinitives from Günther's groups I–VI were entered using COSMAS. All page references are to Günther (1974).

Type I – BEDECKEN The first verb under investigation from this group is the verb *bedecken* itself. There were 949 hits in the public corpus, of which 817 were adjudged to have statistically insignificant collocates. The collocations that are deemed to be most statistically significant are, predictably, in phrases using the adjective *bedeckt* in weather reports. Other instances of *bedecken* do, however, emerge from corpus searches and confirm Günther's comments (p. 101) relating to the breadth of different meanings it and other verbs of this type, such as *behängen* and *belegen*, have. *Bedecken*, for example appears in this group twice and also appears in groups II and VII. Günther's arguments for a purely holistic reading of *bedecken* are supported by evidence from the corpus (e.g. for *bedeckt*, *beklebt*, *behängt*). In a holistic reading the entity represented by the accusative object of a verb such as *belegen* is largely or completely covered, a thesis Günther illustrates by pointing to the anomalous sentence:

(17) ? Ich belege den Tisch mit dem Buche

Consider, for example, the following:

> wir sind auf einem schmutzigen Platz (Erde und ein paar vertrocknete, rote Blütenblätter bedecken den Boden). . .
>
> *ZEIT* (1985, Kultur), 06.12.85

Complete covering of the ground is implicit, and it is clear that only plurals or mass nouns can be the subjects of this variant of *bedecken*. In this case, there were 25 hits with *Boden* as a collocate (with a G score of 71), as compared to 131 hits for *wolkig*, 118 hits for *Schnee,* and 100 hits for *heiter*. Another interesting example is to be found in the spoken language Freiburger corpus, which, despite its factual ambiguity, is still to be interpreted as a holistic reading.

> und dann kommt der Mond vorbei. und dieses Mal wird er die Sonne wenigstens bedecken zwar noch nicht ganz total. . .
>
> *Sonnenfinsternis*, Vortrag. Zweites Deutsches Fernsehen (ZDF), 5.12.1970

The verb *begrünen*, which is the label assigned to a type I subgroup, also displays some interesting behaviour. Günther's assertion that the accusative object is usually 'Boden, Anbaufläche' is confirmed by the G score of 128 for *Dächer* in the public corpus (11 hits out of a total of 127).

> Die Dächer und Fassaden der Bauten werden begrünt, soweit dies technisch möglich ist
>
> *Mannheimer Morgen*, 19.09.1989

He does not, however, predict an (admittedly rare) non-agentive subject such as that in the following example:

> Diese Kletterer begrünen die Wand ganzjährig und halten Wind und Wetter vom Mauerwerk fern
>
> *Mannheimer Morgen*, 18.11.1989

Type II – BEFLAGGEN Günther's assertion that many of these verbs only occur as a past participle is supported by corpus evidence – this is certainly the case for *beflaggen*, where no active sentences such as (11) are to be found. This is also the case for *bepflastern*, for which there were only six hits, all of which were examples of *sein*-passive. There were fifty-nine instances of *beschriften*, of which only a small proportion were to be found in active sentences of the kind cited by Günther. His example (p. 127) is:

(18) Sie beschriftet die Umschläge

and similar sentences are present in the public corpus:

> Etwa 2.000 Luftballons beschrifteten die Dasa-Beschäftigten mit Sprüchen gegen das 'Dolores'-Programm und befestigten sie dann am Werkszaun
>
> *Mannheimer Morgen*, 14.10.1995

There is some counter-evidence for the claim that the subject of the verb *beweiden* is always [–Hum] (i.e. an animal) as shown by the following:

> Sie zogen mit ihrem Vieh nach dem Süden und beweiden heute die Steppenhochländer Kenias an der Grenze nach Tanganjika hin und ihr altes Reich in Tanganjika selbst
>
> *Grzimek*, *Serengeti Darf Nicht Sterben*, Sachbuch. Ullstein Verlag, Westberlin, 1959

Type III – BEARBEITEN The verb *bearbeiten* itself proves to have a wide range of meanings, as Günther (p. 139) himself states. It is to be found in three subgroups of type III and in groups V and VI. There were 1029 hits for *bearbeiten*, but the highest G score (106) is for the collocate *Anträge*, for which there were 20 hits. This 'processing' sense of *bearbeiten* is not the variant under discussion here. Collocates of 1005 of the 1029 hits were deemed to be statistically insignificant. The variant of *bearbeiten* categorized as belonging to type III is specific to technical, medical or agricultural domains, and can be used as a substitute in those cases for a less generic verb. An example of this type III variant of *bearbeiten* is the following:

> Bodenblech, Rückwand und Schüssel werden nach hinten in den Betriebsraum geklappt und von einem ausgeklügelten Bürstensystem bearbeitet
>
> *Mannheimer Morgen*, 05.01.1989

The verb *beackern* occurs ninety-four times in the public corpus and, predictably, tends to collocate with *Feld* (G score of 110 for 14 hits), compounds including *Feld*, and nouns such as *Bio-Bauernhof*. It must, however, be noted that much of the usage found was figurative (all of the 14 hits with *Feld* for example) and should be assigned to groups V and VI; Günther includes *beackern* in these two groups. Literal usage does, however, form part of the corpus as is shown by the following:

> Rund 15 Hektar Land beackert jeder von ihnen im Schnitt, damit können sie als Gemüsebauern ganz gut leben
>
> *Mannheimer Morgen*, 28.01.1989

The occurrences of *bestrahlen*, for which there were 66 hits in the public corpus (no G score returned), confirm Günther's assertions about its usage in technical and medical domains. Indeed, many of the hits come from medical or environmental sections of newspapers. As Günther states, the accusative object of the medical variant can be animate but usually refers to the body part being treated.

> alle drei bis sechs Monate muß sie erneut operiert und bestrahlt werden
>
> *ZEIT* (1986, Medizin), 01.08.86

> wurde beispielsweise die Restbrust nicht bestrahlt, so bildeten sich bei 30 Prozent der Patientinnen binnen fünf Jahren neuerliche Krebsinseln
>
> *Mannheimer Morgen* (1986, Medizin), 06.10.86

Technical/medical usage is accounted for by Günther (although no occurences of *bestrahlen* in the sense of illumination were found), but we also now encounter a usage of *bestrahlen* which was probably not current at the time Günther was writing – that relating to broadcasting from satellites.

> die luxemburgische Societe Europeenne des Satellites (*sic.*)(SES), an der auch die Deutsche Bank und die Dresdner Bank beteiligt sind, will im September 1988 ebenfalls mit der Ariane ihren eigenen Satelliten Astra in den Himmel schießen, der mit seinen 16 mehrsprachigen Programmen halb Europa bestrahlen soll, wenn auch mit geringerer Sendeleistung
>
> *Mannheimer Morgen* (1987, Technik), 06.11.87, S. 57, 'Satellitensignale für jedermann'

Type IV – BESCHAUEN Verbs belonging to this subgroup behave in the way Günther predicts, in that an INSTR is rarely the subject and phrases referring specifically to the sense organs are tautologous and therefore seldom appear. The assertion that *beschauen* (96 hits, no G score returned) can appear in a phrase such as *mit dem X Auge* where X is a qualifying adjective is confirmed by the following:

> der Vierwaldstätter See, die Schwyzer Hocken, Flüelen und Altdorf, auf dem Hin- und Herwege nur wieder mit freiem, offenem Auge beschaut, nötigten meine Einbildungskraft, diese Lokalitäten als eine ungeheure Landschaft mit Personen zu bevölkern, und welche stellten sich schneller dar als Tell und seine wackern Zeitgenossen?
>
> Goethe *'Tag- und Jahreshefte', Hamburger Ausgabe*

Type V – BESPRECHEN Günther points out the difficulty of delimiting the type of accusative objects that occur with these verbs. His assertions regarding accusative objects of *beklagen* being [–Konkr] but often [+Hum] are supported by corpus evidence. Amongst the 2205 hits for *beklagen*, collocates of 2117 were deemed statistically insignificant, but the two nominal collocates for which a G score was returned were *Tote* with a G score of 80 (20 hits) and *Verlust* with a G score of 41 (21 hits).

> in der DDR wird nach Angaben kirchlicher Kreise in West-Berlin der erste Aids-Tote beklagt
>
> *Mannheimer Morgen* (1986, Medizin), 20.12.86

> In der Sozialistischen Partei gibt es eine Reihe von Nostalgikern, die den Verlust an 'ideologischer Substanz' beklagen
>
> *Mannheimer Morgen*, 11.07.1989

As already stated in our treatment of type III verbs, there are more occurrences of *beackern* in its figurative sense than in its literal, agricultural meaning. Consider the following:

> Wesentlich mehr Glück hatten die sechs- bis 15jährigen, die das

Feld des Verkehrs beackerten

Mannheimer Morgen, 07.04.1991

Ein neues Aufgabenfeld hat die IKSR seit vergangenem Jahr zu beackern: den Hochwasserschutz

Mannheimer Morgen, 08.03.1996

Ein lange brachliegendes Thema beackerten die CDU-Sozialausschüsse (CDA) und auch die SPD am Wochenende neu: die Bildung von Produktivvermögen in Arbeitnehmerhand

Mannheimer Morgen, 09.09.1996

Type VI – BEEINFLUSSEN Searches for verbs belonging to this group threw up a large amount of data, but there is a distinct lack of statistical significance as far as their collocates are concerned. For example, the verb *beeinflussen* occurred 1563 times in the public corpus but 1260 of its collocates were deemed statistically insignificant. It could be argued that the type VI distribution of accusative objects (i.e. [+Hum]) is to be found amongst these hits, for example:

Der 1887 in Weißrußland geborene Chagall wurde in seiner Jugend stark von der heiter-mystischen Frömmigkeit des Judentums in seiner Heimat beeinflußt

Mannheimer Morgen 27.01.1989

Of the collocates, adverbs such as *negativ* had the highest G scores (352 for 51 hits). The first nominal collocate to return a G score (71 for 23 hits) was *Entscheidungen* and the next was *Verhalten* (G score of 49 for 15 hits). These complements, however, are categorized by Günther as belonging to group VII and are semantically unrestricted in terms of their selection. On the basis of corpus evidence, these are certainly more significant than those of the variant in group VI. If we consider the 'psych' verbs *befremden* (145 hits) and *bedrücken* (219 hits) we note they do not return G scores and appear frequently in their past participle form (as is noted by Günther (p. 173)).

5.4 Benefits of corpus analysis for the classification of *be-* verbs

Although Günther gives his reasons for not using corpus data as a basis for his taxonomy, he nevertheless felt it was necessary to find a 'Sprachnorm' and to this end consulted a number of dictionaries. If he had been aiming to take frequency of occurrence into consideration, he may have found that dictionaries are not always reliable in their judgement of perceived relative frequencies. In a study of sub-corpora of the Mannheim corpora consisting of economic, technical and environmental texts, Somers and Gupta (1993) found that the frequency of valency patterns of *rechnen* predicted by valency dictionaries and conventional monolingual dictionaries did not tally with their findings. The strongest case that can be made for corpus analysis is the benefit for authors of reference works (particularly those aimed at second language learners, such as Schröder (1992)). The use of 'real' language would certainly make a change from the typical SVO sentences often found in dictionaries (admittedly less frequently nowadays, especially in learner dictionaries of English) and linguistic monographs.

6 Conclusion

It is interesting to note that Günther's intuition-led taxonomy is largely confirmed with minimal counter-evidence. He accurately predicts specialized usage and to this end it may be interesting to look at sublanguage corpora (that is, containing a constrained, domain-specific variety of language) rather than balanced corpora. Such a view is also espoused by Pustejovsky et al. (1993) who argue that homogeneous corpora may provide useful information on lexical preference. The nature of the public corpus is such that it would be possible to build sub-corpora reflecting different genres or text-types. Increased availability of larger spoken-language corpora will enhance work on *be-* verbs, since creative usage would then perhaps be more frequently encountered than in much (non-literary) written language. Finally, it should be noted that quantitative approaches to analysing corpus data (e.g. use of G scores) cannot exclude qualitative analysis; useful as statistical measures of, for example, lexical cohesion are, there is still a place for introspection – a view perhaps shared by Pustejovsky et al., who state:

> We must remember that statistical results in themselves reveal nothing, and require careful and systematic interpretation by the investigator in order to become linguistic data. (1993: 354)

Notes

1 The author wishes to thank Harold Somers, Roel Vismans, Bill Dodd, and the publisher's reader for useful comments. Any mistakes are, of course, the responsibility of the author. This work has been supported by the DAAD.

2 Note that this function was added after the publication of the handbook and is therefore not documented in al-Wadi (1994).

References

al-Wadi, D. (1994), *COSMAS Benutzerhandbuch.* Institut für Deutsche Sprache: Mannheim.

Barnbrook, Geoff (1996), *Language and Computers. A practical introduction to the computer analysis of language* (Edinburgh Textbooks in Empirical Linguistics). Edinburgh University Press: Edinburgh.

Becker, D. A. (1971), 'Case Grammar and German *be*', *Glossa* 5(1): 125–44.

Dunning, T. (1993), 'Accurate methods for the statistics of surprise and coincidence', *Computational Linguistics* 19(1): 61–74.

Durrell, Martin (1996), *Hammer's German Grammar and Usage. Third Edition.* Edward Arnold: London.

Eroms, H.-W. (1980), *Be- verb und Präpositionalphrase: Ein Beitrag zur Grammatik der deutschen Verbalpräfixe.* Carl Winter Universitätsverlag: Heidelberg.

Fillmore, C. (1968), 'The case for case' in E. Bach and R. Harms (eds), *Universals in Linguistic Theory.* Holt, Rinehart, Winston: New York, pp. 1–88.

Günther, H. (1974), *Das System der Verben mit BE-in der deutschen Sprache der Gegenwart.* Max Niemeyer Verlag: Tübingen.

Günther, H. (1986), 'Wortbildung, *be-* verben und das Lexikon', *Beiträge zur Geschichte der deutschen Sprache und Literatur* 109: 179–201.

Helbig, G. and W. Schenkel (1969), *Wörterbuch zur Valenz und Distri-*

bution deutscher Verben. VEB Bibliographisches Institut: Leipzig.

Levin, B. (1993), *English Verb Classes and Alternations – a preliminary investigation*. University of Chicago Press: Chicago.

Lipka, L. (1972), *Semantic Structure and Word-Formation. Verb-particle constructions in contemporary English*. Wilhelm Fink Verlag: Munich.

Manning, C. D. and H. Schütze (1999), *Foundations of Statistical Natural Language Processing*. MIT Press: Cambridge, MA.

McEnery, T. and A. Wilson (1996), *Corpus Linguistics*. Edinburgh University Press: Edinburgh.

Oakes, M. P. (1998), *Statistics for Corpus Linguistics*. Edinburgh University Press: Edinburgh.

Olsen, S. (1995), 'Über Präfix- und Partikelverbsysteme', *FAS Papers in Linguistics* 3: 86–112.

Pounder, A. (1997), 'The semantics of *be-* verbs in German', *Proceedings of the Annual Meeting of the Canadian Linguistics Association – Calgary Working Papers in Linguistics*: 179–91.

Pusch, L. (1972), 'Smear = schmieren/beschmieren Bemerkungen über partitive und holistische Konstruktionen im Deutschen und Englischen', in G. Nickel (ed.), *Reader zur kontrastiven Linguistik*. Athenäum Fischer: Frankfurt, pp. 122–35.

Pustejovsky, J., S. Bergler and P. Anick (1993), 'Lexical semantic techniques for corpus analysis', *Computational Linguistics* 19(2), 331–58.

Schröder, J. (1992), *Lexikon deutscher Präfixverben*, Langenscheidt Verlag Enzyklopädie: Berlin.

Somers, H. and G. A. Gupta (1993), 'A corpus-based approach to the valency analysis of sublanguage texts'. Paper read at Linguistics Association of Great Britain, autumn meeting, Bangor.

Wunderlich, D. (1987), 'An investigation of lexical composition: the case of German *be-* verbs', *Linguistics* 25: 283–331.

A corpus-based study of German accusative/dative prepositions

Randall L. Jones

The nine German prepositions that govern either the accusative or the dative case, *an, auf, hinter, in, neben, über, unter, vor, zwischen*, present an interesting study for both linguists as well as second language acquisition professionals. Unlike the German prepositions which govern only a single case, i.e. accusative, dative, or genitive, the accusative/dative prepositions can govern either the accusative or the dative case, depending on certain conditions. Reference grammars, as well as learning textbooks, often want to make the decision for the choice of the correct case appear simple: accusative if direction is suggested (*in die Stadt*), dative if it is location (*in der Stadt*). When the prepositions deal with simple spatial relationships, the decision is in fact quite straightforward. Learners of German are usually provided with a clear set of examples which illustrate the dichotomous nature of these prepositions.

Representative of the numerous German textbooks used at university level in the US are those by Terrell (1996) for the beginning level and Wells (1997) for the intermediate level. The accusative/dative prepositions are typically treated in two to three pages, mainly with examples such as the following:

an, 'on, at, near'	Sie hat das Bild an *die* Wand gehängt. Das Bild hängt an *der* Wand.
auf, 'on, on top of, at'	Die Katze ist auf *das* Sofa gesprungen Die Katze schläft auf *dem* Sofa.

hinter, 'behind'	Die Kinder sind hinter *das* Haus gelaufen. Die Kinder spielen hinter *dem* Haus.
in, 'in, into'	Frau Bachmann geht in *die* Bäckerei. Frau Bachmann kauft Brot in *der* Bäckerei.
neben, 'next to, beside'	Michael hat die Pflanze neben *den* Tisch gestellt. Die Pflanze steht neben *dem* Tisch.
über, 'above, over'	Susi hat die Lampe über *den* Stuhl gehängt. Die Lampe hängt über *dem* Stuhl.
unter, 'under, below'	Der Hund setzte sich unter *den* Tisch. Der Hund liegt unter *dem* Tisch.
vor, 'before, in front of'	Ich fuhr den Wagen vor *die* Garage. Der Wagen steht vor *der* Garage.
zwischen, 'between'	Ich setzte mich zwischen *meine* Mutter und *meinen* Vater Ich saß zwischen *meiner* Mutter und *meinem* Vater.

It is often pointed out that the accusative choice would respond to the question *wohin?* whereas the dative choice would respond to *wo?* This approach to teaching the accusative/dative prepositions is perhaps satisfactory as a first step, but unfortunately it has a number of problems. First, it leaves the impression that as a rule these prepositions define spatial relationships, i.e. 'under, next to, beside, in front of', etc. Second, it makes it appear that the relationship is generally dichotomous, i.e. there is an 'action and result' relationship between the sentence pairs, e.g. *Er fuhr den Wagen hinter die Garage* (action) and *Der Wagen steht hinter der Garage* (result). Third, most explanations do not point out that there is a significant difference in the frequency of occurrence of these nine prepositions. Some are encountered regularly while others seldom occur. Finally, it is a fact that these prepositions have numerous other meanings which do not allow the case to be predicted by a simple test as illustrated above.

Reference grammars such as Durrell (1991) and larger dictionaries such as the Oxford-Duden German Dictionary (1997) contain more complete information about the accusative/dative prepositions, but they generally list the spatial definitions first and therefore suggest at least implicitly that those are the most common uses. These reference tools are very useful, however, in providing numerous examples. Durrell is especially helpful in listing virtually every conceivable prepositional object construction containing the accusative/dative prepositions.

Folsom (1981, 1984) was one of the first to report on the complexity of German accusative/dative verbs. Based on six published frequency lists of German vocabulary as well as the LIMAS Corpus (of written German) he concluded, among other things, that the dative occurs far more frequently than the accusative, that the relative frequency of the nine prepositions is reasonably stable across the various sources (ranging from 0.53% for *hinter* to 51.14% for *in*), and that based on use the nine prepositions can be grouped into five categories:

1 intralocal/translocal (*Er liegt im Bett, Sie geht ins Haus*);
2 temporal (*Sie spielen am Freitag*);
3 prepositional object (*Er denkt an das neue Auto*);
4 adnominal (*das Buch auf dem Tisch*); and
5 adverbial (*Sie spielt in der Regel gut*).

He also lists the most common verbs that co-occur with these prepositions in either the accusative or dative case.

This paper reports on a recent study of German accusative/dative prepositions based on the Brigham Young University Corpus of Spoken German (BYU-CSG). The corpus is a collection of 400 informal and spontaneous interviews with native speakers of German from Austria, Germany and Switzerland. The interviewees represent a broad spectrum of German speakers with regard to age, gender, geography, and educational background. The interviews are approximately twelve minutes each in length and cover a variety of topics, from current events to recollections of the past. They were recorded in sixty different localities between the years 1989 and 1993. The interviews have been transcribed and the data is accessible through text retrieval programs such as Word-Cruncher and Folio Views (Jones 1997).

A corpus such as the BYU-CSG can be a useful tool for studying authentic examples of a language. A well-designed corpus is a subset of the language and therefore should reflect to a certain degree the language as a whole. Of course it is virtually impossible to construct a corpus of a spoken language that accounts satisfactorily for all demographic factors such as age, sex, education, occupation, geographical location, etc. It is also very difficult to recreate the environment in which speakers naturally communicate, and to gather samples of all types of spontaneous conversations. Although there are weaknesses in the BYU-CSG, some of which will be discussed later, it is nonetheless a reasonably valid body of data on which to base this study. It should be pointed out that in the transcription of the interviews virtually nothing was normalized, thus they reflect much of the reality of spoken language, e.g. incomplete sentences, repetition, use of rhetorical particles, grammatical errors, etc.

Using a text retrieval program such as WordCruncher it is a simple task to determine the frequency of any given word in a corpus. The frequency of the nine German accusative/dative prepositions are listed in Table 1 in ascending order. The 'raw frequency' scores in the first column need to be refined. This is due to two factors. First, some of the instances of the prepositions are not prepositions at all but other parts of speech, e.g. separable verb prefixes or adverbs. This is especially true with *an*, *auf*, and *vor*. But even more important is the fact that in spoken language speakers often repeat themselves, abandon a sentence midway, and even make errors. For example, it is not uncommon to hear a speaker say, *Das haben wir auf, uh, auf, uh, auf einem Bauernhof in Oberbayern gesehen.* Or one might hear, *Das haben wir auf, uh, das war aber wirklich schön.* Duplicate examples and examples that cannot be properly analysed have been removed, yielding the refined frequency scores in the second column.

Based on these occurrences from the corpus each preposition is analysed and classified according to meaning or usage. For the five prepositions with a raw frequency of more than 1000, the analysis was made on a random sample of at least 250 examples. The final frequency fig-

Table 1 Raw and refined frequency of accusative/dative prepositions

Prepositions	Refined frequency
hinter, hinters, hinterm	57
neben, nebenm	76
zwischen	191
unter, unters, unterm	280
vor, vors, vorm	872
über, übers, überm	1036
an, ans, am	1910
auf, aufs, aufm	2508
in, ins, im	14222

ures are then projected statistically. The prepositions are listed in ascending order of frequency, giving the number of occurrences.

HINTER–57

26 **'behind' with dative**

'Die würden nicht mal hören, wenn ein Martinshorn hinter ihnen hupen würde.'
'Wir haben hinterm Haus einen großen Garten.'
'Bleibt ja eigentlich nur noch putzen oder hinter der Kasse zu sitzen.'
'Dann standen hinter unserm Zelt eine Herde mit Bisons.'

'Sie hat es schon faustdick hinter den Ohren gehabt als Mädl.'
'Die Leute glauben, die Bedeutung und Wichtigkeit Deutschlands verstecken zu können hinter dieser kleinen popligen Hauptstadt.'
'Und wir haben das Pech, keinen Großbetrieb hinter uns stehen

zu haben.'

22 ***hinter sich bringen,* (acc.) *hinter sich haben* (dat.)**
'Ich hoffe, daß du das auch jetzt noch gut hinter dich bringst.'
'Die SPD hat eine Phase der Erneuerung hinter sich gebracht.'

'Zwei Wochen haben wir schon hinter uns, . . .'
'Also die Arbeit haben sie halt hinter sich.'
'. . . , daß wir wahrscheinlich unsre beste Zeit hinter uns haben.'

7 **'beyond, on the other side of'** (dat.)
'Das ist hinter Hanau.'
'Faszinierend ist es auch, daß gleich hinter der Grenze in Holland Holländisch gesprochen wird.'

2 **'behind' with accusative**
'Und habe mich also immer so Arme verschränkt hinter ihn gestellt?'

In the corpus *hinter* is by far the least frequent of the nine accusative/dative prepositions, occurring only fifty-seven times. Of the prepositional phrases occurring with *hinter*, forty-six are in the dative case, nine are in the accusative case, and two are not marked for case but would most likely be categorized as dative. There were ten occurrences of the contracted form *hinterm* among the total and one occurrence of *hinters*.

A few interesting facts in relation to *hinter* are worthy of discussion. First, the neat accusative/dative dichotomy is hardly evident. Eighty-four per cent of the examples are dative, and of the nine accusative examples, seven of them occur in the special construction *hinter sich bringen*. The *wo/wohin* test would be applicable in only a small number of cases, and even then it is not always a clear distinction. Furthermore, it is difficult to imagine a plausible accusative/dative relationship for most of the sentences, i.e. similar to a relationship such as *Er fuhr den Wagen hinter die Garage / Der Wagen steht hinter der Garage,* where we can easily see the 'direction' and the 'location' or the 'action' and 'result'. For example, what would be the accusative counterpart to the sentence *Die würden nicht mal hören, wenn ein Martinshorn hinter ihnen hupen würde*?

In the expressions *hinter sich bringen* and *hinter sich haben* the word *hinter* seems less an independent preposition than part of a complex verb construction, similar to *denken an* or *erzählen über*. Although *hinter mich* and *hinter mir* are, technically speaking, prepositional phrases, they don't fulfil the adverbial function that we normally expect. It is also interesting that the usual array of verbs that commonly occur with either the accusative *(stellen, legen, gehen, laufen, fahren*, etc.) or dative (*sein, stehen, sitzen, bleiben*, etc.) is not possible. It can only be *bringen* for the accusative and *haben* for the dative. Another interesting observation is the fact that eight of the twenty-six examples of dative *hinter* in the meaning of 'behind' are figurative, e.g. *hinter dem Rücken* or *sich hinter jemand verstecken*. The dative assignment as 'location' is rather simple to understand, but the relationship is not truly spatial.

NEBEN–76

55 **'besides, in addition to.'** (dat.)
'Ich arbeite also neben dem Studium bei Professor Erdmann.'
'Hast du denn da noch neben dem Muckeltheater Zeit für andere Sachen?'
'Ich habe diesen Schwerpunkt auch beibehalten können neben meiner Altgermanistik.'
'Also neben Russisch und English haben wir auch noch Französisch gelernt.'

19 **'next to'** (dat.)
'Der ist direkt neben unserem großen Zentralfriedhof.'
'Ja, Mettmann liegt also direkt neben dem weltberühmten Neanderthal.'
'Das Haus neben uns wurde abgerissen, . . .'

2 **'next to'** (acc.)
'Also wir [wissen], in welcher Art und Weise die allemanischen

Siedler . . . sich neben die Romanen ins schweizerische Mittelland gesetzt haben.'

Moving slightly up the frequency scale we come to the preposition *neben*, with seventy-six occurrences. Although there are slightly more examples of *neben* than *hinter*, an analysis of its usage is not nearly as complex. Of the seventy-six occurrences with *neben*, seventy-four, or ninety-seven per cent, are dative. There are no occurrences of contractions with *neben* and there are no verb plus prepositional object constructions. Once again, there is no clean division of accusative as direction and dative as location. The majority of examples (seventy two per cent) have the meaning, 'besides, in addition to' and are therefore dative more or less by arbitrary assignment and not because of their function in the sentence. There is no accusative counterpart to these sentences. None of the dative examples is figurative, as was the case with *hinter*.

ZWISCHEN–191

79 **'between' in the sense of relationship, comparison, involvement, etc**.

'Es ist so, daß ich lange Zeit geschwankt habe zwischen Musik und Literatur.'
'Wie ist denn die Beziehung zwischen Schülern und Lehrern an der Realschule?'
'Könnten Sie vielleicht einen Vergleich zwischen Heidelberg und Itzehoe ziehen?'
'Und auch Dialoge zwischen Autoren und ihren Figuren.'
'Und so trennst du ganz klar zwischen Arbeit und Leben?'

38 **'between' involving numerical distance, e.g. age, time, quantity, etc.**

'Also ich bügele halt dann zwischen neun und zwölf abends.'
'Diese ganzen Leute sind alle zwischen dreißig und vierzig.'
'Unterricht beginnt unterschiedlich zwischen 7 Uhr 30 und 8 Uhr.'

32 ***Unterschied zwischen, unterscheiden zwischen***
'Machen Sie einen Unterschied zwischen Ländern und Staaten?'
'Es gibt doch viele kulturelle Unterschiede zwischen England und Deutschland.'
'Ich muß zwischen Menschen und Materie unterscheiden.'

21 **'among', i.e. involving three or more objects**.
'Also es ist recht wenig Kommunikation zwischen den Nachbarn.'
'In Europa ist immer schon ein Konflikt zwischen verschiedenen multikulturellen Einheiten vorhanden gewesen.'
'Da müßt ihr zwischen Leichtathletik, Tanzen, Schwimmen, und noch anderen Sachen was aussuchen.'

17 **'between' in the sense of geographical location**
'Das ist zwischen Heidelberg und Speyer.'
'Das ist ein Ort von 3300 Einwohner zwischen Wetzlar und Gießen.'

3 **'between' (spatial) plus dative**
'Das ist heute zwischen dem Stadtmuseum und der Zicke, da war das Bergtor.'

1 **'between' (spatial) plus accusative**
'Ich lese eigentlich alles mögliche, was mir zwischen die Finger kommt.'

The preposition *zwischen* means 'between' and must by its very nature involve at least two objects. There were a total of 191 occurrences of *zwischen*, of which only one was in the accusative. Its role as an accusative/dative preposition is therefore marginal at best. It could be argued that some of the categories listed above can be combined, as they involve some kind of relationship between two or more groups. However, they were grouped as shown above because of common semantic or structural properties. Once again, we see that the usage most commonly taught in language textbooks and listed first in dictionaries and reference books, i.e. spatial relationship, is by far the least represented in the corpus.

UNTER–280

47 **'among'** (dat.)
'Und dann können sie sich nicht so benehmen, wie wenn sie nur unter Kindern sind.'
Das ist ja ein laufender Wechsel unter den wissenschaftlichen Angestellten.'
'Gibt es besondere Probleme unter besonderen Asylbewerbern?'
'Ja, weil Mageburg unter den Großstädten in der DDR ja die Stadt ist, . . .'

39 ***unter anderem*** (dat.)
Es waren ein Haufen Fragen, unter anderem hat's auch Allgemeinfragen gegeben.'
'Die Kirche ist ja unter anderem auch dafür verantwortlich, daß viele Tabus aufgestellt waren.'
'Und meine Aufgabe ist es unter anderem , diese Teile zu bestellen.

30 **'under' as a category or concept** (dat.)
'Das war sicher eine Bestrebung . . . unter dem Stichwort Emanzipation.'
'Acht Wochen nach der Geburt steht sie ebenfalls unter dieser Schutzvorschrift.'
'. . . , was im Moment ist unter dem Namen Hypertext, Hypermediensystem'

27 ***unter Umständen*** (dat.)
'. . . , und da war's unter Umständen durchaus möglich, daß ich meine Filme mitentwickelt habe.'
'Und diese Nähwerkzeuge, das dauert also unter Umständen ein Vierteljahr bis da Unterlagen erstellt worden sind.'

'Und es kommt immer noch vor, daß ich nach Düsseldorf gehe unter Umständen.'

22 ***verstehen unter, sich vorstellen unter*** (dat.)
'Das vielleicht mal so als erste Definition, was man unter modernem Leben versteht.'
'Nur, ich habe mir eigentlich unter Fijiinseln etwas anderes vorgestellt.'
'Was verstehen Sie unter kinderfreundlich zum Beispiel?'

18 **miscellaneous expressions, idioms, etc**. (dat.)
'Und wenn er dann also ständig unter Hochleistung arbeitet,...'
'Er mußte nach damaligen Erziehungsprinzipien eben unter Kontrolle gehalten werden.'
'Dortmund gehört zum Ruhrgebiet, dort wo eben viele Leute unter Tage gearbeitet haben.' (*unter Tage* = 'to work in or go into a mine')
'Die Mutter war schwerkrank, und der Vater meldete sich dann unter Tränen und weinte und weinte.'
'Die Kinder müssen so lange unter Aufsicht sein und können eben diesen Frühort besuchen.'
'Da war noch gar keine raus, war alles unter der Hand verschwunden.'
'Und unter Anführungszeichen kann man sagen, . . .'

17 **'under' in a spatial relationship** (dat.)
'Und zwar unter mir wohnt eine alte Frau, . . .'
'Das war eigentlich auch sehr schön so mal nur mit Zelt und Schlafsack bewaffnet, unter einem riesigen Sternhimmel zu übernachten.'
'Die Männer müssen halt ja notfalls unter der Brücke schlafen.'

15 **'under someone's command, supervision, direction, etc**. (dat.)
'. . . , daß sie auf der anderen Seite gewohnt haben und all die vierzig Jahre da unter diesem anderen Regime leben mußten.'
'Aber der Staat hatte gemerkt, daß das jahrelange Arbeiten in

großen Betrieben unter staatlicher Aufsicht nicht das brachte, was die Bevölkerung brauchte.'

11 ***unter Druck, unter Zwang, unter Streß*, etc.** (acc./dat.)
'Und ich setzte mich dadurch auch ein bißchen unter Druck, '
'. . . , weil wenn ich nicht unter Zwang stehe.'

11 ***leiden unter*** (dat.)
'Ich denke jeder Mensch leidet in irgendeiner Form unter den unlogischen Dingen, die in der Sprache vorkommen.'
'Die Kleinen müssen jetzt unter Steuererhöhungen leiden.'

10 ***unter Bedingungen, unter Voraussetzungen*, etc.** (dat.)
'Sie kriegt also einen ziemlich brutalen Mann und lebt unter ziemlich schlimmen Bedingungen, . . .'
'. . . , unter den schlechten Voraussetzungen, daß ich mir keinen Fehlstart erlauben durfte.'

10 **'less than' as in age, number, etc.** (acc. or unmarked)
'Die Bevölkerungsstruktur sieht so aus, daß die Hälfte der Bevölkerung unter fünfzehn Jahre als ist.'
'Man kriegt kaum eine Wohnung unter 1000, 1200 Mark.'

10 **'unter einen Hut bringen/kriegen** (acc.)
'Und das läßt sich schon rein zeitlich net unter einen Hut bringen.'
'Es ist manchmal schwer, alles unter einen Hut zu kriegen.'

9 **miscellaneous expressions, idioms, etc.** (acc.)
'Die sprachpraktische Seite fällt sehr viel unter den Tisch.'
'Das waren bestimmt zwanzig Stück, die mir so Zettel unter die Nase hielten.'
'Die fahren dann also unter Tage und gucken sich die Schlächter an.'
'Ich lese alles, was mir unter die Hände kommt außer Zukunftsromanen.'

'Wenn dieser Wirtschaftsbeitritt mal zu unüberlegt und zu leichtfertig gemacht wird, daß sicher ganze Regionen unter die Räder kommen, . . .'
'Das ist aber dann doch uns auch ein bißchen unter die Haut gegangen.'

4 **'under' in a spatial relationship** (acc.)
'. . . und mit Spiegeln fuhr man unter das Auto, um zu kucken, ob sich jemand drunterklammert.'
'Das war ihr sogar vom Arzt verboten, sich unter die Kühe zu sitzen und zu melken.'

Although the preposition *unter* has a frequency just slightly higher than that of *zwischen*, it is far more prolific in its number of usages. Again it could be argued that some of the categories could be combined; however, the sheer number of cases in each usage argues for separate listings. The number of occurrences of *unter* in the dative case is 244 or eighty-seven per cent of the total. The number of examples showing either accusative or dative spatial relationships is twenty-four or 8.5 per cent of the total.

It is interesting to compare the German preposition *unter* with its English counterpart 'under'. A corpus of spoken English would show that a large number of occurrences of 'under', most likely the majority, would be phrases such as 'under unusual circumstances', 'under 100 degrees', 'under a veil of secrecy', 'under her supervision', 'under a different heading', 'to study under a gifted pianist', 'under a new provision', 'under surveillance', 'under lock and key', etc. In some cases the German and English meanings are essentially the same.

VOR–872

348 ***vor allem, vor allen Dingen*** (dat.)
'Ich wandre sehr gern, vor allem im Gebirge.'
'Vor allem, wenn man so an Augsburg hängt und eigentlich gar net weg will.'
'Aber ich bin nicht damit einig, wie sie gegangen ist, vor allen

Dingen mit der Währungsreform.'
'Also jetzt vor allen Dingen mit der Malaria, die ja weit verbreitet ist.'
'Vor allen Dingen freue ich mich besonders, daß ich Sie dazu gebracht habe, . . .'

229 ***vor* + time in the past** (dat.)
'Ich habe auch selber in einem Chor gesungen bis vor kurzem.'
'Unser alter Goethe hatte ja schon vor 150 Jahren oder noch mehr gesagt, die Politik ist ein schmutziges Geschäft.'
'Ich habe vor zehn Jahren an der Uni gearbeitet.'
'Und da haben wir jetzt erst vor einigen Wochen Äpfel geholt.'

95 **'before' + time** (dat.)
'Aber vor den Eisheiligen soll man ja eigentlich nichts aufm Balkon pflanzen.'
'Und bei mir sind eben schon meine Eltern vorm Abitur ausgezogen.'.
'Dann muß man so kurz vor zwanzig Uhr zu den Leuten sagen, ...'
'Und Mark hat vor der Wende zum Glück noch eine Lehrstelle bekommen.'

70 **'before, in front of' spatial** (dat.)
'Also es geht halt dann nur darum, daß du vor Leuten stehen kannst.'
'Sie haben mehrere Bücher herausgebracht und hier vor uns auf den Tisch liegt Ihr neustes Werk.'
'Ich sehe es immer wieder, daß die heutige Jugend nur vorm Fernseher sitzt.'
'Und mittlerweile auch ein Festival vor der Kongreßhalle.'

59 **miscellaneous expressions** (typically dat.)
'Und ich finde es eigentlich toll, wie diese Revolution in der DDR vor sich gegangen ist.'
'. . . , daß er vor der Armee geflüchtet ist.'

'Jetzt stehen die Ferien vor der Tür.'
'Aber das Interesse ist doch größer, wenn ich vor Ort bin.'

42 ***Angst/Respekt haben vor*** (dat.)
'. . . , weil die Leute irgendwie so Angst vor dem Hund hatten.'
'Ich sehe ja den Respekt, den die jungen Menschen heute vor ihren Eltern haben.'

16 **Viertel vor zehn etc**. (unmarked, but most likely dative)
'Wir sind aber schon zwanzig vor sieben hier.'
'Kann ich bis um Viertel vor acht zu Hause bleiben, . . .'

13 **'before, in front of' spatial** (acc.)
'Weil hier der Reichstag von 1521 war, als Luther vor Kaiser Karl den Fünften getreten ist.'
'Und das sind oftmals Gefühle, die ich natürlich aufnehme, wenn ich vor die Tür gehe.'

With the preposition *vor,* the number of occurrences increases dramatically, more than three times that of *unter*. Of the occurrences, 98.5% are in the dative case and only 9.5% show spatial relationships, seventy of which are dative and thirteen accusative. Once again we find that the classical dichotomous relationship exists in only a small minority of cases. This preposition has many other usages in addition to 'before' or 'in front of'.

In view of the overwhelming number of dative constructions with *vor* it should be pointed out that all of the unmarked cases were counted as dative if they fitted the pattern of other occurrences that are clearly marked as dative. For example, the phrase *zwanzig vor sieben* is unmarked, but *zwanzig vor der Stunde* is dative and fits the same pattern. Likewise, *kurz vor acht Uhr* is unmarked but *kurz vorm Abend* is clearly dative.

It is worth noting that there were only two prepositional object constructions among the 872 occurrences of *vor*, viz. *Angst haben vor* and *Respekt haben vor*, which accounted for forty-two examples. Durrell (1991: 378) lists ten verb + *vor* constructions, e.g. *sich ekeln vor, sich fürchten vor, warnen vor, erschrecken vor*, etc., but none of these was found in the corpus.

ÜBER–1036

583 **prepositional objects, e.g. *sprechen/reden/erzählen/sich unterhalten/denken/lesen/erfahren/meinen/sich wundern* etc. + *über*** (acc.)
'Vielleicht können wir damit beginnen, daß Sie uns etwas über Ihre Familie erzählen.'
'Wir haben ja neulich schon mal gesprochen über die Proseminare.'
'Ich würde gerne mit dir über deinen Job reden, über deinen Beruf.'
'Dann unterhalten wir uns noch ein bißchen übers Wetter.'
'Wie denken Sie über die Zukunft der NASA?'
'Man liest viel über die Roma heute in der Zeitung.'
'Und man erfährt dann auch viel über andere Länder.'
'Ich wundere mich aber über den Widerspruch.'

112 ***ein Buch/ein Bericht/ein Film/eine Geschichte* etc. *über*** (acc.)
'Es gibt ein Buch eigentlich über die Wittelsbacher.'
'. . . , meistens Dissertationen über den Konjunktiv, über die Vergangenheitstemporale, über das Adjektiv und so weiter.'
'Es ist eine Geschichte über eine Universität.'
'Und dann gabs noch ein Seminar übers Problemlösen.'

81 **'through, by means of'** (acc.)
'Es kommt auch dazu, daß Sie übers Telefon direkt Kontakt mit fremdsprachigen Sprechern haben.'
'. . . , so daß es über die Krankenkasse finanziert werden mußte.'
'. . . , daß wir über die Kinder eben Eltern von anderen Kindern kennengelernt haben.'
'So müßte man das halt irgendwie über eine Vertrauensperson regeln.

64 **'over, during, throughout' in the sense of time** (acc.)
'Meine Oma ist dort geblieben in Kaufbeuren und wir sind dann übers Wochenende öfters hingefahren.'
'Das geht über den ganzen Tag.'
'Also ich halte die Schafe über den Sommer, im Herbst werden sie dann geschlachtet.'
'Ich habe ein Telefon neben meinem Bett und die Hausglocke ist in mein Zimmer geschaltet über Nacht.

61 **miscellaneous constructions, idioms, etc.** (acc.)
'Ich bringe es inzwischen nicht mehr übers Herz, Schweinefleisch zu essen.'
'Und es ist erstaunlich, in welch kurzer Zeit ein so starker Wandel da über die Bühne gegangen ist.'
'Es Wächst einem eben ab und zu mal über den Kopf.'
'Da wird dann wieder in Mark und Pfennig auch gehandelt, weil die Schriftstücke, die gehen dann auch für teures Geld über den Tisch.'
'In Berlin waren sie bekannt, aber über Berlin hinaus vielleicht gar nicht so sehr.'
'Thomas Bernhard hat Sätzte, die gehen über eine Druckseite hinweg.'

51 **'via, by way of'** (acc.)
'Es ging nichts mehr außer einem Transitweg über die Autobahn nach Berlin.'
'Und wir werden wahrscheinlich sowieso über Madrid fahren.'
'Wir sind über den Kudamm gefahren.'
'. . . , weil ich ja, um nach Zwickau zu kommen, über Leipzig mußte.'

44 **'more than'** (acc.)
'Ich glaube über fünfzig sind es sogar inzwischen.'
'Da kostet eine über 900 Mark.'
'Und es dauert über 100 Jahre, bevor der Entschluß da ist.'
'Und fast jeder fähige Mann, der über 19 ist, sollte Militärdi-

enst tun.'

29 **'across'** (acc.)
'Gleich über die Straße ein paar Meter weiter fing der Wald an.'
'Ja, über die Gleise, also über die Bahnanlage.'
'Ja die geht so vom Ulfer Bahnhof weg quer über die Donau.'
'Man geht dann zurück in die Stadt über die Brücke, über die Nydeggbrücke.'

10 **spatial relationship** (acc.)
'Das heißt fast bis zur Decke, über die Tür, in dieser Höhe.'
'Die Gaststätte ist total renovierbedürftigt, wenn die Ameisen über die Herdplatte spazierengehen.'

1 **spatial relationship** (dat.)
'Es liegt 72 Meter überm Meeresspiegel.'

The preposition *über* represents a dramatic departure from the predominant use of the dative case with accusative/dative prepositions. Only one single example, or approximately 0.1%, of the 1036 occurrences of *über* was in the dative case. About fifty-six per cent of the occurrences were in prepositional object constructions, accounting for all but two of the nineteen examples listed in Durrell (1991: 376). There were eleven examples of spatial relationships, of which ten were accusative.

The unusually high number of prepositional object constructions in the corpus is due in part to the method in which many of the interviews were initiated. The interviewer would often begin by saying something like, *Würden Sie bitte etwas über Ihre Familie erzählen*, or *Vielleicht können wir uns über Ihre Freizeit unterhalten.* This artifact resulted in a high number of prepositional object constructions as well as a frequency listing for *über* that does not reflect typical conversational usage.

AN–1910

693 **'at, on'** (dat.)
'Was für eine Vorbereitung muß man haben, hier an der PH zu

studieren?
'Und wie lange arbeiten Sie an der Universität Passau?'
'Und später habe ich aber Abitur gemacht an einer Jungenschule.'
'Ja, ich sitze an meinem Computer.'
'Ich arbeite auch am Wochenende am Evangelische Krankenhaus.'
'Das war dann eben in Simbach am Inn.'

368 **prepositional objects, e.g. *denken/glauben/sich erinnern* etc. + *an*** (acc.)
'Wenn ich jetzt an die DDR denke, . . .'
'Ich glaube an die katholische Religion ohne die Zusätze, die die Amtskirche der Religion auferlegt.'
'Kannst du dich noch irgendwie an eine ganz besondere Begebenheit erinnern?'
'Ich hatte mich mit einigen Kollegen verständigt, mich nicht ganz genau an das Kurrikulum zu halten.'

190 ***an sich, an und für sich*** (no case)
'Ich würde an sich schon lieber bevorzugen, . . .'
'Ich stamme an sich aus dem Chiemgau.'
'Damit war für mich an und für sich schon alles klar.'
'Ja ich bin an und für sich wohl zufrieden damit.'

181 **miscellaneous *an* + noun** (dat.)
'Dann haben wir einen großen Vorrat an Essenbehältern.'
'Das ist also das Besondere an diesem Haus.'
'. . . und haben noch andere Sammlungen an sehr wertvollen Schriften.'
'Und was gefällt Euch besonders an euren Lehrern?'

172 **'at, on, to'** (acc.)
'Wir sind bis nach Florida runtergefahren und dann quer durchs Land 'rüber an die Westküste.'
'In Deutschland sind sie jetzt gerade dabei, sich mit Medizin-

ern und Linguisten und Psychologen an einen Tisch zu setzen.'

163 **prepositional object, e.g.** ***arbeiten, liegen, teilnehmen*****, etc. +** ***an*** (dat.)
'Ich habe noch nie an einem Computer gearbeitet.'
'Das liegt wahrscheinlich an der Umstrukturierung.'
'Das sieht man ja jetzt an den Wahlversprechen.'
'Als mündiger Staatsbürger sollte man doch schon ein bißchen an der Politik teilnehmen.'

91 ***an*** **+ day or date** (dat.)
'Das soll stattfinden irgendwann nächste Woche an einem Samstag.'
'Das war auch an einem Novembertag.'
'Das wird heute noch gepflegt dadurch, daß an bestimmten Wochentagen plattdeutsche Erzählungen in der Zeitung stehen.'
'Das machen wir dann selber am 15. November.'

30 **noun/adjective +** ***an*** **+ noun** (dat.)
'Das ist der einzige Nachteil an dieser Lage.'
'. . . aber trotzdem weit mehr oder weit häufiger an Krebs erkrankt, als man's geglaubt hat.'
'Das finde ich also sehr vorteilhaft an Schwartau.'

17 **superlative** (dat.)
'Was hörst du denn da am liebsten?'
'Welcher Professor motiviert am meisten?'
'Ach am schönsten ist eigentlich immer noch ein bißchen mit dem Rad herauszufahren.'

5 **progressive** (dat.)
'Und dann natürlich im Moment bin ich gerade am Schreiben.'
'Ich meine, die Immobilien sind im Moment dermaßen am Steigen, daß man eigentlich nur Gewinn machen kann.'

The German preposition *an* is unusual for several reasons. First, for all practical purposes it is pronounced exactly the same, for American speakers, as the English preposition *on*, but it rarely has the same meaning. Second, it has a relatively high number of occurrences that do in fact show spatial relationships (*c*. forty-five per cent), although the relationship is sometimes not easy to define. (More on that later.) Finally, even though sixty-two per cent of the occurrences in the corpus are dative, twenty-eight per cent are accusative, thus approaching a better balance than most of the other accusative/dative prepositions. (Of the examples with *an* 190, or ten per cent, are unmarked.)

English-speaking learners of German probably have more difficulty learning to use *an* correctly than any of the other prepositions. Sentences such as *Sie studiert an der Universität, Er sitzt an dem Computer, Sie steht an der Tafel, Wir machen Urlaub am Plattensee*, all show different relationships between the subject of the sentence and the object of the preposition. In all cases the English preposition *at* could be used, but the spatial relationship is nevertheless more vague than, e.g., *hinter dem Haus, neben dem Bahnhof, unter der Brücke*, etc.

The examples *an (und für) sich, am liebsten* etc., and *am Schreiben* etc. are admittedly problematic. Technically they are prepositional phrases, but *an sich* really shows no case, and although *am liebsten* and *am Schreiben* are obviously dative, they are special constructions that intuitively seem different than the other examples of the preposition *an*. They have nevertheless been included together with the other categories.

As can be seen from the listings above, 531, or twenty-eight per cent, of the examples involve prepositional object constructions. Durrell lists fifteen prepositional object verbs with *an* plus dative and four with *an* plus accusative. All four of the accusative constructions were found in the corpus, *sich erinnern an, denken an, sich gewöhnen an* and *glauben an*, but only six of the dative, *arbeiten an, erkennen an, erkranken an, hängen an, teilnehmen an*, and *verlieren an.*

AUF–2508

737 **prepositional object, e.g. achten/reagieren/stürzen, etc. +** ***auf***

(acc.)
'Wir müssen besonders bei Pflanzenschutzarbeiten aufs Wetter achten.'
'Wir haben uns im vergangenen Jahr vor allem auf die historische Photographie gestürzt.'
'Wie bist du auf die Idee gekommen, Tai Chi zu machen?'
'Es kann aber auch sein so wie heute, daß ich auf eine konkrete Anfrage reagieren muß.'
'. . . , oder wird das sich dann nur auf Paderborn beziehen?'

596 **preposition with dative**
'Ja und die Bergmänner waren auf dem absteigenden Ast.'
'Gab's bei euch ein reges Leben auf dem Campus?'
'Bist du auch auf einer Walddorfschule?'
'Da ist man direkt mit Menschen konfrontiert, die auf der Bühne eben etwas darstellen.'
'Das kann sein, daß die das schon auf einer Diskette haben.'

572 **miscellaneous constructions, idioms, etc.** (acc.)
'Also man sollte auf jeden Fall die Hilfssprachen können der ehemaligen Kolonialherren.'
'. . . , weil auf Dauer war mir das Leben in einer Großstadt doch zu anstrengend.'
'Wobei man jetzt in Bezug auf die Statistik mehr Verbindungen machen kann.'
'Mein Gesprächspartner hat mir aufs Heftigste widersprochen.'

302 **preposition with accusative**
'Ich wußte, daß ich auf die Warteliste komme.'
'Der Weihnachtsmarkt ist wieder an seinen ursprünglichen Platz zurückgekehrt auf den Altmark in Dresden.'
'Die meisten Kinder gehen auf eine Schule, die direkt der Klinik angeschlossen ist.'
'Und wenn meine Enkelin kommt, dann will sie immer zuerst aufs Schloß.'

139 **miscellaneous constructions, idioms, etc.** (dat.)
'Allerdings hat sich meine Situation auf Grund meiner beiden kleinen Kinder geändert.'
'Aber ich finde für die Familie ist das Leben auf dem Land viel schöner.'
'Und auf der anderen Seite . . .'

103 **auf + a language** (unmarked)
'Und viele wollen auch, daß man Teile einer Vorlesung auf Französisch macht.'
'Der hat sogar auf deutsch Gesamtausgaben gekriegt.'

40 **noun/adjective + auf**
'. . . , insbesondere im Hinblick auf die Frage, wie gut man mit seinen Nachbarn auskommt.'
'Als Einzelperson habe ich nicht den Anspruch auf diese zwei Zimmer.'

19 **auf einmal** (unmarked)
'Und auf einmal ist sie gekommen und hat gesagt, . . .'

With 2508 occurrences, the preposition *auf* has a great deal in common with *an*. Of the examples twenty-nine per cent involve prepositional object constructions (cf. twenty-eight per cent for *an*), although no examples of dative were found. (Durrell lists *beharren auf, bestehen auf, basieren auf, beruhen auf*, and *fußen auf* (1991: 373).) The number of occurrences that demonstrate a spatial relationship is thirty-six per cent, compared to forty-five per cent for *an*. The relationship of accusative to dative is, however, reversed, with sixty-six per cent accusative and twenty-nine per cent dative. Unmarked examples (*auf einmal, auf deutsch*) account for five per cent.

Many of the examples showing spatial relationship have to be understood as figurative. For example, the expression *auf die Warteliste kommen* can certainly be imagined as a name on a piece of paper, but in fact the list may be in a computer or it may be in someone's mind. Likewise, *auf einer Diskette sein* may indeed involve a spatial relationship between the magnetic data and the surface of the diskette, but the semantics are not quite the same as the proverbial 'book on the table'.

IN–14 222

12 736 **preposition with dative**
'Und sie lebt in dem Altersheim.'
'Wir müssen immer drum kämpfen, daß in der Bibliothek die Ordnung aufrecht gehalten wird.'
'Ich war erst wieder in Budapest, das war auch wahnsinnig toll.'
'Einmal in der Woche wird sauber gemacht.'
'Ich erinnere mich, daß ich sehr viel Zeit in jedem Semester damit verbracht habe, Altenglisch zu lernen.'
'Ich wollte gerne mal einen längeren Aufenthalt im Ausland machen.'

1372 **preposition with accusative**
'Und wenn man es schafft, in ein sehr gutes Orchester zu kommen, . . .'
'Wenn man da auch wieder in die Supermärkte geht und was einkauft, ist man dann schon beraten.'
'Ja, ich gehe oft in Konzerte.'
'Gehen die noch in die Schule?'
'Ich bin relativ früh ins Bett gegangen.'

114 **miscellaneous expressions, idioms etc.**
'Oder kommt da noch was anderes in Frage?'
'Ich bin also ganz unwissend in Bezug auf Privatschulen.'
'Da kann man nur hoffen, daß es heute noch Eltern gibt, die versuchen, ihre Kindern in der rechten Art und Weise erziehen.'

At first blush the German preposition *in* seems at once overwhelming for its volume and amazing for its simplicity. With 14 222 it accounts for sixty-seven per cent of all the nine accusative/dative prepositions, yet it can easily be listed in three neat categories. It is also worth noting that most of the examples of *in* as a dative preposition correspond to

English *in* and many of the examples of *in* as an accusative preposition correspond to English *in* or *into*.

Further investigation reveals, however, that one could sub-classify the many occurrences of *in* in a variety of ways. For example, the majority of dative occurrences involve a geographic name, e.g. *in Amerika, in Frankfurt, in der Türkei*. That could logically be a separate category. Many of them have time references, e.g. *einmal in der Woche, im Sommer, im November*. And for many of them the spatial relationship is figurative at best, e.g. *in dem Alter, in der Geschichte, in der Freizeit*, etc. However, beyond geographic references and time expressions there are virtually no large logical categories, i.e. there would be hundreds of small ones with just a few members in each.

The category of 'miscellaneous expressions and idioms' was not subdivided into accusative and dative. This is because most of them were unmarked and would result in three very small and insignificant groups. As it is, this category is less than 0.1 per cent of the total.

Of the 14 222 occurrences with *in* approximately ninety per cent were dative and ten per cent were accusative. Most of the cases, however, do not demonstrate the basic *wo/wohin* relationship. For example, the counterpart to *in Deutschland bleiben* is not *in Deutschland fahren*, rather *nach Deutschland fahren* (although countries that use a definite article would have this relationship, e.g. *in die Schweiz fahren, in der Schweiz bleiben*.). Very few of the examples in the corpus were of the type often used to illustrate the accusative vs. dative relationship of *in*, e.g. *in die Bäckerei gehen, in der Bäckerei sein*.

Conclusion

A study of lexical and grammatical categories in a language corpus illustrates that authentic language often reveals information that is sometimes different from what is learned in pedagogical texts, reference grammars, and dictionaries. An analysis of the accusative/dative prepositions in the BYU Corpus of Spoken German is a case in point. Among the interesting findings are:

1 Contrary to what is generally assumed, the determination of case

among these prepositions is rarely based on the simple test of direction vs. location. In the majority of examples case was determined rather arbitrarily by a prepositional object construction or by special idiomatic usage. Even among the clearly defined cases of preposition plus object there was often not a clear spatial relationship between the subject and object of the preposition.

2 For all nine prepositions there is a clear imbalance between accusative and dative (see Table 2). The imbalance is especially significant for *unter*, *neben*, *zwischen*, *vor*, *über*, and *in*. Only *an* and *auf* show any kind of balance.

3 There is also a significant imbalance in the frequency of the nine prepositions (see Table 2). This disparity is not at all obvious in pedagogical texts and reference grammars. It would seem reasonable that in teaching these prepositions there should be some kind of sequencing such that the higher frequency items are taught first. Also, with the exception of the preposition *in*, the prepositional verbs and idiomatic expressions should be taught before the spatial usage, i.e. before the direction/location rule.

Table 2 Relative distribution of accusative and dative

Preposition	**% Accusative**	**% Dative**
hinter	16.0	84.0
neben	3.0	97.0
zwischen	0.5	99.5
unter	12.0	88.0
vor	1.5	98.5
über	99.9	0.1
an	28.0	62.9
auf	66.0	29.0
in	10.0	90.0

This study is just a beginning. It sheds some interesting light on a small piece of the German language, but further corpus-based study of the German accusative/dative prepositions needs to be undertaken in order to compare, e.g., spoken vs. written German as well as spoken German elicited through other techniques. A German corpus similar to the British National Corpus would be useful, as it would include spoken language recorded under a variety of circumstances. This kind of information can be helpful in the learning of German and it can also contribute to a better understanding of the complex workings of the German language.

References

Durrell, Martin (1991), *Hammer's German Grammar and Usage*. Edward Arnold: London.

Folsom, Marvin H. (1981), 'Four approaches to the dative/accusative prepositions', *Unterrichtspraxis* 4: 222–31.

Folsom, Marvin H. (1984), 'Prepositions with the dative or accusative in written and spoken German' in J. Alan Pfeffer (ed.), *Studies in Descriptive German Grammar*. Groos: Heidelberg, pp. 19–32.

Jones, Randall L. (1997), 'Creating and using a corpus of spoken German' in Anne Wichmann et al. (eds), *Teaching and Language Corpora*. Longman: London, pp. 146–56.

Oxford-Duden German Dictionary (1997). Clarendon Press: Oxford.

Terrell, Tracy D. et al. (1996), *Kontakte. A Communicative Approach*. McGraw Hill: New York

Wells, Larry D. (1997), *Handbuch zur deutschen Grammatik. Wiederholen und Anwenden*. Houghton Mifflin: Boston

Translators at play: exploitations of collocational norms in German–English translation

Dorothy Kenny

Introduction

The emergence of a corpus-based approach to translation studies is arguably one of the most promising developments in the area in recent years. The shifts in focus in translation scholarship that prepared the ground for this development have been documented by Baker (1993), while Laviosa (1998) provides a useful overview of the kind of work that is currently being undertaken in the area. Central to much of this work is the idea that there are certain tendencies that are indicative of translation behaviour and that become manifest in repeatedly observed patterns in the linguistic make-up of translated texts. One such tendency proposed in the literature is normalization, the production of target texts that are somehow more conventional (lexically, grammatically, etc.) than their respective source texts. This article focuses on lexical normalization in a specially constructed German–English Parallel Corpus of Literary Texts (GEPCOLT). It is concerned in particular with whether certain creative compounds and collocations in the German source texts are normalized upon translation into English. The study begins with a brief description of GEPCOLT and how data were selected from the corpus. A detailed analysis is then made of individual translation problem–solution pairs with a view to establishing whether source-text creativity is matched by target-text creativity. In evaluating creativity I will have recourse to lexicographical and corpus evidence for German and English,[1] and much of the analysis offered will draw on the analytical categories – including semantic preference and semantic prosody – proposed by corpus linguists to account for both routine and creativity in language use. I will conclude with a brief discussion of some of the limitations of the current approach as well as suggestions for further research.

GEPCOLT and data selection

As already indicated, the data discussed below were extracted from the GEPCOLT corpus. GEPCOLT is an electronic collection of some fourteen works of contemporary German-language fiction, alongside their translations into English. The corpus, which is described in detail in Kenny (1999a), contains roughly one million running words in each language and is aligned at sentence level using the Multiconcord multilingual concordancing package (Woolls 1997). It is currently held at Dublin City University, although many of the English-language target texts are also available to researchers via the Translational English Corpus (Laviosa 1997) web site at UMIST in Manchester.[2] GEPCOLT contains original works by German and Austrian authors, with a spread from more realist to more experimental writing.

The data discussed below are either creative compounds or collocations extracted from the German source texts in GEPCOLT. The creative compounds dealt with represent a mere handful of the thousands of hapax legomena (forms that occur only once) that were identified in GEPCOLT with the help of WordList, one of the programs in Scott's (1997) WordSmith suite of tools. They are singled out because they are considered good examples of forms that embody departures from the normal patterns of combination of their constituent morphemes. The collocations treated all involve the node AUGE. There are 1159 occurrences of this lexeme in GEPCOLT, and a concordance produced using Concord – another WordSmith tool – shows that most of them appear in unsurprising lexical company. The examples given below, however, stand out because they represent creative manipulations of the canonical forms of routine collocations. Although the data are divided into two groups below, we are dealing here with essentially the same phenomenon: the exploitation of norms of combination of free morphemes, whether these free morphemes occur as part of a compound or as independent orthographic words in what are traditionally known as 'collocations'.[3] Given this overlap, I will argue that habitual collocational relations can obtain between parts of compounds, on the one hand, and discrete orthographic words, on the other, and that such habits can be temporarily kicked by writers, usually for comic effect.

Creative compounds in GEPCOLT

(1a) provides a good example of how one manipulation of a collocational norm is used to comic effect in GEPCOLT.[4] In her novel *Violetta*, Pieke Biermann (1990: 238) refers to a group of young men who scurry out of the bushes in a sudden rainstorm, observing that they run for cover even though they do not need to keep their hair dry. In fact, the young men in question do not have any hair to talk about, but rather something resembling *Eintagebärte*, literally, 'one-day beards', on their scalps:

(1a)
bier.de P1908 S9 Sie hatten keine; bloß eine Art **Eintagebärte** auf der Kopfhaut.

(1b)
bier.en P1908 They didn't have any, just a **short one-day stubble** on the scalp.

(1a) is interesting for a number of reasons. For one, beards usually grow on men's faces, not on their scalps. Compare the English 'stubble', which refers to bristly growth on shaven legs, chins, heads, etc. More importantly, in German when a man is unshaven it is normal to say that he has a *Dreitagebart*, 'a three-day beard' not an *Eintagebart*. It is easy to find evidence for this in the Public Corpus where *Dreitagebart* is used some fifteen times – all but three corpus examples come from newspaper articles describing suspects in police investigations – although it does not appear in any of the lexicographical sources consulted.[5] Biermann uses the 'frame' (Leppihalme 1996) provided by this already lexicalized compound for the purposes of comic word-play. Biermann's creation is comical because it is so exaggerated. If normal stubble is three day's growth to a German, then one would have to have a very closely shaven head indeed to sport only one day's growth. Neither this element of hyberbole, nor the collocational clash of 'beard' with 'scalp' has been captured in the English translation of (1a). Biermann's translators, Jill

Hannum and Ines Rieder (1996: 249), have gone for a literal rendering of *Eintage*, the first part of Biermann's compound, and have eliminated the collocational clash in the original by putting 'stubble' on their skinheads' heads. While the expression 'three-day beard' does exist in English – it occurs in Hitchcock's 1954 film *Rear Window* – it is perhaps too obscure to sustain a pun that would reflect Biermann's *Eintage-bärte*. Biermann's translators could have exploited another expression – 'five o'clock shadow' springs to mind – for comic effect, but they opted instead for normalization.

Semantic preference

In example (1a) it is clear that there has been a simple swap in a familiar compound of one free morpheme, *Ein*, for another, paradigmatically related one, *Drei*. (1a) can thus be considered as a straightforward case of lexical substitution (Partington 1998: 126). The analysis of (2a), also from Biermann's *Violetta*, is slightly less straightforward, requiring as it does a degree of abstraction that allows us to talk about the semantic preferences of words.[6] Here Biermann (1990: 35) uses the novel compound *stöckelschuhfreundlich* when complaining that a particular Berlin underground station is not 'high-heel-friendly':

(2a)	(2b)
bier.de P229 S7 Und auch nicht **stöckelschuhfreundlich** genug.	bier.en P229 And it wasn't **high-heel-friendly** either.

At first glance this compound may not appear particularly startling: the adjective *freundlich* can, after all, be used in conjunction with a variety of nouns to create compounds of the form *X-freundlich* meaning, roughly, well disposed towards, good for, or at least not damaging to, X. Such is the combinability of *-freundlich* with nouns that Russ (1994: 231) describes it as a 'suffixoid', a morpheme that lies somewhere between a free and a bound form. *-freundlich* is thus very common as a combining form in German, yet *stöckelschuhfreundlich* in (2a) strikes the reader as somehow humorous. In order to tease out why this might be the case, it is worth looking at lexicographical descriptions of *-freundlich* and other instances of its use in naturally occurring text.

Langenscheidts Großwörterbuch Deutsch als Fremdsprache, for example, gives the following useful information:

> **-freundlich** *im Adj, begrenzt produktiv*; **1** mit e-r positiven Einstellung zur genannten Person / Sache « -feindlich; **kinderfreundlich** <e-e Gesellschaft>, **menschenfreundlich** <e-e Gesinnung>, **regierungsfreundlich** <Truppen> **2** für die genannte Person / Sache gut « -feindlich; **arbeitnehmerfreundlich**, **familienfreundlich** <ein Gesetz>, **umweltfreundlich** <ein Produkt>

What is noticeable in this entry is that although *-freundlich* is defined as meaning well-disposed towards or good for the named person or thing, in all but one example (*umweltfreundlich*, 'environment friendly') it is persons, not things, who are the beneficiaries of whatever it is that is *freundlich*.[7] Thus the prototypical use of *-freundlich* as identified by lexicographers is in compounds that describe something as being good for humans, in one form or another.

Turning now to corpus evidence, just under 2500 instances of the combining form *-freundlich* were downloaded from the Public Corpus, including around 200 instances of nouns derived from adjectives containing *-freundlich*, that is, of the form *X-freundlichkeit*. Just under half of the total is accounted for by the lexeme UMWELTFREUNDLICH, and there is a group of semantically related lexemes including, for example, RECYCLINGFREUNDLICH. Many of the remaining instances tend to involve groups of people on the one hand, as in FAMILIENFREUNDLICH, 'family friendly' (115 adjectival uses), and KINDERFREUNDLICH, 'child friendly' (130 adjectival uses, 30 nominal), RUSSENFREUNDLICH, 'Russian friendly', POLENFREUNDLICH, 'Pole friendly' (two each); or individuals, on the other: CHIRAC-FREUNDLICH, DE-GAULLE-FREUNDLICH, JELZIN-FREUNDLICH (one each). *-freundlich* also combines with abstract nouns like INVESTITION, 'investment', and INNOVATION, to form compounds that indicate the thrust of some agent's policies, as well as with a group of nouns including PFLEGE, REPARATUR, and WARTUNG, to indicate that a product is easy to care for, repair, or maintain. There are very few instances of non-human concrete nouns combining with *-freundlich*.[8] Data from both lexicographical sources and the corpus thus indicate that people and the environment are given pride of place when it comes to combining with *-freundlich*, but that the latter also tends to combine with certain other groups of semantically related, usually abstract, nouns.

Exceptions to this rule-of-thumb in the Public Corpus include BUS-FREUNDLICH, 'bus friendly' (nine instances), and LKW-FREUNDLICH, 'truck friendly' (one instance), which refer either to the convenient access to local transport of certain tourist hotels, or to transport policy in general; and, more notably, BANANENFREUNDLICH. The latter, 'banana friendly', occurs in a newspaper article in the segment: *Zwei Jahre ist es her, da ging die wunderbare "bananenfreundliche" Zeit zu Ende. Anfang Juli 1993 hebelte Brüssel den freien Bananen-Welthandel aus.* 'The wonderful "banana-friendly" days came to an end two years ago when Brussels put a stop to free world trade in bananas' (my translation). The oddness of the form *bananenfreundliche* is emphasized by the use of inverted commas around it. I would like to suggest here that this form is unusual for the same reason that Pieke Biermann's use of *stöckelschuhfreundlich* is unusual: the latter example involves the combination of *-freundlich* with a non-human concrete noun, when *-freundlich* seems to have a semantic preference for people and the environment, and certain sets of abstract nouns. Biermann, like the creator of the lexeme BANANENFREUNDLICH, creates a comic effect by combining *-freundlich* with a far less noble partner than normal: mundane high-heeled shoes.

The English combining form *-friendly* seems to have the same sort of semantic preferences as its German counterpart. The *Collins English Dictionary* entry for this form is as follows:

> **-friendly** *adj. combining form.* helpful, easy, or good for the person or thing specified: *ozone-friendly*.

Evidence from the British National Corpus suggests that this combining form is used most commonly in combinations related to the environment: out of just over 400 instances of 'X-friendly' in the BNC,[9] there are 15 instances of 'eco-friendly', 99 of either 'environmentally-friendly' or 'environment-friendly', and 31 of 'ozone-friendly'. Most other uses refer to benefits to people; the most common example being 'user-friendly', which appears some 125 times in the BNC, especially in connection with consumer goods such as computers. There is also a subset of uses in which something is described as being 'friendly' to some kind of animal, and wildlife in particular, a use that is arguably related to the environment. Even examples like 'car-friendly' (1 occurrence) and 'cycle-friendly' (3 occurrences) can be grouped under the environment heading. There is an interesting set of examples related to the music industry (chart-, club-, dance-, FM-, Hacienda-, indie-, MTV-, NME-, radio-, rave-, studio-friendly), many of which appear to come from popular music magazines, and a smaller set related to the media in general (lens-, media-, television-friendly). Thus the combining form '-friendly' seems to have been embraced in particular by text producers in areas such as the environment, consumer goods, and music journalism. Like its German counterpart, however, it does not combine readily with non-animate concrete nouns that do not refer to the environment (or the music industry) in some shape or form. This makes 'high-heel-friendly' (Hannum and Rieder 1996: 30) as odd in English as *stöckelschuhfreundlich* is in German. Biermann's translators thus exploit the preferences of '-friendly' in much the same way as Biermann exploits the semantic preferences of *-freundlich*, and in doing so they avoid normalization in their translation of Biermann's creative hapax form.

Semantic prosody

As was the case with semantic preference, any discussion of semantic prosody (Louw 1993) requires us to move from the actual words on the page to more abstract notions of the *kind* of collocate a lexical item typically occurs with. If those collocates are predominantly negatively or positively evaluated by speakers, then this can rub off on the lexical item in question. We could argue, for example, that BAJONETT becomes imbued with a negative prosody by virtue of its contact with lexemes like ANGRIFF, 'attack', and LEICHE, 'corpse', in the Public Corpus, not to mention its occurrence in such gruesome contexts as the following, from the same source (translations are my own):

ein blutrotes Plakat, das ein auf ein Bajonett aufgespießtes Baby ...	a blood-red poster, with a baby speared by a bayonet ...

die von Krüppeln, zermanschten Leichen, Bajonetten, uniformierten Sadisten ...

by cripples, mashed corpses, bayonets, uniformed sadists ...

If BAJONETT is deemed to have negative semantic prosody, then its co-occurrence with the seemingly neutral *Andenken* in (3a), taken from Elfriede Jelinek's *Die Ausgesperrten* (1980: 205) can be regarded as something of an oddity:[10]

(3a)
jelinek2.de P543 S6 Halt, Anni, ich weiß etwas, um das klägliche Ergebnis zu verbessern, nämlich das **Andenkenbajonett** unseres Vaters, das er wiederum von seinem eigenen Vati hat, man glaubt nicht, daß dieses Ungeheuer Eltern besitzt, die es einmal geboren und gezeugt haben, er hat aber doch, Beweis: das Bajonett, welches noch aus dem Ersten Weltkrieg stammt.

(3b)
jelinek2.en P543 Hang on, Anni, I know how we can make it look less pathetic, Father's **souvenir bayonet**, which he in turn had from his Dad, you wouldn't believe this monster had parents who begat it and gave birth to it once upon a time, but he did, the bayonet is the proof, it dates back to the First World War.

If we consider compounds in the Public Corpus containing the form *Andenken* in first position (there are nineteen in all), we can see that they usually pertain either to some kind of commercial activity as in *Andenkenverkäufer*, 'souvenir sellers' and *Andenkenladen*, 'souvenir shop', or to photos (*Andenkenbilder*) sold in such shops. *Andenken*, as it occurs in the Public Corpus, can be said to combine with fairly neutral collocates related to commerce. The combination of *Andenken* with *Bajonett* in (3a) is thus unexpected given the normal behaviour of the former, and might call for a special interpretation. The association of a bayonet with the souvenir industry establishes an incongruity, a clash of prosodies that is perhaps intended to reveal a perversion in the psyche of the father in Jelinek's novel. The same disturbing clash of prosodies is evident in Michael Hulse's (1990: 196) English translation in (3b):

data from the British National Corpus would suggest that 'souvenir' usually collocates with lexemes such as SHOP and SELLER, although one instance of 'souvenir' in the BNC has the same gruesome quality as *Andenkenbajonett*, namely when it is in collocation with the form 'shrapnel' in a *Daily Mirror* article.

(4a) contains another example of a clash of prosodies, this time involving the intensifier *stink-* and the adjective FREUNDLICH in Biermann's *Violetta* (1990: 88):

(4a)	(4b)
bier.de P691 S3 Er versuchte ein **stinkfreundliches** Lächeln, aber es blieb im Schmerz stecken.	bier.en P691 He attempted a **super-friendly** smile, but it faltered because of the pain.

In *Langenscheidts Großwörterbuch Deutsch als Fremdsprache* (Götz et al. 1997), the use of the intensifier *stink-* is summarized as follows:

> **stink-** im Adj, begrenzt produktiv, gespr pej; verwendet, um bestimmte Adjektive zu verstärken » sehr; **stinkfaul, stinkfein** (=übertrieben vornehm), **stinklangweilig**, **stinknormal**, **stinkreich**, **stinkvornehm**, **stinkwütend**

Stink- is thus characterized by lexicographers as a morpheme of limited productivity used pejoratively in spoken language to intensify certain adjectives. The examples given translate roughly as 'bone idle', 'dead posh', 'deadly boring', 'boringly normal', 'stinking rich', and 'raging'. A concordance of the morpheme *stink-* in the Public Corpus reveals just how common these compounds are: STINK(E)SAUER occurs forty-three times; STINKNORMAL seventeen times; STINKLANGWEILIG eight times; STINKREICH four times; and STINKFAUL once. Three other instances of *stink-* occur in the Public Corpus, namely in the compounds STINKBOURGEOIS, STINKKONSERVATIV, and STINKREAKTIONÄR, all of which come from a single source that aims to illustrate the use of such intensifiers in political discourse. What is remarkable about the data supplied both by lexicographical sources (the *Collins German Dictionary* (Terrelletal 1997) also lists all the *Langenscheidt* examples with the exception of STINKFEIN) and the corpus, is that many of the adjectives intensified by *stink-* already describe unpleasant attributes. Given that *stink-* regularly co-occurs with such adjectives, its association by text producers with other adjectives describing less obviously negative attributes inevitably reveals such text producers' negative evaluation of richness, finery, etc., states that may be considered excessive or distasteful. This is the case with Biermann's description of a character's smile as STINKFREUNDLICH. While friendliness would not normally be presented as a negative characteristic, it is clear that in this case the sincerity of the attempted friendly smile is very much in doubt.

Hannum and Rieder's translation of *ein stinkfreundliches Lächeln* is 'a super-friendly smile' (1996: 87). Here the translators have chosen to use the prefix 'super-' to intensify the adjective 'friendly'. The *Collins English Dictionary* describes this use of the prefix 'super-' as indicating that something is 'beyond a standard or norm', and suggests as synonyms 'exceeding' and 'exceedingly'. The character in Biermann's novel thus attempts an exceedingly friendly smile, but is it an *excessively* friendly smile? Evidence from the British National Corpus suggests that 'super-' is used to intensify predominantly positive adjectives such as 'clean', 'confident', 'efficient', 'smooth', 'snug' and 'strong'.[11] Its use in advertising texts, in particular in combinations like 'super deluxe' and 'super luxury', also suggests that 'super-' is used to portray objects referred to in a very positive light. The prefix 'super-' carries none of the negative prosody that the German *stink-* would appear to have. The translation of *stinkfreundliches Lächeln* as 'super-friendly smile' thus captures the intensity, and perhaps exaggerated nature of the smile (given the circumstances in which the character smiles; he is, after all, in pain), but it does not embody a clash of prosodies like Biermann's creative compound does, and so does not represent as disruptive a 'switch point' (Sinclair 1991: 114) as the original author's word choice.

Creative collocations in GEPCOLT

The kind of analysis applied thus far to compounds in GEPCOLT can, of course, be extended to multiword collocations in the corpus. In (5a), for example, Biermann (1990: 144) again uses lexical substitution to humorous effect, this time within a familiar collocation. In this case Lang, a police officer, boasts of the quality of intelligence gathered by his department. Their information is better than that supplied by *die Jungs mit den zwei linken Augen*, literally 'the boys with the two left eyes':

(5a)	(5b)
bier.de P1175 S2 »Ich sag dir doch, wir sind besser als die Jungs **mit den zwei linken Augen**.	bier.en P1175 "I told you, we're better than the boys **with two left eyes**.

Lang's assertion is a play on the conventional collocation ZWEI LINKE HÄNDE HABEN, 'to have two left hands', a colloquial expression that means 'to be clumsy'.[12] The canonical form of this conventional collocation is manipulated through a process of substitution of *Augen* for *Händen*. Biermann thus exploits a common collocation used to indicate lack of dexterity to suggest that some of Lang's peers lack skill in observation. Hannum and Rieder's translation (1996: 147) is literal, and difficult to interpret, given that the only analogous conventional collocation in English against which the reader can evaluate 'two left eyes' is the expression 'two left feet'. Although the latter is a common collocation in English,[13] it is so associated with lack of dancing skill that it does not spring to mind easily in the context of a police investigation. The translation in (5b) cannot be said to recreate the effect of the unusual source text collocation, as it is not obvious what canonical form of what collocation, if any, is being exploited, and so readers of the translation cannot share the 'smugness effect' (Partington 1998: 140) enjoyed by readers of the original upon recognition of the manipulation of a familiar collocation. At the same time, the collocation 'with two left eyes' is remarkable in itself, and so it is difficult to speak of lexical normalization here.

In (6a), taken from Erich Loest's *Völkerschlachtdenkmal* (1984), lexical substitution is evident once more:

(6a)	(6b)
loest.de P57 S12 Ein Volksstamm mußte **sämtliche Augen zudrücken**.	loest.en P57 A whole tribe had to **turn a collective blind eye**.

In this case, the canonical form of the collocation is EIN AUGE ZUDRÜCKEN, literally 'to close an eye', or the more emphatic BEIDE AUGEN ZUDRÜCKEN, 'to close both eyes', both conventionally translated into English as 'to turn a blind eye'.[14] In (6a) Loest (1984: 26) uses hyperbole to poke fun at the Saxons who chose to 'close *all* eyes' (*sämtliche Augen*) to the fact that they had fought on the side of the vanquished in the Battle of the Nations, and so to the fact that they had collaborated with the Napoleonic forces. In so doing, they obviate the need for 'de-Napoleonification' of their territory. In the context of a book that follows the fortunes of Leipzig from the early 1800s through to the Nazi era and its aftermath, with its attendant concern with de-Nazification, the satirical tone is clear. It should be noted here that Loest's collocation is not completely novel: it occurs four times in the Public Corpus, twice in a single work by Heinrich Böll (*Ansichten eines Clowns*), and once in two separate newspaper articles from the 1990s. Nevertheless, the use of *sämtliche Augen* can be considered as marked, given the dominance of the canonical form EIN AUGE ZUDRÜCKEN and the availability of the more emphatic BEIDE AUGEN ZUDRÜCKEN. Loest's translator, Ian Mitchell (1987: 18), translates *sämtliche Augen zudrücken* with a similarly marked collocation formed by inserting the modifier 'collective' into the normally fixed expression TURN A BLIND EYE.[15] The result, (6b), like (6a), emphasizes the massive scale of the collusion involved in ignoring inconvenient aspects of the recent past. Mitchell's target text collocation is as marked as the source text one; normalization does not take place.

In example (7a) the canonical form of a familiar collocation is manipulated in another way, namely through a process of 'rephrasing' (Partington 1998: 127) or 'transposition' (Baker and McCarthy 1990):

(7a)	(7b)
bier.de P2 S1 **DAS GESETZ DES AUGES**	bier.en P2 **THE LAW OF THE EYE**

(7a) is the title of the 'prelude' to Biermann's *Violetta* (1990: 9). In this short chapter, an eye witness gives a necessarily selective account of events surrounding an assault on a young man in Berlin. Given the co-text, the title can be taken at face value, but most readers of the German text will recognize that it is also an inversion of *das Auge des Gesetzes*, literally 'the eye of the law', an informal, but conventional name for the police.[16] Knowledge of the canonical form of this common collocation may force the German reader to posit extra motivation for its manipulation. Given that in the novel the police hunt a mysterious serial killer, who is also a photographer and hence concerned with what can be suggested to the eye, the German reader may infer, even retrospectively, that the conflict between the forces of law and order and the photographer in question finds expression in the competition between norm and exploitation in the heading *Das Gesetz des Auges*. Similarly, Hannum and Rieder's translation (1996: 1) can be considered a manipulation of the collocation '(in) the eyes of the law', although the allusion to this familiar collocation might have been more effective had the translators left the lexeme EYE in the plural. This said, in both original and translation there is competition between the canonical form of a collocation, and the manipulated form that replaces it, and this helps to set up a tension that will underlie the entire detective story.

Conclusion

This study has been concerned with the question of how a number of creative compounds and collocations have been translated into English, and in particular with whether they were normalized upon translation. A crude summary of the discussion so far would suggest that in two out of the seven cases dealt with, normalization did indeed take place, but it would be foolhardy to generalize from such a small sample to the whole of the corpus, or, for that matter, to German–English literary translation in general.[17] Nor do I wish to suggest that a study of lexical patterns that is limited to hapax legomena and collocations involving a single node can hope to account for all the lexical creativity in a parallel corpus. It is clear that the type of investigation reported on here would have to be extended to cover, for example, forms that occur more than once in GEPCOLT but whose distribution in the corpus is remarkable in some other way (they might appear in the writings of only one author for instance), and collocations involving other, common and uncommon, nodes, before we could begin to have anything like a full picture of lexical creativity in GEPCOLT. These extensions are obvious candidates for future research. What studies such as the present one make clear, however, is that translation-oriented investigations of lexical creativity can benefit greatly from both the use of comparative corpus evidence and the integration of corpus-linguistic notions of collocation, semantic preference and semantic prosody, and that these concepts can find application below as well as above word level.

Notes

1 The lexicographical sources consulted for the purposes of this research are the Wahrig (1986) *Deutsches Wörterbuch*, *Langenscheidts Großwörterbuch Deutsch als Fremdsprache* (Götz et al. 1997), the *Collins German Dictionary* (Terrell et al. 1997), and the *Collins English Dictionary* (1994). The corpora used to provide comparative data for German and English are contained in the Public Corpus of the Institut für Deutsche Sprache (al-Wadi 1994), which contains nearly 63 million words of written German, and the 100 million word British National Corpus (Aston and Burnard 1998).

2 UMIST's URL is <http://www.umist.ac.uk/>.

3 The 'traditional' understanding of collocation referred to here can be defined as 'the occurrence of two or more words within a short space of each other in a text' (Sinclair 1991: 170). But while analysts of English collocations are mostly concerned with syntagmatic relations that hold between discrete orthographic words, linguists dealing with German and Dutch have maintained that collocational relations may obtain between elements below the level of the orthographic word. See, for example, Lehr (1996: 139–40) who treats *ad hoc* German compounds as collocations, and van der Wouden (1992: 452–4) who argues that collocational analysis can be applied even to lexicalized noun-adjective compounds in Dutch.

4 As is the case with all aligned source- and target-text segments given in this article, (1a) and (1b) were produced using Multiconcord. The software's display options allow segments to be preceded by the name or number of their host file, paragraph and sentence.

5 The *Collins German Dictionary* entry (Terrell et al. 1997) for BART does, however, include *ein drei Tage alter Bart*, which it translates as 'three day's growth (on one's chin)'.

6 The 'semantic preference' of a lexical item can be described as its tendency to co-occur with other lexical items that share a particular semantic feature (see, for example, the discussion of the idiom NAKED EYE in Sinclair 1996).

7 Such persons are designated by the words *Kinder*, 'children', *Menschen*,

'people', *Regierung*, 'government', *Arbeitnehmer*, 'employees', and *Familien*, 'families'.

8 There is a small set of adjectives, such as ZAHNFREUNDLICH, RÜCKENFREUNDLICH, KREUZFREUNDLICH and AUGENFREUNDLICH, that indicate that something (for example, a product or sitting position) is good for or easy on a human being's teeth, back or eyes. These are considered here as still referring to humans, albeit a part of them.

9 There are 404 instances of 'X-friendly' in the BNC. A further ten instances of 'X-unfriendly' are ignored here.

10 *Bajonett* might, of course, be considered a 'negative' word even before its collocates are considered. As a weapon it might automatically be negatively evaluated by many native speakers.

11 'Super-' is also used very frequently as an intensifier in sports, in particular boxing ('super lightweight', 'super middleweight', etc.) and skiing ('super giant slalom'), where it further specifies the class in which athletes compete.

12 The German expression is listed in the *Wahrig Deutsches Wörterbuch* (1986), and is found five times in the Public Corpus.

13 'Two left feet' occurs sixteen times in the BNC. On two occasions it is the name of a racehorse; on five, the name of a film. In the remaining nine cases it describes the predicament of a person who cannot dance very well.

14 Both *ein Auge zudrücken* and *beide Augen zudrücken* are listed in the *Collins German Dictionary* (Terrell et al. 1997) and *Langenscheidts Großwörterbuch Deutsch als Fremdsprache* (Götz et al. 1997). The former expression occurs thirty-nine times and the latter eighteen times in the Public Corpus. There are also four variations on the second expression: *die Augen zugedrückt*, *zwei Augen zudrücken*, *ein Paar Augen zudrückte*, and *meine Augen zugedrückt*.

15 There are 157 instances of TURN A BLIND EYE in the BNC, the overwhelming majority (149) of which appear in the canonical form. Of the remaining eight, two are contractions (e.g., 'UN 'will not turn blind eye to rights violations'), three demonstrate grammatical substitution (Partington 1998:126) in the replacement of 'a' by 'the' or 'that' (e.g., 'nobody here today can turn that blind eye'), one is a nominalization ('the blind eye treatment'), and two involve the insertion of modifiers ('many others turned a conveniently blind eye to their arms merchants' activities' and 'they are hoping that the authorities will turn their customary blind eye').

16 *Das Auge des Gesetzes* is listed in all the lexicographical sources consulted, and occurs fifteen times in the Public Corpus.

17 The examples of source-text creativity dealt with in this paper are actually taken from a more extensive study of lexical normalization in GEPCOLT (Kenny 1999), in which it was found that normalization was a feature of the translation of creative hapax legomena in the corpus (occurring in fifty

two (44%) of 117 cases investigated), but was uncommon given creative collocations involving the node AUGE (occurring in six (16%) of thirty seven cases).

References

al-Wadi, Doris (1994), *COSMAS Benutzerhandbuch.* Institut für Deutsche Sprache: Mannheim.

Aston, Guy and Lou Burnard (1998), *The BNC Handbook: Exploring the British National Corpus with Sara.* Edinburgh University Press: Edinburgh.

Baker, Mona (1993), 'Corpus linguistics and translation studies. Implications and applications', in Mona Baker, Gill Francis and Elena Tognini-Bonelli (eds), *Text and Technology: in honour of John Sinclair.* John Benjamins Publishing Company: Amsterdam and Philadelphia, pp. 233–50.

Baker, Mona and Michael McCarthy (1990) 'Multi-word units and things like that', unpublished research paper, Birmingham: University of Birmingham.

Biermann, Pieke (1990) *Violetta.* Rotbuch Verlag: Berlin.

Collins English Dictionary (1994), 3rd edn. HarperCollins Publishers: Glasgow.

Götz, Dieter, Günther Haensch and Hans Wellmann (eds) (1997), *Langenscheidts Großwörterbuch Deutsch als Fremdsprache* 8th edn. Langenscheidt KG: Berlin and Munich.

Hannum, Jill and Ines Rieder (1996), *Violetta.* Serpent's Tail: London and New York.

Hulse, Michael (1990), *Wonderful, Wonderful Times* Serpent's Tail: London.

Jelinek, Elfriede (1980), *Die Ausgesperrten* Rowohlt Verlag GmbH: Reinbek bei Hamburg.

Kenny, Dorothy (1999) 'Norms and creativity: lexis in translated text' Unpublished Ph.D thesis, UMIST.

Kenny, Dorothy (1999a) 'The German–English Parallel Corpus of Literary Texts (GEPCOLT): a resource for translation scholars', *Teanga* 18: 25–42.

Laviosa, Sara (1997), 'How comparable can 'comparable corpora' be?',

Target 9(2): 289–319.

Laviosa, Sara (ed.) (1998), *L'approche basée sur le corpus/The corpus-based approach*. Special issue of *Meta* 43 (4).

Lehr, Andrea (1996), *Kollokationen und maschinenlesbare Korpora: Ein operationales Analysemodell zum Aufbau lexikalischer Netze*. Niemeyer: Tübingen.

Leppihalme, Ritva (1996) 'A target-culture viewpoint on allusive wordplay'. *The Translator* 2(2): 199–218.

Loest, Erich (1984), *Völkerschlachtdenkmal*. Hoffmann und Campe Verlag: Hamburg.

Louw, Bill (1993), 'Irony in the text or insincerity in the writer? The diagnostic potential of semantic prosodies' in Mona Baker, Gill Francis and Elena Tognini-Bonelli (eds), *Text and Technology: in honour of John Sinclair*. John Benjamins Publishing Company: Amsterdam and Philadelphia, pp. 157–76.

Mitchell, Ian (1987), *The Monument*. Martin Secker & Warburg Ltd: London.

Partington, Alan (1998), *Patterns and Meanings: using corpora for English language research and teaching*. John Benjamins Publishing Company: Amsterdam and Philadelphia.

Russ, Charles V. J. (1994), *The German Language Today*. Routledge: London and New York.

Scott, Mike (1997), *WordSmith Tools version 2.0*. Oxford University Press: Oxford.

Sinclair, John (1991), *Corpus, Concordance, Collocation*. Oxford University Press: Oxford.

Sinclair, John (1996), 'The search for units of meaning', *Textus* IX: 75–106.

Terrell, Peter, Veronika Schnorr, Wendy V. A. Morris and Roland Breitsprecher (eds) (1997), *Collins German Dictionary* 3rd edn. HarperCollins Publishers: Glasgow and New York:

van der Wouden, Ton (1992), 'Prolegomena to a multilingual description of collocations' in Hannu Tommola, Krista Varantola, Tarja Salmi-Tolonen and Jürgen Schopp (eds), *Euralex '92 Proceedings*, studia translatologica ser. A. vol. 2. Department of Translation Studies, University of Tampere: Tampere, pp. 449–56.

Wahrig, Gerhard (1986), *Deutsches Wörterbuch*. Mosaik Verlag: Munich.
Woolls, David (1997), *Multiconcord version 1.5*. CFL Software Development: Birmingham.

'Die schöne Geschichte': a corpus-based analysis of Thomas Mann's *Joseph und seine Brüder*

Ann Lawson

Preliminary remarks

Since form and content are inherently linked in language, it would seem essential for any study of literature to pay close attention to textual and linguistic evidence. This paper explores the practical role of analysis techniques from corpus linguistics in literary studies. While it is now commonplace for corpus analysis to be used in linguistics, language teaching and lexicography, computational methods are still a relatively new line for investigations in literature teaching and research. Methods of analysing text adapted from the sphere of computational linguistics can, however, highlight many aspects of language, especially language patterning, not only more quickly and efficiently, but also more accurately and objectively than human readers. Through corpus linguistics and the sophisticated tools it offers, we can now gain access to unprecedented insights into the linguistic patterning of literary works.

This paper has arisen from my earlier research on Thomas Mann's great novel of the 1920s and 1930s, *Joseph und seine Brüder* (*Joseph*) (Lawson 1995). This was based on a 'traditional' reading of the text. My initial investigation led inevitably to more questions, particularly regarding the status of the work in the context of Mann's political engagement during the time of writing. *Joseph* is Mann's response to and reckoning with the political and socio-historical trends of the time. A large index of file-cards with repeated themes, images and phrases, while invaluable as a preliminary resource, highlighted the subjective, even random nature of such manually undertaken studies. If a word, phrase or image attracted sufficient interest upon reading page 1500 of the novel, a new card was started. If the word occurred again and if I remembered that it might be interesting, I could manually add the new example context to the record. However, all previous occurrences of that word or phrase would be lost to me. Potentially, a new reading of the text would be necessary on each new discovery of something interesting. Clearly, extremely painstaking reading would be necessary to ensure that nothing slipped through the net which had been woven by these manual searches. I realized after immersion not only in Mann's writing but in some of his extensive reading that the phrases which attracted my attention were sometimes not found elsewhere in his text, but rather in the author's reading. Koopmann has already pointed out the echo of Edgar Dacqué's *Urwelt, Sage und Menschheit* in the opening line of the novel (Koopmann 1984: 81), but other echoes and partial quotes abound throughout.

While the indexing of file-cards described above could feasibly be undertaken manually, the scale of Mann's work and his extensive reading would make it a lifelong and wearying task. It makes sense to leave repetitive and tedious tasks to machines which cannot become weary, careless or disheartened. Quantities of text can quickly be analysed on a scale and with an accuracy not otherwise feasible. But corpus research is more than a fast and efficient access tool or repository of research techniques; it can also address new types of questions. Although not a linguistic theory in itself, corpus research techniques offer an exploratory tool to assist in the identification and description of language behaviour in literature and to aid literary criticism in the broader sense. Detail, language and style peculiar to a text can also attain focus in a systematic and comprehensive way. Corpus statistics and word frequencies can be used to obtain preliminary and often very telling information on the texts to be explored. Concordance lines then offer the opportunity to view the immediate context of words, phrases or sets of words, thus providing insight into the patterns built up around words. Such patterns can be further analysed through collocational analysis which displays the words occurring with most significance around the search word and highlights possible semantic prosodies. This paper describes briefly the above technical options and shows the results obtained in practical work on *Joseph*.

It is improbable that a student or researcher would approach a corpus-based study of a text with no idea of what they expect, or perhaps would hope, to find. Indeed, such an approach would suggest that the researcher is not familiar with the text. In practice, analysis tends to stem partly from hypotheses to be explored and partly from noticing and following up unexpected findings. Any computational analysis of language requires extensive pre- and post-processing and this would be largely impossible without thorough familiarity with the texts. The word 'evidence' is often used and would seem to suggest that corpus research claims to discover some objective 'truth' about language and texts. This is no more likely than a seminar of engaged students agreeing that they have all had the same experience of reading a text. However, using corpora can provide objective stimuli for further exploration and possibly challenge the researcher's preconceptions about the text. The search process is highly interactive as an initial search leads to further questions and searches, possibly with altered parameters.

It is argued by some that linguistics runs the risk of reducing literature to 'mere' language. This argument appears to suggest that any form of discourse could be independent of meaning, context and culture. I would certainly not want to argue that individual human agency can be dispensed with in interpreting texts – quite the contrary. On the other hand, I do believe that corpus techniques provide the interpreter with a marvellous tool for making language use transparent as the carrier of meaning and culture. While any supposed 'meaning' of a text is clearly not to be found in linguistic patterns alone, and cannot be satisfactorily explained by statistical measures, language is the medium used and clearly an exploration of it will be fruitful. Of course, no computational examination of a text is made without human intervention. Searches are undertaken, criteria chosen and decisions made about what is to be looked for within the current possibilities; undeniably, what is found is to some extent what is looked for. Corpus research is no machine to be fed text and churn out results in dismantled, easily digestible segments. Rather, it has the potential to highlight specific aspects of language use which are otherwise hard to locate and isolate. It provides only data which then have to be interpreted, and thus always leads back to the text as a whole, which is the best evidence there is. Corpus analysis neither can nor should replace thorough 'manual' textual analysis but is a tool for further exploration and reading. Of course the computer can only search for what it is told to search for and cannot evaluate the results. It is often the case that the researcher has to adapt searches. However, what the computer lacks in intuition and understanding it makes up for in the speed, consistency and accuracy of its searches.

The novel

A brief introduction to the *Joseph* tetralogy, one of Mann's lesser-known works, is apt at this point. Writing began in 1925 and the volumes were published separately in 1933 (*Die Geschichten Jaakobs*), 1934 (*Der junge Joseph*), 1936 (*Joseph in Ägypten*) and 1943 (*Joseph der Ernährer*).[1] In *Joseph*, Mann retells in almost 2000 pages the Old Testament tales of Joseph and his ancestors, his brothers and his ambitions, beginning in the first volume after the prefatory *Höllenfahrt* with the stories passed on to Joseph by his father Jaakob. The second volume describes Joseph's upbringing and childhood hubris, culminating in the attack by his brothers. The third volume follows Joseph's progress in Egypt as he rises to an honourable position in Potiphar's house and is subsequently accused of attempted rape by Potiphar's wife. The final book describes Joseph's eventual success as adviser to Pharaoh, ending with the family reunion in times of famine and Jaakob's death.

Mann's self-professed aim from the start was to make *Joseph und seine Brüder* 'leicht, humoristisch und intellektuell' (Letter to Ernst Bertram of 28 December 1926 in Mann 1960:154). He emphasized that the novel was 'in erster Linie ein Sprachwerk und zugleich Menschheitsgedicht' (XI, 680). Such comments should not, however, be taken as an indication that the work was merely a pleasant distraction in turbulent times. Mann's turning to mythical stories was no mere escape from the political demands of the day. On the contrary, *Joseph* was Mann's artistic, ironical response to the simplification of history he saw being made around him by the 'Fanatiker der Einfalt' (IX, 233). Although the rise of fascism forced him to become politically engaged in a way the writer of the *Betrachtungen eines Unpolitischen* may not have imagined, Mann's most eloquent and passionate political debates took place within the sphere of *Geist*, in his literary writings and essays on great *Erzieher* such as Lessing, Goethe and Nietzsche.

In *Joseph*, Mann directly discusses what he considered the burning issues of the day, rather as Jaakob asks in the closing pages of the novel: 'ist's nicht ein Mißbrauch der Gabe, Dinge zu künden, die gar keinen Bezug haben zum Wirklichen?' (V, 1710). In turning to ancient history and myth, Mann was confronting the political demands of the present in the way with which he ultimately felt most comfortable. *Joseph* responds to the characteristic German phenomenon of *Kulturpolitik*, whereby even such apparently abstruse issues as the nature and authority of myth can reflect and help to shape political attitudes and choices. The naturally conservative author was deeply sensitive by the early 1920s to the tendency in Germany towards the mythologizing manipulation and simplification of history for ultimately political purposes. The 'humanization of myth' undertaken in the novels aims to educate the reader in the uses and abuses of appeals to authority, whether mythical or traditional, as a means of evading individual responsibility or justifying self-interest. In *Joseph*, Mann sought to expose the 'Fiktionen voller Tagestendenz' (X, 263), the influence of which he recognized early as a danger. In rewriting the familiar biblical story Mann is playing with the concept repeated throughout the novel of 'es steht geschrieben' (IV, 449) and illustrating that nothing is in fact cast in stone: instead, 'es steht *so gut wie* geschrieben' (V, 1592, my emphasis) and can be rewritten, if the situation demands.

I was delighted to discover that an electronic text of *Joseph* was included in the corpus holdings of the Institut für Deutsche Sprache. I had considered manually scanning the text during doctoral work. The poor quality of paper used in the editions made scanning impossible and typing necessary, which was not feasible with limited resources and a book of this length. As soon as I had the chance to work with the electronic text, I set about it, using the IDS COSMAS tools. First some customization of the existing text was necessary. The 'Thomas Mann Korpus', which had been keyed in by hand, was split into its component parts to make examination of the separate parts possible either individually or in groups of sub-corpora.[2] For instance, the four volumes of *Joseph* (which total over 660 000 words) could be compared and contrasted, the complete text of *Joseph* examined, or solely the volumes of 'Reden und Aufsätze'. I have initially examined chiefly the word level, although it is now widely acknowledged that the unit of meaning often does not correspond to the word (Sinclair 1996). Since reliable ways of identifying and analysing multi-word units have yet to be developed, such units of meaning have been found via the searches rather than forming search queries of their own.

Corpus statistics and word frequencies

Preliminary, relatively unsophisticated information already provided interesting findings. A comparison of sentence length in the various sections of *Joseph* illustrates, for instance, the complex syntactic structures of the introductory *Höllenfahrt*. The average sentence length in the dense and complex essay is 49.4 words, compared with 34.9, 27.6, 35.4 and 31.4 for each volume respectively (average 32.9).[3] A comparison with similar statistics in the rest of Thomas Mann's work reveals that Mann's average sentence length varied dramatically between his early work (*Buddenbrooks* 21.6 words per sentence) and his mature work (*Doktor Faustus* 34.7 words per sentence). The essays and speeches average 32.6 words per sentence, very similar in length to *Joseph*. As a guideline for comparison the average sentence length in a German corpus of general written language is just over 21 words.[4]

Word frequencies can be used to obtain a general picture of the shape of the text. A list of raw word-form frequencies can be easily obtained for the text as a whole and for the separate volumes. This then forms a useful basis for further exploration and searches. The first thirty or so words of such lists are grammatical words. Only then do the most frequently occurring lexical words begin to appear, and it is on lexical words that this study focuses. In *Joseph*, the first of these words in the frequency list of the whole book was, rather unsurprisingly, 'Joseph', with just under 2000 occurrences. More interestingly, 'Auge(n)' appears rather unexpectedly as the first noun on the list with 875 instances. Such frequency lists can offer a snapshot of the subject matter and vocabulary of the individual books. 'Jaakob' occurs, for instance, as the most common name in the first volume, while in the third volume 'Herrin' as a designation for Mut, Potiphar's wife, predominates. Pharaoh's name occurs increasingly frequently as his presence in the story becomes greater.

Frequency lists are often most useful when lemmatized, that is, when word-forms are grouped together under the lemma; singular, plural and various case forms of a noun would be grouped, and 'schön', 'schöne', 'schönen' etc would be grouped under 'schön'. COSMAS presents the user with a list of grammatical words suggested by the programme, which can then be edited as required. This procedure is clearly more useful in German than in English. It can, however, be useful to view frequency lists both with and without lemmatization. On the other hand, the true picture of the frequency of a lemma is only evident once the word-forms have been grouped. The frequency of 'Sohn' (449) rises when 'Sohn', 'Söhne', 'Söhnen' and 'Sohnes' are grouped together to make it the second most frequently occurring lexical word or lemma. The subject matter is significant, of course. In the book in question, whether the sons of Jaakob act as a collective, or individually, is of great import to Mann's argument (809).

Frequency lists can provide absolute (raw) frequencies, that is, how many times the words or lemmas occur in any given text. Relative frequencies, on the other hand, provide information on the significance of the occurrence of a word in this text. This shows up the specialization of a text when compared with a general language corpus or any specific sub-corpus. What constitutes 'general language' and what should and could be in a corpus of general language is a topic for heated debate. A balanced general language corpus would ideally include a range of the different text-types of language in proportions reflecting their levels of use in the language community at large. The difficulties with this ideal are clear, especially as regards spoken material. In addition, the frame of reference relevant for literature of the 1920s is rather different to that for recent texts. Nevertheless, such comparisons are useful to highlight deviation from the given norm.

Looking at pairs or groups of frequently occurring related words can highlight patterns. In *Joseph*, the patterns of occurrence of 'Sonne' and 'Mond' reveal that 'Mond' predominates in the first volume, as the familial stories are recounted during Joseph's education. Joseph is first introduced to the reader as he displays himself in the 'reine und weiche Blendung' of the moonlight (IV, 64). The chief influences in Joseph's early life are related to the sphere of the moon, in turn representing certain cultural influences such as the work of Spengler and Bachofen whose misuse of myth, in Mann's opinion, was profoundly disturbing. Mann's diary entries trace his initial sympathy with much of this work and his subsequent rejection of their fatalistic claims as facile and untenable because of their potential effects. Mann's marginal comments in his copy of Alfred Baeumler's extensive introduction to Bachofen's *Mythos von Orient und Occident,* for instance, are telling:

> Das Ganze schmeckt arg nach Dunkelmännerei und ist in historischer Form auf kleine Art zeit-tendenziös und feindselig. Den Deutschen heute all diese Nachtschwärmerei vorzureden ist abscheulich.

Baeumler offered absolute oppositions and disapproved strongly of the position 'zwischen den Gegensätzen' advocated by Mann. Baeumler attacked the mixture of myth and enlightenment which is found in Nietzsche's *Geburt der Tragödie* and investigated by Mann in *Joseph.* The opening lines of the novel dispute a view which claims stability for myths and seeks ultimate authority in the past, and they challenge implicitly those who base their arguments on such a view. In the *Höllenfahrt*, for instance, when the narrator suggests that the 'Brunnen der Zeit' is unfathomable, Mann is responding to Baeumler's claims to offer the fundamental truth. Mann detected in such 'Dunkelmänner' the destructive aims infusing their authoritative claims. Mann questioned such claims in essays published at the time he began on *Joseph*:

> Aber ob es eine gute und lebensfreundliche, eine pädagogische Tat ist, den Deutschen von heute all diese Nachtschwärmerei, diesen ganzen Joseph Görres-Komplex von Erde, Volk, Natur, Vergangenheit und Tod, einen revolutionären Obskurantismus, derb charakterisiert, in den Leib zu reden, mit der stillen Insinuation, dies alles sei wieder an der Tagesordnung, wir ständen wieder an diesem Punkt, es handle sich nicht sowohl um Geschichte als um Leben, Jugend und Zukunft - das ist die Frage, die beunruhigt. (XI, 48)

The stringency, unpleasantness and aggression of such doctrines are displayed by certain characters in the novel, most memorably Beknechons, the chief priest of Egypt and Pharaoh's arch enemy in matters of reform. This reactionary and deeply xenophobic figure takes advantage of the population's insecurity and the fear of destabilization and represents the 'Geist trotziger Rückständigkeit' (V, 1500). Potiphar recognizes the dangerous influence the teachings of the unpleasant Beknechons have on his suggestible wife: 'er ist nicht mein Freund, und ich mag ihn nicht leiden mit seiner störrigen Wörterliste' (V, 1039). One of Beknechons' chief followers in the novel is the ugly, devious and ultimately vilified Dudu, who spies on Joseph in Potiphar's house. Mann thus directly responds in the novel to the contemporary influences exerted by the 'Geistesfeindlichkeit' (X, 158) of the likes of Spengler, Baeumler and Bachofen, whom he specifically associates with the influence of the moon. As Joseph learns from his mistakes and creates his own individual story in maturity, the clear bright light of the Egyptian sun, representing reason and democracy, becomes more evident in the later volumes. Although Joseph retains an increasingly suppressed longing for the moonlight of his youth, he lives his later life in the reason and caution symbolized by the sunlight.

Concordance lines

The major drawback of simple frequency lists is clearly the lack of context. Polysemous words, or those used in a variety of ways by an author, cannot be distinguished in simple frequency lists. Concordance lines of selected words can show their behaviour in a linguistic context which can vary in size from a few words either side of the node (keyword) to several sentences. Such a concordance makes the text more accessible, restructuring it to highlight the words of interest and thus providing data with which the researcher can formulate, test, corroborate or reject hypotheses. Concordance lines are generally most useful when they are sorted, either by the word immediately to the left or to the right. Patterns of usage then become evident.

Vital for the process of change central to *Joseph* is the realization that the stories passed down through the generations may have become unsuitable for current times. Characters complain that the story or myth they feel obliged to fulfil is now out of date:

> Ist aber doch manches Mal ein Fallstrick mit des Alten Ehrwürdigkeit, wenn's nämlich einfach bloß überständig ist in der Zeit und verrottet - dann tut's nur ehrwürdig, ist aber in Wahrheit ein Greuel vor Gott und ein Unflat. (688)

The concordance lines of 'Greuel' ('abomination', 'atrocity') in *Joseph* are presented below, sorted chronologically. The lines are here cut off at the screen width but more context can be examined online. The characters after the line number show the origin of the example (HV = Höllenfahrt, J1–J4 are the four books). For reasons of space, only half of the lines are shown, chosen randomly out of forty-eight:

1/HV	... ihnen gut scheint, den Himmlischen ein	Greuel	ist? Die blöden Mensc...
2/J1	... r, aber meinesteils bin ich leider ein	Greuel	vor euch und heute beson...
3/J1	... ht tun sollst, weil es schlechthin ein	Greuel	ist vor meinem Angesicht...
4/J1	...erdienst gleichkomme und vielleicht ein	Greuel	sei vor dem Herrn und ei...
5/J1	... m ihre Überzeugung stehe, würde es ein	Greuel	und eine Schande in ihre...
6/J1	... eine wird, denn es wäre uns anders ein	Greuel	vor unserm Gott. Sie...
7/J1	... nd, das war allein schon ein Ärger und	Greuel	für Lea, nach deren rüs...
8/J1	... en Menschen, das ist auf die Dauer ein	Greuel	vor mir . Du hast mir ge...
9/J2	... er drunten in Blüte stand, war ihm ein	Greuel	und eine Narrheit, - di...
10/J2	... wir ärgern uns alle gleichmäßig ob des	Greuels	, und Ascher nimmt unse...
11/J2	... rfeigte, das wäre das Rechte, und der	Greuel	unter meinem Magen käme...
12/J2	... und nach ausdrücklichem Beschluß einen	Greuel	tun und die Hand wider...
13/J2	... nicht, dennoch zu kommen, das ist ein	Greuel	in meinen Augen und ist...
14/J3	... ur ehrwürdig, ist aber in Wahrheit ein	Greuel	vor Gott und ein Unflat...
15/J3	... was noch ehrwürdig und was schon ein	Greuel	? Da gäbe es bald nich...
16/J3	... Verehrung zu: es war ein merkwürdiger	Greuel	und lustig übrigens auch...
17/J3	... re. der Begriff der Unreinheit und des	Greuels	war keine Erfindung de...
18/J3	...n und den Leuten Ägyptens gemeinsam ein	Greuel	: zum Beispiel das Sch...
19/J3	... em, wie weit etwa schon der Brauch zum	Greuel	geworden. Aber die ent...
20/J3	... nicht zu weit gehen. er ist uns kein	Greuel	, doch eine Scheu und ei...
21/J3	... sternheit. Dies ist nun der Gipfel des	Greuels	, und besonders deswege...
22/J3	... um meiner Liebe Lust; es ist etwas von	Greuel	darin und paß...
23/J4	... ein Ärgernis, um nicht zu sagen: ein	Greuel	! Läßt man es dahin ko...
24/J4	... anz vergaßen, daß es grundsätzlich ein	Greuel	vor ihnen war, mit den...

It is clear that this concept is a matter of deep and urgent concern for characters in *Joseph*. The question of what should now be rejected in favour of something more suitable is formulated throughout the work. The pattern which emerges even in the relatively narrow context shown corresponds directly to the gradual process of change within the novels. This progress is observed as characters realize that the mythical templates may no longer suit them, and furthermore that only they can alter the pattern to one with which they are happy to live.

Characters in the early volumes often suggest tentatively ('vielleicht', in apparently rhetorical questions) that traditions may have become a 'Greuel' to a third party, chiefly God (lines 1, 4, 6). They are unable or unprepared to admit that they themselves do not approve and seek to evade responsibility for the decision that older ways are now outdated and should be revised. Jaakob, for instance, describes in conversations with Joseph his reluctance to play the mythical role and sacrifice his beloved son. He explicitly claims that he would refuse God the sacrifice demanded of and offered by Abraham, but when the time comes to send Joseph to his brothers, Jaakob does so in full awareness of his actions: '[er] blieb entsagend stehen, das Herz schwerer, als passen wollte' (IV, 529). He is faced with the same decision in later years when the remaining brothers take Benjamin to Egypt and again Jaakob finds the mythical templates compelling; 'ich willige drein' (V, 1638). He merely attempts to avert what is in his opinion 'in Erz geschrieben' by explicitly exclaiming to God 'ich opfere ihn dir nicht...ich will ihn zurückhaben' (V, 1639). Although attracted by progress, Jaakob is pulled more towards the mythical patterns which claim his sacrifice 'mit Recht, wenn auch gegen die Zukunft' (IV, 105). His inability to break the pattern makes his loss all the more painful. Jaakob finds that being able to claim mythical support for his actions does not ease his distress. Rather, his knowledge that he had been aware and would have wished to alter the story 'die geschrieben steht' compounds his pain:

> Siehe, die Überraschung ist glaubhaft. Daß aber kommt das Geahndete und scheut sich nicht, dennoch zu kommen, das ist ein Greuel in meinen Augen und ist wider die Abmachung (IV, 637).

The number of personal pronouns appearing in the vicinity of 'Greuel' in the concordance lines is striking (my emphasis in all examples): 'meinesteils bin ich leider ein Greuel vor *euch*' (line 2), 'weil es schlechthin ein Greuel ist vor *meinem* Angesicht' (line 3), 'das ist auf die Dauer ein Greuel vor *mir*' (line 8) and '(es) war *ihm* ein Greuel und eine Narrheit' (line 9). It is even claimed: 'denn es wäre *uns* anders ein Greuel *vor unserm Gott*' (line 6), as characters define what they consider to be acceptable to their God. The feeling that something is no longer tenable emerges as something very personal; 'Greuel' is what characters would not choose to happen to themselves or their loved ones. This process illustrates the assertion of individuality in a world of meshed mythical identities.

The experience of 'Greuel' can even be physically uncomfortable: 'unter meinem Magen' (line 11). Further exploration of concordance lines of 'Magen' shows that of sixteen instances, the majority (thirteen) describe the physical discomfort of acting in schemes which are no longer suitable: 'da kehrte sich Herz und Magen mir um, und ich zweifelte an meiner Seele' (V, 1793). This is, quite literally, a gut reaction to actions and situations which are unpleasant to the individual. Joseph's brothers find themselves feeling deeply uncomfortable after their collective action of throwing Joseph, whom they individually remember with tenderness, into the dry well. They are taciturn, sleepless, cannot look each other in the eye and even turn to drink to relieve their anguish (IV, 595 ff.). Like Jaakob, they find that their guilt gnaws at them and mythical justifications do not help their personal suffering, although communal guilt eases the burden somewhat.

Such emotional crises lead braver characters originally given to following the patterns of myth to seek and eventually to create alternative patterns as they assert their individual choice in a gradual and often painful process. The chapter 'Jaakob muß reisen' in which Esau and Ismael plot revenge is one of the great scenes of the novel.[5] Esau, cheated of the paternal blessing by his brother Jaakob, and Ismael, likewise cast aside by Isaak, are fully aware of the mythical footsteps in which they are treading: 'in denselben Fußstapfen gingen sie, unangenehm, ausgeschlossen' (IV, 214). Esau and Ismael are unwilling, however, to fulfil their perceived mythical roles by killing their respective brothers: 'er [Esau] scheute die Kainstat, scheute sich, durch sie noch mehr und deutlicher er selbst zu werden' (IV, 214–15). Fond feelings for their 'zarte' brothers make both Esau and Ismael unwilling to commit fratricide although they find justification for it in the myth of Cain and Abel. They discuss this issue at such length that Jaakob can make his escape, as they are aware he would (IV, 215), thus neatly avoiding the fulfilment of the old pattern, and indeed murder, while also avoiding making a new pattern for the future.

Yet more imaginative and creative characters in the context of the novels not only avoid the mythical templates which they no longer find suitable but produce new patterns: 'ich weiß nicht, wo es geschrieben steht, aber es läßt sich nicht tun' (IV, 489). Again, the process of change is based on emotions and subjective perceptions of what is honourable and what is now a 'Greuel'. The travelling merchant who rescues Joseph from the well criticizes him for the arrogance of such decisions:

> Und wo kämen wir hin, wenn jeder Gimpel sich zum Mittelpunkt setzen wollte der Welt und sich wollte zum Richter aufwerfen darüber, was heilig ist in der Welt und was nur alt, was noch ehrwürdig und was schon ein Greuel? Da gäbe es bald nichts Heiliges mehr! (V, 695)

However, each character who effects a change does in fact set himself or herself as the centre of their own world, as Ruben exclaims; 'ich werd nicht gegen meine Überzeugung handeln, ich will gerecht und billig sein, das ist meiner Seele zuträglicher' (IV, 497). Such decisions are ultimately selfish as characters opt to feel good about themselves rather than uncomfortable and guilty.

Tradition and myth are not, however, wholly rejected in *Joseph*, which describes in detail the comfort and freedom from responsibility offered by mythical patterns. The motivations for calling upon mythical templates are nevertheless exposed as arbitrary, political and potentially dangerous. The concordance lines show that the criteria used in the definition of 'Greuel' at any given time are personal and subjective. Mann exposes the potential for manipulation to show that what is 'ehrwürdig' and suitable for the times must be revised according to the current situation. This decision must be based on personal feelings.

Collocational information

Collocational searches provide a further step in analysis by examining the context of a word in a systematic way in order to find the words with which it co-occurs. They build up a picture of an author's idiosyncratic use of language. This in turn can be used to investigate when the pattern differs from the norm built up in the author's work. These searches too are best calculated using relative frequencies to show the significance of the appearance of a word in the given context. It is, for instance, of relatively little interest that the word 'der' collocates frequently with a given search word, since it occurs frequently in the vicinity of every word.[6] Of more interest is that, for instance, 'rot' collocates often with 'Zahlen', 'Teppich' and 'Faden' in a corpus of general language, or with 'Esau' and 'Zotteln' within *Joseph*.

Collocational analysis is one of the key areas where extensive work would be impossible without computational support. Most query tools in general use have been created for relatively large-scale lexicography. They are highly efficient at searching for what are considered to be statistically significant items in large corpora of at least several million tokens. The precise nature of such significance is often hard to determine, as the user is presented with the results of complex algorithms but not the method used to reach those results.[7] They are not, however, well suited to smaller-scale data sets and very specific tasks. The minimum cut-off point of what the tools regard as statistically significant is often never reached in relatively short literary texts. This needs to be borne in mind as tests are undertaken and results examined. Some customization of tools may be necessary to adequately capture the peculiar nature of literary texts. Initial collocational analysis of key words in *Joseph* led to inconclusive results, chiefly because the text is relatively short in computational linguistic terms and absolute frequencies thus too low to be considered of significance by the program. For the present study results were obtained by lowering the cut-off point for presumed significance.

Investigation of a *leitmotif*

The concept of 'Geschichte' as story, history and narration is pivotal in the novel. Mann emphasized in essays and speeches the 'verspielte Wissenschaftlichkeit' of the text (XI, 625). In essays about *Joseph*, Mann explicitly points out to the reader the folly of imagining that the stories of the novel represent truth. Mann challenges the reader to realize the game that is being played: 'die Erörterung gehört hier zum Spiel' (XI, 656). Mann's narrative method undermines excessive claims to authority, whether in the form of myth or of (hi)stories, as the dogma of fascist ideology is parodied by the ironic narrator.

'Tief ist der Brunnen der Vergangenheit. Sollte man ihn nicht unergründlich nennen?' (IV, 9); so the narrator of *Joseph und seine Brüder* begins his epic retelling of the biblical story. The narrator claims to be impressively well-informed but it is clear from the start that he is playing with the reader, with the story and with story-telling. The narrator brings the reader back to the present with the closing lines:

> 'Und so endigt die schöne Geschichte und Gotteserfindung von *Joseph und seinen Brüdern*.' (V, 1818)

The status of the story as fiction is underlined by the formal repetition of the title by the tongue-in-cheek narrator. I was struck by those words because the semantic prosody of 'schön' in the novel seemed to me to suggest an element of unreliability, even deception. The first search I undertook when I could access the electronic version of the text was for more examples of 'schön' and 'Geschichte' appearing together. I was certain that I would find other instances but upon analysing the corpus, I was amazed to find that the combination in fact occurs only once, in that final sentence. I then undertook analysis of 'schön' to see whether my intuition about the colouring effected by the use of 'schön' was well-founded.

The collocates of 'schön' highlight the process of change during the novels as what is considered beautiful alters during Joseph's life. In the first volume, the statistically strongest collocates of 'schön' (in a range of five words before and five after the node) are 'Gespräch', 'Monde', 'Rede', 'Kopf', 'Augen' and 'Spiel'. These collocates form a set important to Joseph at this stage in his life. Joseph is often described as 'hübsch und schön', implying hubris and immaturity. At this stage in his life Joseph trades on his physical appearance and similarity to his mother, Rachel, beloved of Jaakob, to find favour in the world. Beauty is explicitly criticized as superficial and deceptive by the mysterious stranger who leads Joseph to the brothers' camp (IV, 541f.). The use of the adjective 'schön' here implies superficial beauty but underlying ignorance and confusion, or even an element of bias and duplicity.

The 'schöne Gespräche' of *Die Geschichten Jaakobs* illustrate vividly the gratification and satisfaction gained from formalized modes of behaviour, the repetition of known patterns and phrases, well-rehearsed gestures and formulaic language as each recites his given part, as in a litany. Characters repeatedly prompt each other by asking questions to which they already know the answers (e.g. IV, 83). Joseph soothes his father's distress by flattering and reassuring him. The son's tactics towards his father involve recounting seasoned and familiar stories which suggest ironically the distraction and placation of a child by tales. Both father and son play this game in their *Zwiegesang*, reciting well-known events ['weißt du von ihm?', 'wohl weiß ich', 'ich weiß es genau', 'das weiß ich wie du'] in order to provide consolation and cheer. Such conversations serve neither for functional communication nor information:

> Joseph verstand, daß das Gespräch schön werden sollte, ein 'schönes Gespräch', daß hieß: ein solches, das nicht mehr dem nützlichen Austausch diente und der Verständigung über praktische oder geistliche Fragen, sondern der bloßen Aufführung und Aussagung des beiderseits Bekannten, der Erinnerung, Bestätigung und Erbauung, und ein redender Wechselsang war... (IV, 116)

Such conversations occur regularly throughout the novels. The narrator frequently protests that 'schöne Gespräche' are unreliable, confused, forgotten, remembered only partially or inaccurately, even deliberately misleading or deceptive 'Lügenmärlein' (IV, 282):

> genau ist hier die wahre Reihenfolge der Geschehnisse zu beachten, die anders war, als später die Hirten im Schönen Gespräch sie anordneten und weitergaben (IV, 171).

Such 'zweckhafte Hirtenmärlein' (IV, 173) often contain 'späte und zweckvolle Eintragungen' (IV, 13). The reader is encouraged by this framework of scepticism to consider independently whether any version offered may be accepted as true. It is thus suggested that what is described as 'schön' in the novel should not be taken at face value but should be critically examined for potential manipulation to advance a hidden agenda.

Joseph recognizes in his father that people are overwhelmed, even scared, by unpleasant or challenging information and the idea that they must accept responsibility. He learns that status and success can be attained by giving people the comfort and reassurance they require. He couches important and novel information in familiar and comforting words in order to disguise revision of myth in traditional costume. It is important, then, that such conversations are 'schön' not only to be suitable and pleasant but also in order to be effective. The semantic prosody of 'schön' is gradually built up in the novels to suggest something pleasant but potentially deceptive.

In the second volume, Joseph's preoccupation with himself and his appearance is further instanced by the most frequent collocates: 'Augen', 'Gestalt', 'Gott', 'Kopf', 'Gespräch' and 'Rede'. In the third volume, *Joseph in Ägypten*, the focus of Joseph's life changes as he assumes the cloak of responsibility rather than favoured beauty: 'Range', 'Ordnung', 'Dienst'. However, some collocates illustrate the danger his remaining hubris poses: 'Figur', 'Sünderin' and he is repeatedly described as 'schön von Angesicht/Antlitz/Gesicht/Gestalt'. In the final volume, Joseph's role in government is clear in the appearance of new collocates: 'Befehl', 'Wille', 'Lehre', 'Förmlichkeit'. The strong collocative clash of 'schön' with 'Befehl 'and 'Wille' in the final volume is especially striking. In a search of all written corpora held at the IDS, 'Befehl' collocated solely with words related to military action, and not once with 'schön'. 'Befehle' collocates early in *Joseph* with 'Gott' and 'Vater' as the mythical patterns are re-enacted, but by the third volume they are secular: 'königlich' and 'mild'. In the final volume, with by far the most occurrences in total, they are predominantly 'schön'. It is a slogan that Pharaoh's orders are 'schön'. They are effective and successful, indeed, but the decadent and sensitive monarch would not accept them were they not also pleasant and painless for him.

The collocation of 'schön' and 'Geschichte' at the end of *Joseph* explicitly draws upon the semantic prosody of 'schön' built up throughout the book. The final words of the tetralogy subvert the narrator's ironic claims for his narration as truth or facticity because all the 'schöne

Gespräche' the reader has heard have been unreliable, manipulable and more reassuring and entertaining than objectively true. The reader is encouraged to challenge all apparent truths and to look especially suspiciously on those who would claim to offer the truth. The use of 'schön' is not, however, purely ironic. It is vital that the stories told and the history created should be 'schön'. Again and again, characters realize that unpleasant stories cause pain to themselves and others. For stories to be accepted and thus effective, they must be pleasant, humorous and well-told.

Mann presents in *Joseph* a beautiful, enjoyable, convincing, self-aware and difficult story with no easy choices or sharply defined lines. Mann offered irony and ambivalence instead of absolute authority, complications rather than the easy solutions of the 'Fanatiker der Einfalt'. Mann thus challenged the self-professed certainty and authority with which writers such as Spengler, Baeumler and Klages staked out their reactionary doctrines, offering in their place scepticism as his philosophy of history. He not only argues that the truths offered by such writers are wrong, but that they have no right to claim to have reached the truth. Mann's most complex and passionate discussion of contemporary politics and the dangers inherent in such argumentation is embedded in his apparently non-political creative writing.

The value of a corpus-based approach

The corpus exploration techniques described above have provided otherwise unobtainable information for a detailed study of the portrayal of the gradual process of change within *Joseph*. Initial searches provided preliminary information which in turn led to more detailed concordance and collocational analysis. Immersion in the data often led to successive searches and exploration, quickly resulting in a mass of data, only a fraction of which has been interpreted here. The narrator and narration of the text provide a particularly rich field of investigation, again inherently bound up with the subject matter, which cannot be futher described here. Analyses from different sections of work, periods, characters and genres can be compared; for instance the literary work with Mann's essays and speeches of the same time.

Corpus analysis never strays from the undiluted original text. It does, however, offer us ways of manipulating the text in rich and suggestive ways, both prompted and being driven by the researcher's imagination; indeed it leads the researcher again and again back to that text. Fast and easy access to the patterns of the language of the text at every stage and an increased range of questioning techniques mean that more can be discovered and measured than is possible through traditional reading. Often corpus exploration provides evidence to support hypotheses formed through initial reading. Texts are sometimes, however, subsequently viewed from a new perspective as preconceptions and subjective perceptions are challenged. While corpus data provides only results originating from the text, the value of objective, fast and reliable searches to display the patterns of language cannot be underestimated. The benefits of a corpus-supported reading of literature are manifold. It is clear that we stand at the beginning of further development and study in this field.

Notes

1 All references to Mann's works are in the format (II, 237), referring to the appropriate volume of the *Gesammelte Werke in dreizehn Bänden* (Mann 1974). Volume IV contains the first two volumes of *Joseph und seine Brüder*, Volume V the remaining two volumes.

2 For assistance in accessing the texts, my thanks go to Cyril Belica of the Institut für Deutsche Sprache. In addition, Eva Breßler provided valuable assistance with computer searches.

3 Unfortunately the standard deviation measure, which provides a more accurate picture of sentence-length distribution and variation, cannot be accessed via COSMAS.

4 For this analysis the collected written holdings of the IDS were consulted.

5 Mann commented on the scene in *Freud und die Zukunft* (XI, 498).

6 A lemmatized frequency list shows that the definite article in all its forms is the most frequently occurring word in German, followed by 'in', 'und' and 'sein'.

7 For a comparison of the main statistical tests see Barnbrook (1996: ch. 5) and Oakes (1998).

References

Barnbrook, Geoff (1996), *Language and Computers. A practical introduction to the computer analysis of language* (Edinburgh Textbooks in Empirical Linguistics). Edinburgh University Press: Edinburgh.

Koopmann, Helmut (1984), 'Aufklärung als Forderung des Tages. Zu Thomas Manns kulturpilosphischer Position in den zwanziger Jahren und im Exil' in Wulf Koepke and Michael Winkler (eds), *Deutschsprachige Exilliteratur*. Bouvrer: Bonn, pp 75–91.

Lawson, Ann (1995), 'The Humanisation of Myth: a study of Thomas Mann's 'Joseph und seine Brüder' in the context of contemporary cultural politics in Germany', Ph.D. dissertation, University of Birmingham.

Mann, Thomas (1960), *Thomas Mann an Ernst Bertram: Briefe aus den Jahren 1910-1955*, edited by Inge Jens. Neske: Pfullingen.

Mann, Thomas (1974), *Gesammelte Werke in dreizehn Bänden*. Fischer: Frankfurt.

Oakes, Michael P. (1998), *Statistics for Corpus Linguistics* (Edinburgh Textbooks in Empirical Linguistics). Edinburgh University Press: Edinburgh.

Sinclair, John (1996) 'The search for units of meaning', *TEXTUS* IX(I): 75–106.

Towards a corpus-based comparison of two journals in the field of business and management German

April Mackison

1 Introduction

This study details preliminary findings from the analysis of two small corpora of approximately half a million words each[1] which I have compiled from two German management periodicals, *Wirtschaftswoche* and *technologie & management*, with particular emphasis on the frequency and distribution of two groups of German terms which equate to the English terms 'manager' and 'management'. These are, respectively: *Leiter, Führer, Manager, Boß, Chef*; and *Leitung, Führung, Management*. The analysis also investigates all the 'lexical sets' of which these terms form a part, i.e. all relevant compound nouns formed with these words. The findings reported here demonstrate various advantages of a corpus-based approach to such a comparative study, illustrating in particular the way in which standard concordancing techniques can help to illuminate differences in lexis, semantics and style. In evaluating this data I argue that these linguistic differences reflect different assumptions about each journal's readership, and also provide the kind of evidence on which a subsequent, linguistically founded, comparison of register could be based, perhaps applying a typology of register variation such as that developed by Biber.[2]

The first corpus was compiled from *technologie & management* (hereafter TM), the 'Fachmagazin' or trade journal of the Verband Deutscher Wirtschaftsingenieure (Association of German Industrial Engineers). This periodical was chosen for its focus on contemporary developments in management theory, with the anticipation that it would contain a high concentration of up-to-date management and business vocabulary. It also contains articles on the most recent theories and trends in management strategy, pieces of a philosophical nature for managers who wish to develop their personal qualities, and reviews of new books on management practices. The periodical is published four times a year (in March, June, September and December), and is privately circulated to members of the association.

The second corpus was compiled from *Wirtschaftswoche* (hereafter WW), the approximate German equivalent of *Business Week*. Although *Wirtschaftswoche* is a weekly publication, it was decided to follow the pattern dictated by TM and to select four issues from each year, these four being the first issues of March, June, September and December. It was hoped that in this way a roughly equivalent amount of text would be obtained. Unfortunately this was not the case, because, unlike TM, WW contains many full page advertisements, a large number of photographs and illustrations, and therefore less text per page. For this reason extra issues were scanned in, approximately equidistant between those already selected, in order to obtain a corpus which was broadly comparable to that compiled from TM.

2 The external evidence

Before embarking on a discussion of the corpus-based analysis, let us consider the 'external' evidence, that is to say, what is already known about these two periodicals without reading them intensively. It is clear that there are certain basic differences between them. First, they differ in their distribution. WW is freely available for purchase from newsagents and other sales outlets. TM, however, is privately circulated to a restricted number of readers by post, and is not available to buy off the shelf. Second, WW is a weekly publication, while TM appears only four times a year. Finally, a brief examination of the contents of the two periodicals reveals that WW consists mainly of news items, articles about actual occurrences and the latest developments in the world of business, and interviews with managers of companies, while TM contains articles about current management issues and the most recent developments in management theory written by leading academics, economists, engineers, and managers. TM also contains reviews of the latest management publications.

Halliday's (1978) functional model of register views register variation as a product of the situations speakers and writers find themselves in, and identifies three influential factors: field (the subject matter of a communication), tenor (the relationship between the communicator and the individual or individuals communicated with), and mode (the channel of communication). In the case of this study, the field would appear to be broadly similar for both periodicals – issues relating to business and management. In so far as both are printed journals, the mode would also appear to be the same. At least in these first two respects one might say that the similarities are more immediate than any differences. However, there do seem to be significant differences in respect of the tenor, or relationship between sender and receiver, for each periodical, given the contrasts in the frequency of publication, manner of distribution, and size of readership. Even on this 'external' evidence one might deduce that TM addresses a much smaller and socially more distinct readership than WW. A question which I wished to explore in compiling these corpora was whether, and to what extent, corpus evidence could test and hopefully flesh out the hypothesis that the two periodicals have different implied readerships. The term 'implied readership' here is not used in the sense in which it has been used in literary studies, but in the more straightforward sense that, as Stubbs observes, 'all texts make assumptions about their readers' (Stubbs 1996: 91).[3]

These 'external' considerations were thus influential in the choice of periodicals for this study. The question was how the two journals would compare in terms of the frequency and distribution of these key management terms, which are after all central to any discourse on business and management; and whether the data would shed any light on questions of differing implied readerships and register differences between the two.

3 The corpus evidence

The corpus data do indeed help to illuminate a substantial pattern of differences between the two corpora. This is immediately apparent from the figures for the occurrence of each lexical set in the two periodicals (see Figure 1). In this section I will review the main findings regarding differences in frequency, in semantics, and in type-token ratios. I will also explore the contrast in the use of the 'low register' vocabulary items *Chef* and *Boß*.

3.1 Differences in frequency

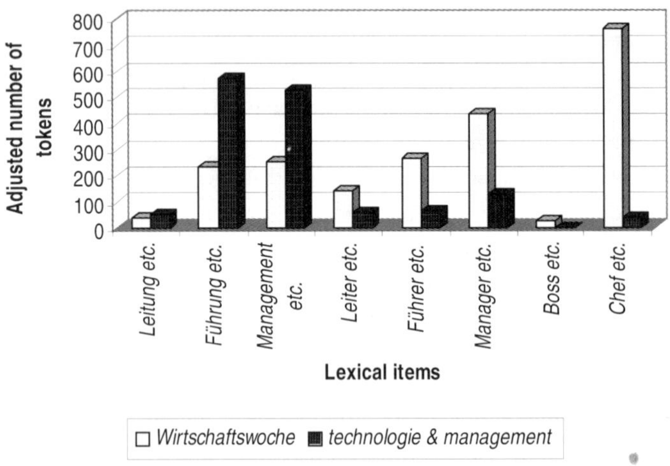

Figure 1 Graphical representation of all lexical sets in both corpora

Figure 1 shows a marked and consistent mirror-image pattern, whereby 'management' words occur with much greater frequency in TM than in WW, and 'manager' words occur with much greater frequency in WW than in TM. This is true not only of the words in their independent forms but also of each lexical set as a whole. The set '*Manager* etc.', for example, includes compound words in which the term is the head (**manager*) or the qualifier (*Manager**). There are only a few minor exceptions to this 'mirror image' pattern, and these are discussed later in this section.

Various points are immediately striking about the patterns of distribution revealed in Figure 1. Turning first to the 'management' words, we can see that the *Leitung* lexical set is numerically quite similar in both corpora. This is clearly the third and least popular choice of 'management' term in both periodicals, possibly because *Leitung* can be used in many other different contexts which are unrelated to the field of management. *Führung* is the most frequent lexical set by a small margin in TM, and second choice by a small margin in WW. This pattern is reversed for *Management* etc.; it is the most frequent lexical set in WW and comes a close second to *Führung* in TM. Many examples of the independent form of *Management* are in fact excluded from the TM statistics due to the frequent occurrence of this term in references to the title of the periodical itself, and if these were included the evidence would be violently skewed in favour of TM. As a group, the 'management' words occur more than twice as frequently in TM than they do in WW, as can be seen from Table 1 and Figures 2 and 3.

Table 1 Statistics for 'management' lexical sets

	TM – 441 429 words		WW – 524 952 words	
Word	No. of tokens	Approx. % of total tokens	No. of tokens	Approx. % of total tokens
Leitung	18	0.004	7	0.001
Leitung*	0	0	3	0.0005
*leitung	27	0.006	33	0.006
Führung	133	0.03	46	0.009
Führung*	258	0.058	139	0.026
*führung	113	0.026	61	0.012
Management	197	0.045	128	0.024
Management*	109	0.025	70	0.013
*management	162	0.037	65	0.012
% of total tokens		0.231%		0.1035%

Referring to the distribution of the 'manager' words as displayed in Figure 1, it is immediately clear that the lexical set of *Leiter* is of lesser importance in both periodicals: it is fourth choice in WW and third in TM, although in the latter corpus the actual number of occurrences is quite close to that found for *Führer*. The *Führer* lexical set is the third choice for WW and the second choice (by a small margin) in TM. The

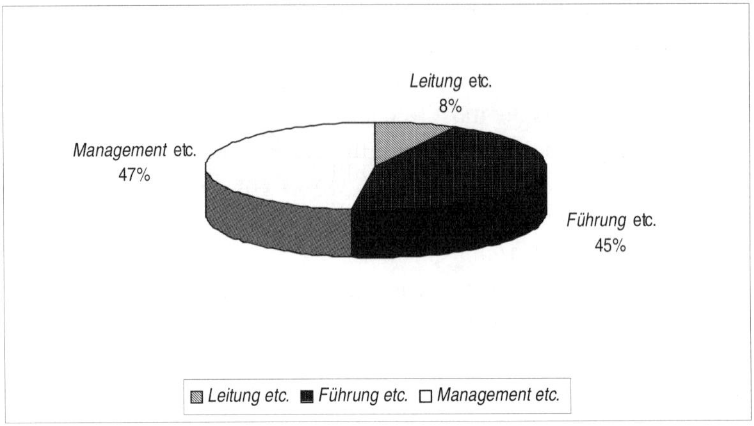

Figure 2 Graphical representation of 'management' words in WW

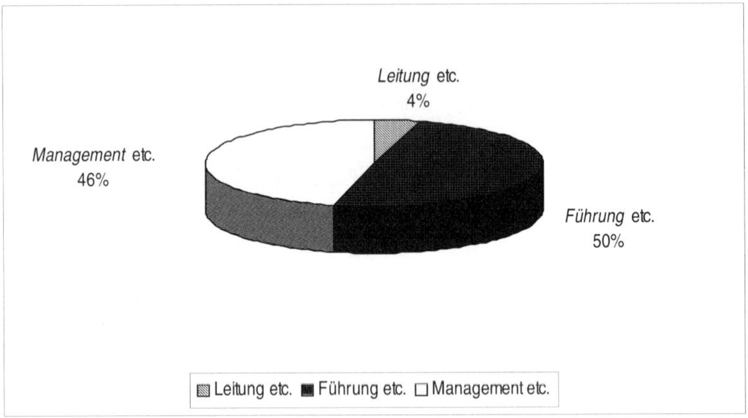

Figure 3 Graphical representation of 'management' words in TM

overall amount of evidence found in WW for the *Führer* lexical set looks quite large; however, very little of this is accounted for by the word in its independent form – it occurs predominantly in compound forms, such as *Geschäftsführer, Unternehmensführer* and *Branchenführer*. In TM, however, *Führer* occurs quite often as an independent word, a fact which deserves further investigation. On closer inspection of the data, we find certain 'safety features' which allow the use of this word in its independent form in TM, and these will be discussed below. The most frequently used lexical set in TM is, predictably perhaps, *Manager*. This is also commonly used in WW, where it occupies second place, but significantly, it comes a rather poor second to the runaway leader, *Chef*. The least frequent of the five 'manager' terms is *Boß*, which is found only twenty-six times in WW and is not found at all in TM. But the most striking indicator of the difference between the two corpora is surely the evidence for the lexical set *Chef*. *Chef* is by far the first preference for 'manager' in WW, occurring almost as often as all the other 'manager' terms put together. In stark contrast, it occupies a poor fourth place in TM. Indeed, *Chef* as an independent word does not really form a significant part of the lexis found in TM. In contrast to this marginal status, the independent word *Chef* is the most frequent of all five independent 'manager' words in WW. And finally, the scale on which 'manager' words occur in the two corpora is also significantly

Table 2 Statistics for 'manager' lexical sets

	TM – 441 429 words		WW – 524 952 words	
Word	No. of tokens	Approx. % of total tokens	No. of tokens	Approx. % of total tokens
Leiter	27	0.006	53	0.01
Leiter*	1	0.00002	5	0.00009
*leiter	24	0.005	92	0.017
Führer	17	0.003	9	0.001
Führer*	7	0.001	4	0.00007
*führer	35	0.007	267	0.05
Boß	0	0	5	0.00009
Boß*	0	0	10	0.001
*boß	0	0	12	0.002
Chef	14	0.003	177	0.03
Chef*	16	0.003	102	0.01
*chef	3	0.00006	521	0.09
Manager	67	0.01	213	0.04
Manager*	32	0.007	57	0.01
*manager	15	0.003	190	0.03
% of total tokens		0.058%		0.327%

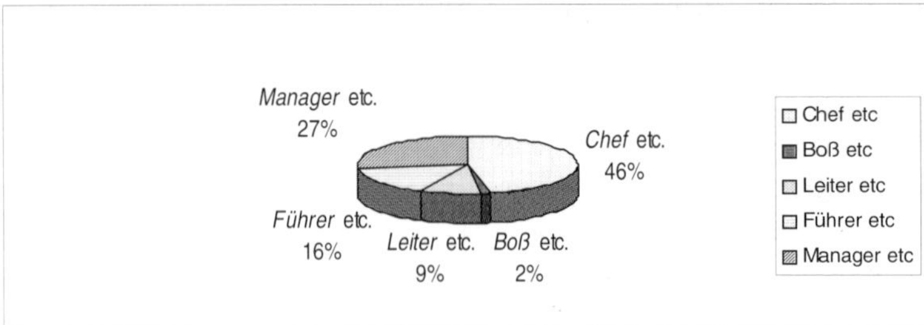

Figure 4 Graphical representation of 'manager' words in WW

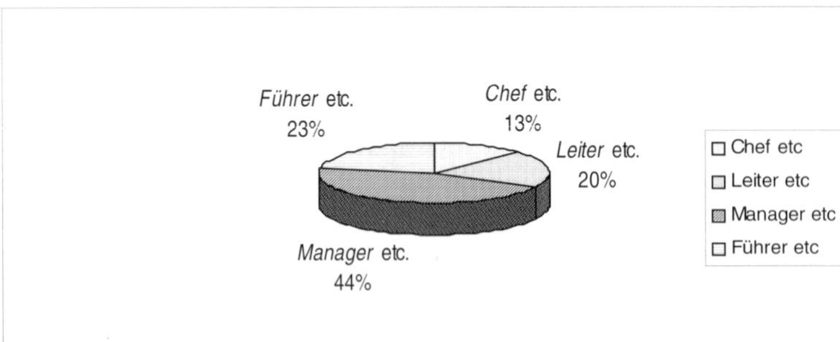

Figure 5 Graphical representation of 'manager' words in TM

different. As a group, they are more than five-and-a-half times more frequent in WW than in TM. The distribution of 'manager' words in the two corpora is shown in Table 2 and Figures 4 and 5.

Together, these findings demonstrate a consistent and substantial difference between the journals in the frequency with which the concepts of 'manager' and 'management' occur and in the choice of lexical item to express these concepts. By extension, these findings suggest that interesting distinctions in register are to be found between the two periodicals.

The graph in Figure 6 reveals the way in which the lexical sets differ from each other numerically, both within the same corpus, and between the two corpora. In WW, as we have seen, *Chef* etc. is a long way ahead of every other set. After an extremely large gap, this lexical set is followed by that of *Manager*, which is in turn separated from the *Führer* set by another large gap. *Führer* is quite close numerically to the sets of

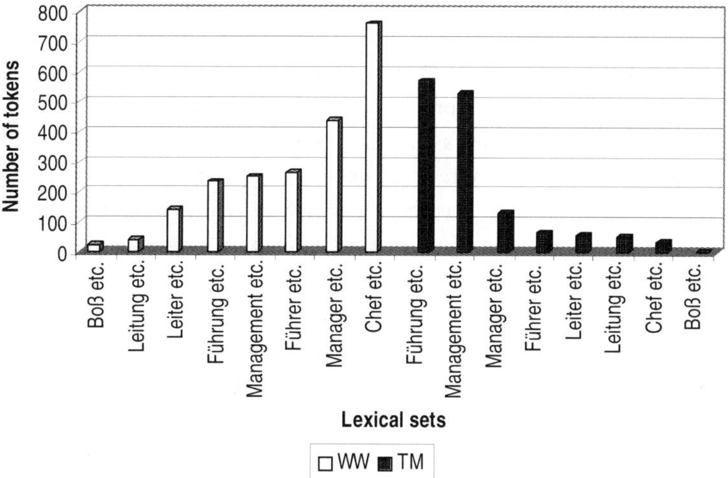

Figure 6 Comparison of relative frequency of occurrence

Management and *Führung*, but another smaller gap separates the latter from the next set, *Leiter*. At the bottom, separated from *Leiter* by a similar gap, are the sets of *Leitung* and *Boß*. In TM, by contrast, the largest set is *Führung*, followed closely by *Management*. There is then an extremely large gap separating these two sets from *Manager* and then, another step down, come *Führer, Leiter* and *Leitung* in reasonably close order. A small gap then separates off the sets at the bottom of the TM scale, *Chef* and the non-occurring *Boß*.

It is interesting to note that the majority of the lexical sets in WW are much larger numerically than the majority of those in TM. The big differences in frequency can be seen instantly: the sets of *Führung* and *Management* occur twice as often in TM as they do in WW. In contrast, *Manager* etc., *Führer* etc. and *Leiter* etc. each occur between twice and four times as often in WW as they do in TM. And as we have seen, the enormous difference between the two corpora with regard to the *Chef* lexical set could scarcely be more pronounced.

It seems clear that the evidence presented thus far for both 'management' and 'manager' lexical sets points to consistent differences in focus between the journals, and indeed in register. However, there are certain relatively minor exceptions to the 'mirror-image' pattern established so far. For instance, among the 'management' lexical sets, *Leitung** actually occupies a rather peripheral place in this study, as no relevant examples of this compound are found in TM, and indeed very few in WW. However, the case of *Führer* as an independent word, highlighted earlier, is rather more revealing. There are almost twice as many instances of *Führer* in TM as there are in WW, and two reasons for this can be observed. First, in TM, the word *Führer* often occurs in the sense of 'leader' in articles about the application of Chinese philosophical teachings to modern day management theory. It is most frequently found in direct quotations from ancient Chinese texts. Thus, the use of this problematical word is in a specific context which is safely distanced both in terms of geography and history from the connotations which are still very much attached to it in contemporary German contexts. There is no equivalent set of contexts in WW for this type of 'safe' temporal and geographical distance, since WW consists primarily of news reportage, dealing with actual, as opposed to abstract, issues. It is not surprising, therefore, to find the use of the *Führer* lexical set severely constrained and the use of the independent word generally avoided in WW. In parenthesis, it is interesting to note that wherever *Führer* is used in TM, it tends to collocate with adjectives which are semantically very positive and which stress the ethical dimension of leadership, such as *mutig, treu* and *ehrfürchtig*.

3.2 Differences in semantics

I will focus in this section on the semantics of the concept of 'management', as illustrated by my findings from WW and TM. In German, as in English, 'management' can denote either a group of people, in which case the word form can be classified semantically as (+human), or it can denote an activity or function, in which case the word can be classified as (+abstract). In these two corpora there is, interestingly, a general tendency for 'management' words to be (+abstract) in TM and (+human) in WW. In the majority of contexts it is also quite clear to which of these semantic categories each instance belongs; there are relatively few contexts in which the semantics remain unclear, and in most cases a decision can be made on the basis of the contextual evidence contained within the KWIC line.[4] Consider, for example, the following twenty or so lines from each of the concordances for *Management* from TM and WW:

1	ietsch diskutiert zahlreiche Konzepte für das	Management	von Softwareprojekten- einschli	\tm19344a.new
2	-Merbach, Heiner: Philosophie-Splitter für das	Management	- 16 praktische Handreichungen	\tm39119a.new
3	in den NBL tragfähig. Aus ihnen istdurch das	Management	die unternehmensbezogeneAnw	\tm49132a.new
4	-Merbach, Heiner: Philosophie-Splitter für das	Management	-16 praktische Handreichungenf	\tm394128.new
5	rbeiter Neben der Unterstützung durch das	Management	ist die Einbindung des Betriebsr	\tm49457a.new
6	rend die vorhandeneUnterstützung durch das	Management	als wichtiger fördernderUmsetz	\tm49456a.new
7	ei im engen Sinne. Demgegenüberist für das	Management	das Handeln durch Nicht-Handel	\tm49136a.new
8	sten einen hohen Rang einzuräumen und das	Management	darauf auszurichten. Ohne die	\tm49129a.new
9	r zur Entdeckung der weichen Faktoren. Das	Management	der Humanressourcen wird zum	\tm29467a.new
10	kationswerkzeuge. Dies ist besonders für das	Management	hilfreich, denn Management ist i	\tm39144a.new
11	lsweise die fehlende Unterstützung durch das	Management	hemmend auf die Umsetzung ei	\tm49456a.new
12	ehmen die Großunternehmen Einfluß auf das	Management	und die Personalpolitik der abhä	\tm39243a.new
13	Der Autor zielt auf das	Management	von Wissen in dem (eher engen)	\tm29394a.new
14	en, 98,- DM. Mintzbergs Ansichten über das	Management	von Organisationen sind in vielerl	\tm19233a.new
15	. JETZTNEU! Philosophie-Splitter für das	Management	16 praktische Handrechnunge	\tm19145a.new
16	ärkte stellen neue Herausforderungenan das	Management	vieler Unternehmenim technisch	\tm29493a.new
17	schließbar sein, insbesondere wenn sich das	Management	den Markterfordernissenstellt u	\tm49130a.new
18	ubiläum des WIV: Dr. Wagner, WIV: Das	Management	der vergangenen30 Jahre (Der	\tm19440a.new
19	enken. Die Idee der Natur als Vorbild für das	Management	schimmert indes nur ansatzweis	\tm49383a.new
20	zbergs Buch bereichert die Literatur über das	Management	von Organisationenin dreifacher	\tm19238a.new
21	gnalisieren den Bedarf nach Wissen über das	Management	von Organisationen, ob groß ode	\tm19233a.new
22	diesjährigen Serie Philosophie-Splitter für das	Management	mit dem Thema Führen durch S	\tm29356a.new

In the lines from TM above, it is clear in the majority of cases whether *Management* is semantically (+human) or (+abstract); in this particular concordance, the ratio is approximately fifty-fifty. It is self evident that this finding does not concur with the argument made out above for more (+abstract) occurrences in TM; however, certain of the (+human) occurrences can be explained away as repetition (lines 2, 4, 15, 22, and lines 5, 6, 11), and on taking this into consideration, the majority of the remainder are clearly (+abstract). Lines 8 and 19 are the only two which are not simple to categorize, and despite consulting the wider context, the semantics remain unclear – in other words, these two examples could be either (+human) or (+abstract).

In the lines from WW below, it is immediately clear in most cases that *Management* is semantically (+human) – in other words, that it is referring to a group of people. It was necessary to consult the wider context for lines 4, 12, and 18, but it transpires that these are also (+human). Only two lines are (+abstract) – lines 11 and 15, and there are no cases in which the semantics are unclear.

1	Dollarverdienenwürde, provoziertedas Managementeinen Kurssturz an der Bör	\ww591177.new
2	erten Autoren verweisendarauf, daß das Managementder betroffenenRüstungsge	\ww69180.new
3	rsetzen. So stellt es sich jedenfallsdas Managementder Haas-Laser GmbHim	\ww49185.new
4	glaubtensie verzichtenzu können. Das Managementsetzte auf den vermeintlich	\ww49243.new
5	ken pro Jahrgesenkt werden. Doch das Managementdrückt sich vorunbequeme	\ww591202.new
6	g neuen Wechselbädernaus: Wenn das Managementmit guten Nachrichtengera	\ww591177.new
7	weiter rollen. Die Treuhandwill jetzt das Managementin ihren Unternehmensyst	\ww69147.new
8	menkontofließen. Mit dem Geld will das Managementdas Wachstum in den neu	\ww491156.new
9	cht ist. Auf dem Ertragsgipfelhat es das Managementversäumt, so Jörg Schlüter,	\ww692142.new
10	SA. Bei allen unseren Partnernhat das Managementzum Teil ja mehrfachgewe	\ww593148.new
11	r von GreenpeaceInternational, über das Managementder Umweltschutzorganisat	\ww59466.new
12	e, daß es keinen Grundgibt, warumdas Managementeiner ZeitschriftanderenRe	\ww492193.new
13	nkreter und verdichtensich, so daß das Managemententsprechendreagierenka	\ww69496.new
14	ze Flut neuer Aufträgereinbringen. Das ManagementvonArianespacekontert. U	\ww193156.new
15	d schon völligvoneinandergetrennt. Das Managementliegt heute und in Zukunfti	\ww292144.new
16	ühaufklärungdazu geführt, daß sich das Managementeingehendmit dem Thema	\ww69497.new
17	er. "Manche Unternehrnenmüssen das Managementausdünnen, wollendie Leut	\ww59349.new
18	tzten Umsatzpotentialemacht MSR das Managementaus. Um Lohnkostenzu kü	\ww694104.new
19	esentlich verschlechternwürde. Um das Managementauf die Auswirkungendiese	\ww69498.new
20	anzierung- zu fallen. "Früherwußte das Managementnicht mehr, was es mit de	\ww39150.new

Once again, the two periodicals display divergent tendencies. I calculate that, in total, there are four times more (+abstract) examples of 'management' words in TM than (+human). The difference is less pronounced in WW, but in general, (+human) examples tend to outnumber (+abstract), as can be seen from the figures for **führung* in Table 3.

Table 3 Comparing the occurrence of (+human)/(+abstract) compounds of **führung*

**führung*	No. of occurrences in TM (113)	% of total occurrences	No. of occurrences in WW (61)	% of total occurrences
(+human)	17	15	42	69
(+abstract)	94	83	19	31
unclear	2	2	0	0

3.3 Differences in lexical variety

I will focus in this section on some initial findings on differences in lexical variety between the two periodicals, with particular reference to two points: type-token ratios, and specific lexical items.

3.3.1 Type-token ratios

Type-token ratios were calculated for the various word-forms, including their presence in compounds, in each corpus. Looking at the type-token ratios for the compound forms in both the 'management' and 'manager' groups, one finds that the number of types occurring in WW is, for almost every category, greater than in TM, even when the overall number of tokens is greater in TM than in WW. This suggests that WW uses a more varied lexis than TM in respect of the word families denoting 'manager' and 'management'. A much greater amount of what appears to be *ad hoc* creation of new types is seen in WW, such as *Ex-VW-Chef*, *Schwäbisch-Hall-Vertriebschef*, and *BP-Shipping-Chef*, in comparison with TM where, if an unusual compound is featured, it is often a specialized management term (e.g. *O.I.-Führung*[5]).

Table 4 Comparison of type-token ratios

'Qualifier' words	Type-token ratios		'Head' words	Type-token ratios	
	TM	WW		TM	WW
Leitung*	0	1:1	*leitung	1:4.5	1:3
Führung*	1:3	1:3	*führung	1:7.5	1:3
Management*	1:2.5	1:1.5	*management	1:4	1:2
Leiter*	1:1	1:5	*leiter	1:1.5	1:2.5
Führer*	1:1.5	1.1	*führer	1:3	1:4
Manager*	1:4	1:4	*manager	1:1.5	1:1.5
Boß*	0	1:3	*boß	0	1:1.2
Chef*	1:2	1:2.5	*chef	1:1	1:2

Table 4 illustrates the difference between the two corpora. These findings suggest that the use of the expressions investigated in this study is characterized by a greater degree of lexical variety in WW (relative to TM, at least) and, conversely, TM has a relative tendency towards lexical repetition. In other words, the more specialist publication appears to be lexically rather conservative, while the weekly magazine appears to be lexically more adventurous. My first reaction to this implication was that it was counter-intuitive – rightly or wrongly, I had anticipated that the 'higher', specialist publication would contain a more varied and complex range of vocabulary than the 'lower', journalistic publication. However, the type-token ratios for the lexical items investigated in these two corpora suggest that, here at least, the reverse is the case. One possible explanation, which would naturally require further investigation, is that TM displays a preference for terminological exactness and/or orthodoxy over stylistic considerations.

A cautionary note needs perhaps to be sounded at this point with regard to the interpretation of type-token ratios. For almost every lexical item there are more types found in WW, despite the fact that sometimes the type-token ratio may appear to favour TM. In other words, although in some cases the type-token ratio seems to be higher in TM than in WW, this may be due to the fact that the actual number of tokens found in TM is very low – perhaps only one or two instances. For example, there are only three tokens of **chef* in TM, each one representing a different type, so the type-token ratio is 1:1, or 100 per cent, the highest level of variety. But in WW, there are 521 tokens of **chef*, representing no fewer than 233 types. The type-token ratio for WW is therefore around 50 per cent. But it is a moot point whether we can meaningfully say that WW has half the type-token ratio found in TM. Common sense tells us that the evidence found in WW is on a completely different scale to that found in TM.

3.3.2 Specific lexical items

One of the more obvious differences in lexical variety is that TM generally avoids 'low' register words for 'manager'.[6] *Boß* is not found at all in TM, and this makes the occurrence of *Chef* in the TM corpus sufficiently interesting to prompt a closer look at the contexts in which it occurs. On closer inspection, we find that *Chef* is used in several passages in which the author is adopting the perspective of a *Mitarbeiter* – in other words, of an employee lower down the ladder. I have already noted that *Führer, Leiter*, and *Manager* are the preferred items for denoting managers in TM. It would appear that *Chef*, by contrast, is a marked item, not the kind of word a TM author would use with reference to himself or his peers (at least not in print) – these being the implied readers of the periodical. This point can reasonably be deduced even from the often rather scant evidence of the KWIC concordance lines:

1	n. Früher hatten wir die Weisheit beim Chef konzentriert, und der verließ sich a	\tm29467a.new
2	r ab. Angeführt von Jaques Calvet, dem Chef des PSA-Konzerns, formierten sic	\tm29222a.new
3	einem Menschen übrigbleibt, wenn der Chef den Raum betritt." Erfolgreich wird	\tm29239a.new
4	ar und wird von einem Chef geführt. Der Chef ist die Schlüsselfigur der Organisa	\tm19235a.new
5	tigen ist. Aber niemand anderer als der Chef des Unternehmens kann diese Auf	\tm49452a.new
6	n Job. Was aber im Fall des Falles der Chef denkt, das lasse ich mal offen." N	\tm49452a.new
7	die Franzosen sagen: "Il a une tete du chef ", d. h. " er wirkt einfach wie ein Ch	\tm39304a.new
8	und überschaubar und wird von einem Chef geführt. Der Chef ist die Schlüsself	\tm19235a.new
9	Satz eines Exil-Ungarn kommentieren: "Chef weiß selbst nicht, was soll mach	\tm4927a.new
10	noch bei ESSO tätig war, wollte mein Chef mich durch ein Lob motivieren und	\tm29234a.new
11	erschein benutzen, wohl aber ungeprüft Chef von tausend Mitarbeitern werden d	\tm29239a.new
12	Nein, diese Klarstellung kann nur vom Chef selbst erfolgen. ò Die zweite Antw	\tm49452a.new
13	u chef ", d. h. " er wirkt einfach wie ein Chef", ohne daß man um seine konkret	\tm39304a.new
14	; ich bin dafür v., daß ...; er ist nur dem Chef, dem Vorstand [gegenüber] v.; ich	\tm49226a.new
15	den Umsatz verdoppelt",lobt sich der Chef. Leise Rückfrage: "Und was haben	\tm29239a.new

Note, for example, the presence of words such as *mal, Job, dich* in some of the co-texts, words which suggest informal, colloquial, even spoken language. Line 1 comes from a text which discusses the lateral spread of responsibility within management, and refers specifically to the support of the *Kundenberater* by the entire organization, not leaving it to the *Chef*. Lines 2, 7 and 13 are either in French, a translation of French, or referring to a Frenchman. Line 14 is a citation from the *Duden-Stilwörterbuch* (1970), defining the word *verantwortlich*. Lines 5, 6 and 12 come from the same article, and, fairly conclusively, as the wider context reveals, the author is *in einem imaginären Gespräch mit einem Mitarbeiter*. Lines 4 and 8 refer to the structure of a typical company with the *Chef* at the top. Lines 7, 8, 13 and 14 come from an article on making management more 'human'; line 3 is a quotation from Wernher von Braun, and line 10 details a personal experience of the author (when younger and lower down the ladder). Finally, line 9 comes from an article on the amusing mistakes that foreigners make when trying to speak or write German. Clearly, none of these examples refers explicitly to specific people (with the exception of line 2), in contrast to the evidence for *Chef* from WW, where 114 of the 177 examples of *Chef* as an independent word are followed by the genitive article and a company or department name.

Perhaps it is possible to see an extension of this point in the evidence for *Führung* from both corpora. The collocation *unter Führung* is often found in WW, but virtually absent from TM. Returning to the notion of an implied readership, one might ask whether this finding might reflect different assumptions which are being made about the readers of each periodical. It could be that the stereotypical WW reader belongs to the middle to lower echelons of management rank, and might therefore be accustomed to think of him/herself as *unter Führung*; whereas TM assumes a rather different, and more elevated, readership, more likely to belong to the middle to upper ranks of management, who might therefore be less accustomed to think of themselves as *unter Führung*. TM readers, in other words, tend to see themselves as the leaders rather than the led. This is, admittedly, speculation, but speculation which is shaped by the general findings of this study.

4 Conclusion

The corpus-based analysis of these two periodicals, centred on their use of a defined set of key vocabulary items, has produced the following findings:

1. The distribution of these lexical items, both as independent words and as constituents in compounds, is radically different in the two corpora. The relative distribution of 'manager' words and 'management' words, as distinct groups, in one corpus is virtually a mirror image of their distribution in the other.
2. 'Manager' words significantly outnumber 'management' words in WW, the reverse being the case in TM.
3. Where words for 'management' occur, they tend to be semantically (+human) in WW, denoting a group of people, and (+abstract) in TM, denoting a function.
4. Certain major differences concern the use of 'low register' items such as *Chef* and *Boß*. Where *Chef* is used in TM, it often coincides with an implied invitation to adopt the perspective and linguistic habits of individuals who are lower down the employment hierarchy.

As I have suggested at various points in this paper, these findings suggest that a more detailed study of these two periodicals might produce further data which cumulatively would build a linguistic profile of what in effect are differences in register. I have further argued that these differences in register should also be viewed in terms of the different assumptions being made about the readership of each publication. A logical next step would seem to be to explore the possibility of expanding the linguistic evidence of systematic variation between the two corpora, informed, for example, by Biber's 'factorial' model of register variation (1988), to produce a more differentiated linguistic profile based not on external or functional concepts of register variation but on the 'internal evidence' of the corpora themselves.

Notes

1 The *technologie & management* (TM) corpus consists of 441 429 tokens; the *Wirtschaftswoche* (WW) corpus consists of 524 952 tokens. It is obviously essential to be able to compare corpora on equal terms, and so a simple method was devised of adjusting the figures up or down as if the total number of words per corpus were exactly 500 000. Figures from TM are divided by 88.28 and then multiplied by 100; figures from WW are divided by 104.99 and then multiplied by 100. This creates statistical data which are exactly comparable, and all figures used in this study are adjusted in this way. A point worth noting is that these corpora are completely 'clean'; they have no marks or codes whatever attached to them. This was a deliberate decision, since the corpora were compiled primarily to provide semantic and lexical information; therefore there was not much to be gained from the time-consuming process of inserting codes.

2 Biber has written extensively on register variation; see, for example, Biber (1988; 1995) and Biber et al. (1998), particularly Chapter 6.

3 See also Iser (1974).

4 See Fox (1990: 280). Fox states that overlaps and gaps between 'meanings' of words are normal. However, in this study there seem to be very few cases where overlaps occur; most occurrences of the words under investigation can be allocated clearly either to the (+human) or (+abstract) category.

5 *O.I.-Führung*: this stands for Organizational Intelligence, a term coined by Takehiko Matsuda, president of the SANNO College in Tokyo, and is used to define the process of interaction of human and artificial intelligence in an organization.

6 The 'low register' words referred to here are *Chef* and *Boß*. To confirm that these are regarded as low register words, see the following dictionary definitions from the *Duden Fremdwörterbuch* (1990).

Chef *der*; -s, -s: 1.a) Leiter, Vorgesetzter, Geschäftsinhaber; b) (ugs) Anführer. 2. (ugs) Saloppe Anrede (als Aufforderung o. ä.) an einen Unbekannten. (p. 141)
Boß [*niederl.-engl.-amerik.] der*; Bosses, Bosse: derjenige, der in einem Unternehmen, in einer Gruppe die Führungsrolle innehat, der bestimmt, was getan wird; Chef; Vorgesetzter. (p. 122)

References

Biber, Douglas (1988), *Variation across Speech and Writing*. Cambridge University Press: Cambridge.

Biber, Douglas (1995), *Dimensions of Register Variation: a cross-linguistic comparison*. Cambridge University Press: Cambridge.

Biber, Douglas, Susan Conrad and Randi Reppen (1998), *Corpus Linguistics. Investigating language structure and use*. Cambridge University Press: Cambridge.

Duden Fremdwörterbuch (Band 5) (1990). Dudenverlag: Mannheim.

Fox, A. (1990), *The Structure of German*. Clarendon: Oxford.

Halliday M. A. K. (1978), *Language as Social Semiotic: the social interpretation of language and meaning*. Edward Arnold: London.

Iser, W. (1974), *The Implied Reader*. Johns Hopkins University Press: Baltimore and London.

Stubbs, M. (1996), *Text and Corpus Analysis*. Blackwell: Oxford.

The ASTCOVEA German Grammar in conText Project

Peter Roe

Background to the project

The project reported on here provides language learners, or others interested in exploring the German language, with a corpus and a flexible browser. Although conceived primarily in terms of its pedagogic function, it also permits general queries regarding what the German language, as exemplified by this corpus, is like. It formed part of a larger project entitled Computer-Assisted FL Grammar Learning (CALL at ASTCOVEA), which itself formed part of TLTP Project 65.[1] From the beginning the aim of the programme was to make teaching and learning more productive and efficient by harnessing modern technology. ASTCOVEA (originally the Universities of ASTon, COVentry and East Anglia, subsequently only the first two of these) focused on improving the command of French and German grammar by undergraduates in British universities. This essay reports more particularly on the corpus-based software for German developed by the University of Aston, and more recent developments.

The pedagogic perspective

The view was taken that two complementary principles are at work when undergraduate students of foreign languages develop their grammatical competence: the explicit and the implicit. The explicit principle suggests that the underlying regularities of a language need to be specifically modelled, using named parts and relationships, rules and possibly transformations, to provide conscious insight into those regularities, thus enabling us to ensure that our own performance in the target language conforms with the prescriptions and proscriptions of that model. The implicit view argues that we know intuitively whether or not a stretch of discourse conforms with such a model by virtue of its familiarity derived from a great number of exposures *in vivo*, which subconsciously engram a multiplicity of possible templates, collectively referred to as *Sprachgefühl*. This perspective was formulated by Bolinger as

> the gradual EMERGENCE of meaning, for the speaker, through a long process of decontextualization in which a word is only dimly grasped at first, and slowly, as it gains in contexts, cancels its overextensions, one by one. (Bolinger 1965: 446)

The same principle applies even more strongly to structures than to words. Propounders of the implicit view point back to Malinowski (see his supplementary essay in Ogden and Richards 1949), Vygotsky (1934) and beyond, more recently to Krashen (1982) and Prabhu (1987), and currently – and with the greatest immediate relevance – to the conclusions of such work as Alderson et al. (1996), e.g.:

> There is no evidence to support the belief that students with higher levels of metalinguistic knowledge perform better at French, or that they improve their French proficiency at higher rates than other students. (Alderson et al. 1996: 13)

The thinking which informed this project was not of the extreme form that one or other of these principles alone would suffice, but that the best formula for success was a judicious balance between the two, not forgetting that the formula for a judicious mixture would vary significantly from individual to individual. For Altmann (1997) code and context are inseparable and mutually interactive. The learners

> use the structure of the events they see in the world to aid in their interpretation of the structure of the sentences they hear. Conversely, they use the structure of the sentence they hear to guide what

> they should be attending to in the world they see. It is a two-way process.
>
> (Altmann 1997: 40)

The next stage in the argument was provided by my Aston colleague Frank Knowles taking the extreme (but only partly humorous) view: 'The best way to learn Russian is to go away and read twenty million words.' Yes, but there are at least two major disadvantages to this approach (apart from problems of alphabet). Which twenty million words? And if the instances of these regularities of language are perversely scattered throughout, what are the chances that the learner will notice them? The omens are not good unless we weight the odds in the learner's favour. This we do in three stages:

1. Select the texts used from sources which the learner is most likely to encounter and feel 'at home' with.
2. Arrange for a computer to group and cluster regular patternings of language.
3. Allow learners to explore these at their own speed, and to follow their own interests, rather than follow a prescribed *a priori* menu.

The first of these three steps was realized by the decision to create a corpus consisting entirely of texts presented to learners by university tutors, either as examination passages or classroom exercises, plus a few A-level examination papers. This was the world of discourse most likely to match their needs, and to incorporate and instantiate just those regularities they are likely to encounter, and for which they need to develop the necessary *Sprachgefühl*. The second was to commission an educational software company, Forwords Limited, to produce the necessary learner interface. Professor Nigel Reeves was in overall charge, assisted by Dave Pollard, the Aston CAL specialist. I was responsible for the detailed design, for which I drew on the work I had already done in connection with the Lexical Studies programme offered as part of the Aston Masters degree in the Teaching of English, and various French and German projects.

Implementation

Professor Reeves invited the heads of all departments of German to submit samples of the texts they used in first-year undergraduate classes and examinations. Relevant examining authorities were also asked to supply recent texts for translation at university entrance level. The response was most rewarding, and of the order of a million words of text were received. It was decided that, based on our experience with other corpora (*Le Monde*, *Handelsblatt*, *Financial Times*, etc.) a corpus of the order of 100 000 tokens would be appropriate for the purposes outlined above. The complex nature of the significant morphological differences between the three languages analysed (French, German, and English) precludes simplistic comparisons, such as word length versus morphological variation. But more words might well have swamped the regularities we wished to bring into prominence. If the aim had been use and variability of lexis, clearly a much larger corpus would have been indicated.

Selection criteria

In the event, the corpus statistics for French and German were as follows:

	Characters	Tokens	Types
German	701 109	94 864	18 545
French	664 983	106 941	16 004

Thus a larger German corpus, in terms of characters, has fewer tokens than the French. The difference would have been greater given a different definition of 'token', which is simply that of any string of non-punctuation characters bounded by spaces, provided the string contains a letter of the alphabet. This results in e. g. the French *qu'arrive-t-il* and the German *Bundesverfassungsgerichtsurteil* both being counted as a single token, but <'Franchise'-system> being counted as two.

Much of the text received covered topics, and contained language, which not everybody saw as 'suitable' for young people. The decision on this was that if we were to start bowdlerizing, we would not know where to stop, and that this would defeat the initial assumptions about the nature of the discourse which learners would be faced with. Consequently, no text was either selected or excluded on the grounds of content. The only criteria of selection were:

- Take at least one item from every source.
- Favour texts not heavily dependent on visuals.
- Avoid poetry which does not observe sentence boundaries.

A small amount of verse, and one instance of text in note form, were included.

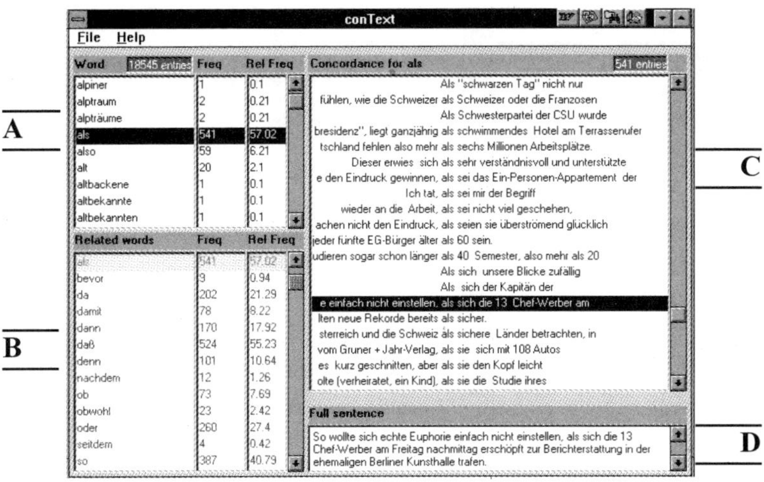

Figure 1 General view of the Grammar in conText screen, with the type 'als' selected

The learner interface

The screen which controls the learner interface is shown in Figure 1. The four sections of the screen are labelled A, B, C and D and serve as follows. Section A shows all types in the corpus, together with the raw and relative frequency (out of 10 000). If the word highlighted in this frequency list is seen as belonging to a pedagogically useful category, or 'family', this family is listed in section B. Double clicking on a type in Section A produces a concordance for it in Section C. The full sentence containing the line highlighted in Section C is shown in Section D. The total number of lines in the frequency list and the concordance is shown above the appropriate listing. These are shown as 18 545 and 541 respectively in Figure 1.

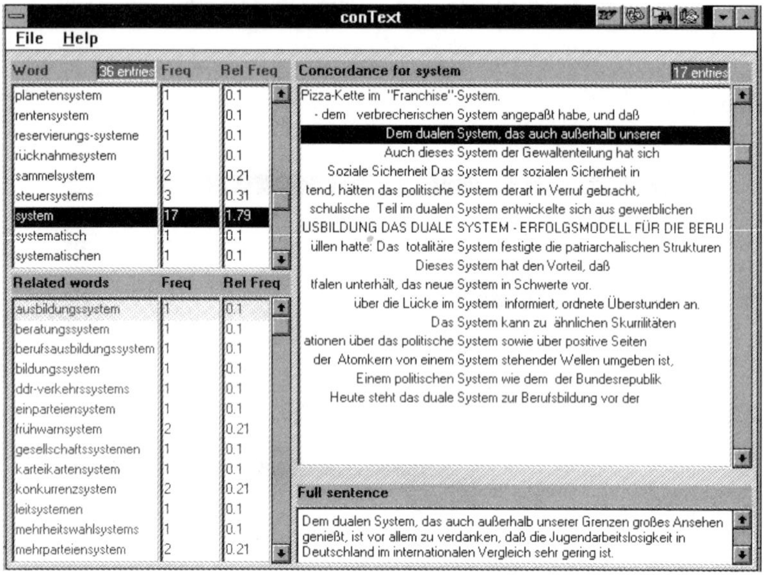

Figure 2 As for Figure 1, except that the frequency list now shows only those types which contain the substring 'system'

The user can modify these screens as follows:

Section A The frequency listing of the types can also be displayed in alphabetical order. The list can also be filtered for a substring, specifying word-initial, word-final, or anywhere. In Figure 2 the string 'system' has been specified.

Section B Clicking on a word locates that type in Section A.

Section C The concordance listing can be ordered alphabetically left or right of the keyword. It can also be filtered by a substring left, right or both. The example in Figure 2 (system) has been ordered right but not filtered.

Section D Sentences too long for the box can be scrolled as necessary.

Table 1 The first 150 lines of the frequency list showing raw scores and relative frequencies (out of 10 000)

die	3614	382.16	werden	335	35.42
der	3048	322.31	bei	325	34.37
und	2529	267.43	aber	324	34.26
in	1777	187.91	nur	320	33.84
das	1153	121.92	man	295	31.19
den	1113	117.69	haben	292	30.88
zu	1025	108.39	um	280	29.61
sie	987	104.37	mehr	279	29.50
sich	837	88.51	wird	271	28.66
von	822	86.92	über	264	27.92
nicht	817	86.39	zum	263	27.81
mit	813	85.97	oder	260	27.49
ich	808	85.44	wir	258	27.28
ist	750	79.31	vor	255	26.97
es	733	77.51	am	249	26.33
ein	719	76.03	einen	249	26.33
auf	703	74.34	einer	247	26.12
für	649	68.63	einem	212	22.42
im	632	66.83	prozent	203	21.47
eine	605	63.98	durch	202	21.36
dem	594	62.81	da	202	21.36
als	541	57.21	ihre	198	20.94
daß	524	55.41	wenn	196	20.73
des	507	53.61	schon	192	20.30
auch	493	52.13	was	174	18.40
an	488	51.60	deutschland	172	18.19
er	423	44.73	immer	171	18.08
aus	404	42.72	dann	170	17.98
so	387	40.92	hatte	170	17.98
sind	380	40.18	zur	169	17.87
nach	368	38.91	sein	167	17.66
wie	361	38.17	deutschen	161	17.02
noch	351	37.12	doch	160	16.92
war	347	36.69	kann	157	16.60
hat	336	35.53	mich	153	16.18

Table 1 cont.

diese	147	15.54	nichts	87	9.20
wurde	146	15.44	millionen	84	8.88
habe	143	15.12	heute	83	8.78
mir	141	14.91	ja	81	8.57
wieder	138	14.59	neue	81	8.57
bis	135	14.28	eines	80	8.46
keine	133	14.06	hab	80	8.46
ihr	132	13.96	sagte	80	8.46
waren	132	13.96	ddr	78	8.25
seit	125	13.22	damit	78	8.25
alle	123	13.01	leben	78	8.25
menschen	123	13.01	ihm	78	8.25
gegen	122	12.90	fast	77	8.14
viele	121	12.80	frauen	77	8.14
unter	120	12.69	andere	75	7.93
zwei	117	12.37	ersten	75	7.93
jahr	116	12.27	weil	75	7.93
können	116	12.27	ihren	74	7.83
jetzt	114	12.05	ab	73	7.72
uns	114	12.05	bundesrepublik	73	7.72
dieser	113	11.95	drei	73	7.72
sei	111	11.74	gut	73	7.72
vom	106	11.21	ihnen	73	7.72
ihrer	104	11.00	müssen	73	7.72
ganz	103	10.89	ob	73	7.72
jahren	102	10.79	selbst	72	7.61
denn	101	10.68	wurden	72	7.61
deutsche	100	10.57	kein	71	7.51
jahre	100	10.57	etwa	70	7.40
ohne	100	10.57	frau	70	7.40
muß	100	10.57	viel	69	7.30
hier	98	10.36	jeder	68	7.19
seine	98	10.36	nun	68	7.19
sehr	98	10.36	ihn	67	7.08
zeit	94	9.94	ins	67	7.08
alles	92	9.73	seiner	67	7.08
etwas	92	9.73	wollen	67	7.08
gibt	91	9.62	diesem	66	6.98
mark	90	9.52	geht	65	6.87
zwischen	88	9.31	kinder	65	6.87
neuen	87	9.20	mal	65	6.87
machen	87	9.20			

Frequency lists

The first 150 types in the frequency list, in descending order of frequency, are shown in Table 1. This gives the learner an overview of some of the main building blocks of the German language at the atomic level of 'type'. What it fails to highlight is the 'gluons' (tied morphemes or micromolecules, by analogy with the gluons which hold quarks together in subnuclear physics) of German morphology and the characteristic macromolecular patternings of German syntax. But it does enable the learner to ask to see the molecules associated with a certain 'atom', or even 'gluon'. For example, the frequency list can be reduced to only those types which end in the morpheme '-heit' or '-ung'. An overview of all types in the corpus containing a given morpheme can give the learner a sense of the range of what can be expected, thus contributing to the desired *Sprachgefühl.* But the full list of which Table 1 is just a small portion cannot bring out the importance and function of those individual morphemes, frequent in themselves as elements in a range of different types, which are cumulatively numerous but individually too infrequent to figure in a frequency list of simple types. One such example is the element '-system-'. In its 'root' form it occurs only sixteen times, but the total occurrence of the string in all types is nearly four times as great (sixty-three), which would place it only just off the end of the scale of Table 1. The full list of all types containing the substring 'system' is shown in Table 2.

Table 2 All types containing the substring 'system', with frequencies

16 system	4 systems	3 steuersystems
2 frühwarnsystem	2 konkordanzsystem	2 konkurrenzsystem
2 mehrparteiensystem	2 sammelsystem	2 zweiparteiensystem
1 ausbildungssystem	1 beratungssystem	1 berufsausbildungssystem
1 bildungssystem	1 ddr-verkehrssystems	1 einparteiensystem
1 'franchise'-system	1 gesellschaftssystemen	1 karteikartensystem
1 leitsystemen	1 mehrheitswahlsystems	1 mehrwegsysteme
1 mischwahlsystem	1 parteiensystems	1 pfandsystem
1 planetensystem	1 rentensystem	1 reservierungs-systeme
1 rücknahmesystem	1 systematisch	1 systematischen
1 systeme	1 verteilungssystem	1 vielparteiensystem
1 vielparteiensystems	1 wahlsystem	1 wertesystem
1 wertsystem		

As they do not fall together in either numerical or alphabetical order, they need to be seen as a concentrated list in their own right. This gives the learner the opportunity to form an overall impression of the characteristic way in which the morpheme combines with others, leading to Bolinger's 'gradual EMERGENCE of meaning', and contributing to the 'long process of decontextualization' by which word structure 'is only dimly grasped at first', slowly becoming more familiar.

Pedagogically useful 'families'

This notion, linked to that of Alderson et al. quoted earlier, led to the conviction that metalanguage should be kept to a minimum, if what we are interested in is more learners' ability to produce correct German than to parse it. This relates likewise to the Barthesian notion of intertextuality and the *déjà lu*, the sense of awareness of many thousands of snatches or 'chunks' of text we know we have encountered, without knowing where, which form the basis of our *Sprachgefühl*. As Culler puts it,

> Barthes warns that from the perspective of intertextuality 'the quotations of which a text is made are anonymous, untraceable, and nevertheless already read'; they function – this is the crucial thing – as 'already read'. (Culler 1981: 103)

An ability to parse or construe will never amount to this sense of familiarity, of an intuitive awareness of which such 'texts' are in current use in the community, and above all of the range of contexts and co-texts in which they are considered appropriate. Parsing, and the associated 'tagging', carry with them the excessive overhead of learning a labelling system, which needs to be further and further refined to cater for all the syntactic distinctions and subdistinctions natural language is heir to. Parallel to his article referred to above, Bolinger might well have written another entitled 'The Atomization of Syntax'. Against which, learners can be saved a lot of timewasting wonderment by having it pointed out not only that *bin*, *ist*, *sei* and *war* are all in some way related, but that so are, in different ways, *zu* and *von*, *mein* and *ihr*, in ways that learners as researchers are invited to explore, thereby enriching their intertextual store. It is a purely pedagogic decision as to what members are put into each category, or family, the important thing being that they are labelless. The families arrived at in the Grammar in conText project are a (hopefully judicious) mixture of lemmas, derivatives, and semantic and syntactic affinities. They are not based on any formal system of analysis.

Concordances

Thus emerge the beginnings of a sense of grammaticality at word level. The next stage is to allow the same gradual emergence of an awareness of the rich range of possibilities of German word order through a similar 'long process of decontextualization', this time in a context (or at least sufficient co-text to provide a glimpse of context). A simple double click on an item in the frequency list, itself possibly reduced by a 'gluon' search, leads to a full concordance of the item in question in a span of four words to left and right. By ordering these alphabetically according to the text to left or right of the keyword, left-associative and right-associative patternings stand out, highlighting regularities in the German language as exemplified by the corpus. In the case of long concordances, these can be filtered for collocates of interest, even when these are not adjacent to the keyword. The judicious use of filters, and left and right ordering, can quickly foreground syntactic patternings not otherwise apparent. Figure 2 gave a simple example for *System*. Figure 3 shows the first lines of a concordance for *doch* after 'Sort left' has been selected. The effect of this is to place all instances of sentence-initial *Doch* at the top, since the left-hand side is always blank in such cases. (Case is preserved in concordances, but not in the frequency lists.)

Sentence level

A superficial inspection immediately reveals that there is no inversion after *doch*. A closer look, however, appears to provide conflicting evidence in the shape of the line highlighted which also appears to give *Grund* the wrong gender. This demonstrates how, although the short plus/minus four word contexts suffice for the recognition of common regularities, the text of the full sentence, available on demand, is sometimes necessary for syntactic disambiguation.

Many aspects of German syntax, particularly the discontinuous verbal group or subordinate clause structure, are of course invisible to a four-by-four contextual span. For this reason, any line of a concordance can instantly be expanded to full sentence level, as illustrated in Figure 2 and Figure 3.

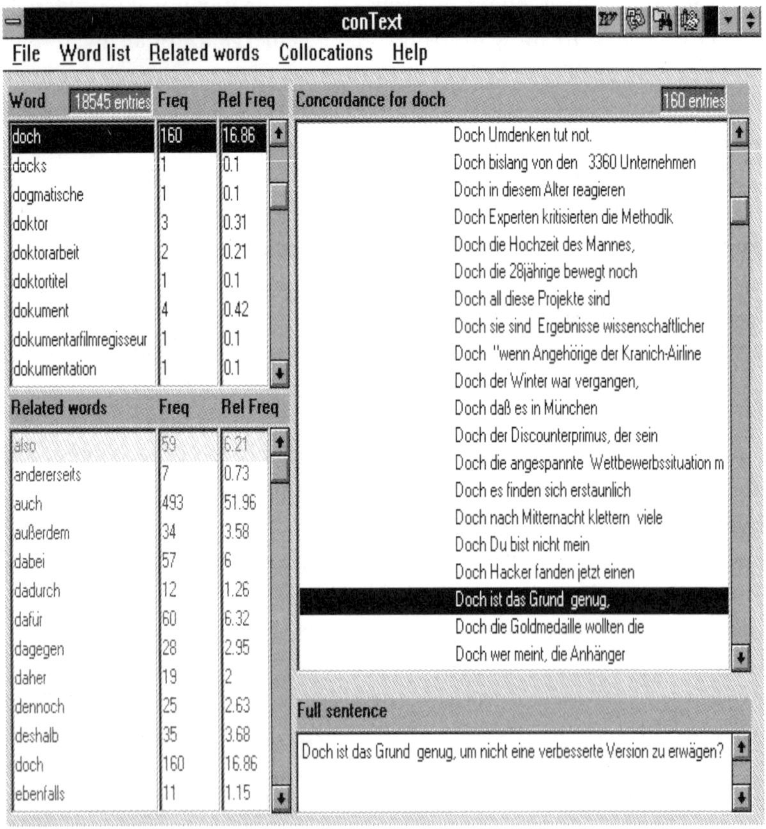

Figure 3 The first twenty lines (of 160) of the concordance for *doch*, after left-hand alphabetical ordering

Obtaining your copy of Grammar in conText

Grammar in conText is freely available to educational institutions in the United Kingdom, and can be downloaded from <http://www.aston.ac.uk/cal>. There is also a manual and a set of exercises available at the same site. For further information, please e-mail me at <p.j.roe@aston.ac.uk>.

Further developments

In spite of the success of Grammar inContext, there was a natural tendency to wish it could achieve more. It was seen as a useful tool for the learner as researcher, of some help to the teacher as researcher, but less so for the linguist as researcher. So the search was on for an interface designed to provide more power, without losing any of the existing benefits. The Language Studies Unit of Aston University therefore commissioned an entirely newly programmed (by Forwords Limited) Windows-based suite of functions which would add significantly to the functionalities available, particularly the ability to export screens and to summarize lexical distribution in a long concordance in the form of a 'synoptic profile'. Thus Language inSight was born, and applied to a number of languages. In the case of German, the main text used was a quarter of a million words scanned from *Handelsblatt*, by kind permission of the proprietors.

The new screen

This appears as shown in Figure 4.

The reference corpus

This new feature enables at-a-glance comparison with lexical distribution in other corpora. The third column in the word frequency list shows the relative frequency (to the same base of 1/10 000) of the type in another corpus of the user's choosing. In the above case, the ASTCOVEA corpus has been used. The 'Filter' options have been designed to display only those types of greater or lesser frequency than the reference

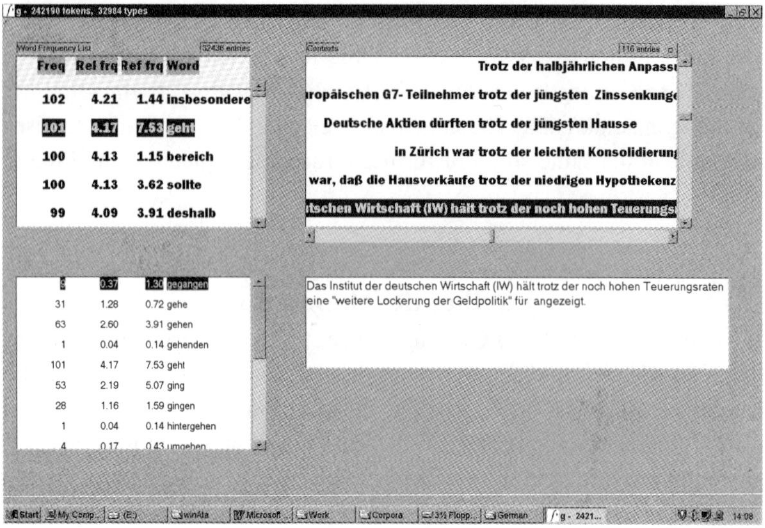

Figure 4 The Language inSight screen

corpus. This function has many possible applications of interest, not so much to learners as to researchers wishing to establish comparisons and contrasts across authors, genres or periods.

The frequency filter

Grammar in conText already had a filter for types in the word frequency list, but could not search on the frequencies themselves. Language inSight has now made this possible, enabling the researcher to call, for example, for all hapax legomena (types occurring only once) in alphabetical order, and to see at a glance how many there are of these.

The synoptic profile

Perhaps the most significant advance in terms of Language inSight as research tool is the provision for converting the concordance into a synoptic summary (see Figure 5) of all tokens in a concordance. It can often be tedious to search manually through a concordance of a thousand lines for regularities, especially when these are discontinuous. For example, *unter Umständen* may appear as a (perhaps relatively infrequent) phrase. All instances will appear together under a right-sorted concordance for unter. But it is harder to observe the numerous instances of *unter* [*diesen/den heutigen/solchen* ...] *Umständen*. This relationship can readily be seen in a synoptic profile. To take another example, if one suspects *allerdings* of being sensitive to pejorative or negative semantic prosody,[2] the display in Figure 5 may prove helpful, at least to the initiated.

g - 242190 tokens, 32984 types
Profile | 171 entries

5 der	7 die	7 die	10 ist	16 nicht	22 die	14 die	8 der
4 nach	5 der	4 ist	5 sei	8 nur	13 sich	11 der	7 von
3 in	4 und	4 des	5 der	8 noch	9 es	4 in	6 die
3 im	4 ist	4 der	4 sich	7 die	7 in	3 von	5 daß
2 zum	3 von	4 das	3 wird	6 wird	7 der	3 und	4 und
2 r	2 sich	4 Das	3 sind	6 sei	6 zu	3 einer	4 nicht
2 mit	2 sei	3 in	2 wurde	5 wieder	6 das	3 auch	4 in
2 käme	2 fr	3 d	2 wolle	5 mit	5 nicht	2 r	4 im
2 ein	2 einiger	3 Es	2 wobei	5 ist	5 daß	2 noch	4 es

Figure 5 A synoptic profile for *allerdings*

The user needs to know that the eight columns represent the eight positions, four to the left and four to the right, of the keyword in a set of contexts. The figure against each type is the number of occurrences for it in that position in the concordance. A cursory examination of Figure 4 reveals that *nicht* is the commonest word to follow *allerdings* (sixteen occurrences), but that it also occurs frequently in positions +3 and +4 after the keyword. The frequency of *nur* and even *noch* would send the researcher back to the full concordance, and possibly full sentences, in search of evidence of these items functioning as restrictions on the scope of a proposition, if not a fully negative sense.

Maximized screens, font selection and cumulative filter

A further innovation is the option to maximize the concordance screen, whether in concordance or synoptic profile mode. Figure 5 shows an example of a profile in full-screen mode, while Figure 6 presents part of a full-screen concordance for *je*. This shows the further option of over-printing the sentence containing the highlighted concordance line, and the pedagogically useful device of successive filters being added to the screen. In this case, all instances of *je* preceded by *denn* have been added to those for *als,* thus highlighting the structural ambiguity of *denn je*.

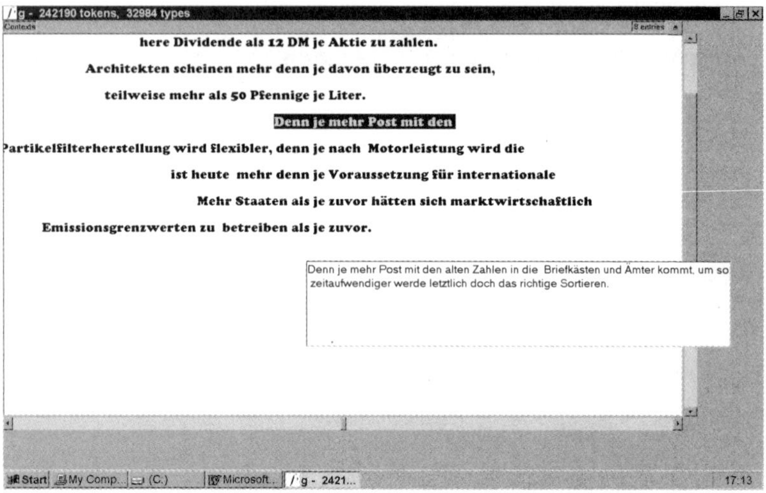

Figure 6 Full-screen display of contexts for *je* preceded by *denn* and *als*

Crystal gazing

It is as yet a little early to evaluate the success of this approach with learners of German, and a fully fledged methodology has yet to be elaborated and tested. But Aston University doctoral students are currently producing exciting results using comparable techniques with learners of English. Kirkgöz, whose results are now available as an unpublished thesis (Kirkgöz 1999), has transcribed the protocols of Turkish students working on concordances of economic texts, studying the ratiocinative processes involved.

A working hypothesis

As a result of work so far by students at Masters and doctoral level in a number of countries, it is currently felt that success in developing the elusive *Sprachgefühl* will lie in the direction of tilting the scales more in favour of the intertextuality principle, at the expense of the conventional emphasis on grammatical system and metalanguage. But as a well-known figure in the field remarked to me: 'Intertextual chunks – there must be thousands of them! You can't teach them all!!' No indeed. So the answer once again seems to lie in the aphorism: Don't try harder, try different. And that difference surely lies in the common experience of asking an average German 'What is the gender of *Lied*?'. According to the working hypothesis, our average German will not in fact 'know', but will be able to work it out. Call up a few intertextual chunks, such as *das klagende Lied*, *ein anderes Lied*, etc. and s/he knows it is a *das*-word, that *das*-words are neuter, and that the answer to the question asked is 'neuter'. But it is the *Sprachgefühl* which generates that knowledge, not the other way about.

Conclusion

I end with a reminder of the words of Bakhtine (1977) in the French translation from the Russian of a work which appeared originally in 1929.

> La langue, en tant que produit fini («ergon»), en tant que système stable (lexique, grammaire, phonétique) se présente comme un dépôt inerte, telle la lave refroidie de la création linguistique, abstraitement construite par les linguistes en vue de son acquisition pratique comme outil prêt à l'usage. (Bakhtine 1977: 75)
> Language, seen as a finished product ('ergon') as a stable system (lexis, grammar, phonetics), appears as an inert deposit, the solidified lava, as it were, of linguistic creation, abstractly constructed by linguists with a view to its practical acquisition as a ready-to-use tool. [My translation]

The *Sprachgefühl* argument is certainly not new.

Notes

1 For further detail see <http://www.icbl.hw.ac.uk/tltp/>.

2 See the Introduction to this volume.

References

Alderson, J., C. Clapham and D. Steel (1966), *Metalinguistic Knowledge, Language Aptitude and Language Proficiency.* Working Papers Series 26, Centre for Language in Language Education: Lancaster (End-of-Award Report to the Economic and Social Research Council).

Altmann, G. (1997), *The Ascent of Babel: An exploration of language, mind and understanding*. Oxford University Press: Oxford.

Bakhtine, M. (1977), *Le Marxisme et la philosophie du langage* (originally published under the name *Volochinov* in 1929). Les Editions de Minuit: Paris.

Bolinger, D. (1965), 'The atomization of meaning' in Jakobovits & Miron (eds), *Readings in the Psychology of Language*. Prentice Hall: New Jersey.

Culler, J. (1981), *The Pursuit of Signs*. Routledge & Kegan Paul: London.

Kirkgöz, Y. (1999), 'Knowledge acquisition from L2 specialist texts', unpublished Ph.D thesis, University of Aston, Birmingham.

Krashen, S. (1982), *Principles and Practice in Second Language Acquisition*. Pergamon: Oxford.

Prabhu, N. (1987), *Second Language Pedagogy.* Oxford University Press: Oxford.

Ogden, C. and I. Richards (1949), *The Meaning of Meaning*. Routledge and Kegan Paul: London.

Vygotsky, L. (1934), *Language and Thought*. Gosisdat: Moscow.

An electronic corpus of Early New High German

Jonathan West

1 Early New High German and corpus linguistics

Early New High German (ENHG) denotes the German language from c.1350 to c.1750. Between these two rather arbitrary dates,[1] German is characterized synchronically by marked regional, social and text-typical variation in orthography, grammar and vocabulary and diachronically by the emergence of a supraregional, standardized, written idiom, which ultimately becomes the New High German (NHG) standard language. In broad terms, the process takes place in two phases. The first is one of unplanned convergence of regional written usages, in which the early years of the sixteenth century seem to be particularly significant. The second is one of conscious planning and codification which sees a demand for, and finally the emergence of, genuinely standard works of lexicography and grammar. Running parallel to this standardization process in German is a gradual change in the relative position of German and Latin. In the early period, Latin functioned as the standard written language: writing in German was relatively rare. Indeed, many of the texts of the earlier period, even those apparently independent of Latin, cannot be read or understood outside their wider Latin context. As the period progressed, German gradually supplanted Latin in an increasing number of text-types and emerged as a language of extraordinary versatility and power. However, the importance of Latin for the period as a whole cannot be over-emphasized. One indication of this are Schirokauer's figures, to date unchallenged, which report that German imprints outnumbered Latin ones for the first time as late as 1681 (König 1994: 99; von Polenz 1994: 20). The heterogeneity of ENHG, and its dependence on Latin, make the problems associated with corpus definition and use particularly acute.

Electronic corpora of German have existed for many years and have formed the basis for a number of indices and concordances.[2] The most important for the present discussion is the Bonn corpus, used to provide basic data for the Bonn volumes of the *Grammatik des Frühneuhochdeutschen* (Wegera 1987; Dammers et al. 1988; Solms and Wegera 1988).[3] This Bonn corpus has been described extensively elsewhere (Hoffmann and Wetter 1985). Briefly, it comprises two sub-corpora consisting of texts of roughly comparable length (40 *Normalseiten*, '40 normal pages') reflecting written prose usage in ten High German dialect areas in four fifty-year periods (see Table 1).

Table 1 The Bonn corpus

	1350–1400	1450–1500	1550–1600	1650–1700
EUG (Vienna)	111 (HC73 theological)	113 (HC320 chronicle)	115 (HC329 chronicle)	117 (HC1 theological)
WUG (Swabian)	121 (HC188 devotional)	123 (HC141 literary)	125 (HC376 chronicle)	127 (HC310 chronicle)
NUG (Nuremberg)	131 (HC319 devotional)	133 (HC266 devotional)	135 (HC106 devotional)	137 (HC45 devotional)
ECG (Upper Saxon)	141 (HC426 devotional)	143 (HC440 devotional)	145 (HC301 devotional)	147 (HC 518 literary)
WCG (Cologne)	151 (HC60 chronicle)	153 (HC88 chronicle)	155 (HC177 devotional)	157 (HC399 theological)
WUG (Alemannic)	211 (HC364 factual)	213 (HC116 chronicle)	215 (HC271 devotional)	217 (HC195 literary)
WUG (Augsburg)	221 (HC112 literary)	223 (HC206 literary)	225 (HC8 devotional)	227 (HC133 devotional)
WUG (Strasbourg)	231 (HC272 devotional)	233 (HC96 factual)	235 (HC527 literary)	237 (HC328 literary)
WCG (Hessen)	241 (HC445 theological)	243 (HC97 factual)	245 (HC374 chronicle)	247 (HC5 chronicle)
ECG (Thuringian)	251 (HC117 theological)	253 (HC282 chronicle)	255 (HC480 chronicle)	257 (HC170 devotional)

The Bonn corpus was designed to provide data on inflectional morphology and the resulting volumes are now standard works. The *Grammatik des Frühneuhochdeutschen,* which carried on the pioneering work of Moser (1929, 1951), remained faithful to an essentially neogrammarian plan and did not envisage sections on word formation or syntax, let alone text structure. However, a syntax section is included in the new *Frühneuhochdeutsche Grammatik* in the *Sammlung kurzer Grammatiken germanischer Dialekte* series (*Frühneuhochdeutsche Grammatik* 1993, abbreviated *FG*).[4]

Clearly, other variables could have been incorporated into the data as well. Text-type is an obvious one, but there is no evidence that text-type correlates in any significant way with inflection, and it is therefore not surprising that the Bonn corpus did not reflect it. However, the texts chosen were all in prose and relatively homogeneous (eleven chronicles, five theological texts, fourteen devotional, seven literary, and two factual). For its purpose the corpus is probably large enough. With additional tagging, it could probably also be used for some aspects of syntax (e.g. sentence patterns). But to elicit meaningful information on word formation (now a focus of research activity in several centres), other aspects of lexical organization, and areas of syntax which interface with the lexicon (e.g. valency), a larger, more differentiated corpus is needed. We should also consider whether more than one text should be included for each category,[5] although it can be extraordinarily difficult to find accessible data of unambiguous date and provenance, especially for the earlier time periods. The remainder of this paper reports on steps taken to remedy this deficit using texts collected for the *Frühneuhochdeutsches Wörterbuch* and addresses some of the theoretical and practical problems which arise.

2 The *Frühneuhochdeutsches Wörterbuch* and the Heidelberg corpus

There is at present no complete dictionary of ENHG apart from glossaries like Götze's (1971), which is, as its title suggests, intended primarily for seminar work. Serious lexicographical access to the period has been for many years via the dictionaries of Middle High German (MHG), which cover the late medieval period and occasionally the early sixteenth century (Lexer 1872–78; Benecke et al. 1963), historical dictionaries of NHG (for example, Grimm and Grimm (1984); *Deutsches Rechtswörterbuch* (1914–1983), and a battery of sundry reference works, largely written in the nineteenth century. Of these, the most important are Diefenbach and Wülcker (1965), which contains material which Diefenbach had collected in his work on late medieval glossaries (1857; 1867); Kehrein (1965), which lists vocabulary from his collection of hymns; and Schade (1966), which contains a range of short theological texts from various dialect areas reflecting sixteenth-century usage. Although these early works have recently been supplemented by a series of studies on individual authors (e.g Tauber 1983; Wetekamp 1980; West 1989), and the publication of key lexicographical works of the fifteenth century (e.g. Bremer 1990; Schmitt 1983; Grubmüller et al. 1988ff), the replacement of this gallimaufry of lexicographical endeavour with a scholarly reference work is an urgent desideratum.

Compared with earlier historical periods of German (Schwarz 1984–85; Kästner and Schirok 1984–85), the ENHG textual base is immense and would require a major dictionary project to describe its lexicon in the degree of detail which standard dictionaries of modern languages achieve. While recognizing this as a desirable long-term goal, the scholars who conceived the *Frühneuhochdeutsches Wörterbuch* (*FWB,* Early New High German Dictionary), the first detailed dictionary of ENHG, sought to reflect the diversity inherent in a non-standardized language during a period of significant change in a reference work of manageable size which would appear within a reasonable period of time. Bearing these constraints in mind, the impracticality of compiling and excerpting a text corpus from scratch was immediately apparent. The solution was to access the language through the glossaries of edited texts and to accept the shortcomings entailed by this methodology in a provisional dictionary, but one which will nevertheless be acceptable for the foreseeable future. The resultant database is a corpus of over 500 primary texts (referred to hereafter as the Heidelberg corpus, abbreviated HC), which reflects diachronic, diatopic and text-typical variation in the way detailed briefly in the following sections. The application of what are largely traditional methods on this corpus has already resulted in several volumes of the dictionary; others will follow at regular intervals and the whole project is scheduled for completion in c.2005.

As far as the *Frühneuhochdeutsches Wörterbuch* is concerned, the Heidelberg corpus is being used to generate slips which are then used to compile dictionary entries in the traditional fashion. Briefly, the method is to use the glossaries of the edited texts to produce dictionary slips. A slip is produced for each example noted in the glossaries, assigning it to a headword (lemma), time period, dialect area, and noting meaning, syntactic features and possible synonyms. For each example, a portion of the edited text is photocopied and pasted onto the slip. Because even this is too large a project for a single scholar to handle, the work has been split between a number of scholars who have each undertaken to work on a portion of the alphabet. Each participant in the project is committed to the methodology underlying the volumes already published (*FWB*:10–164) so as to ensure that the dictionary remains as homogeneous as possible. Naturally, this leaves little scope for experimentation or development in the primary task – and also produces, in the form of boxes full of index cards, an inflexible database which can only be used for the production of the dictionary. However, a condition of local finance for the Newcastle part of the project was that the data collection should not produce a static collection of dictionary slips and it was therefore decided to begin to store the corpus in machine-readable form. While the primary aim of the Newcastle project is therefore to complete Volume Q–SR, a secondary goal is to use the corpus for further linguistic study of ENHG. The two chief desiderata in this area are syntax and word formation.

Two problems must be tackled if the Heidelberg corpus is to be used for further computer-assisted analysis. First, there is the storing of the data in electronic form and its subsequent retrieval. Equally important, however, is the extent to which an essentially random corpus of texts – chosen on no other basis than that their editors saw fit to append a glossary – can be adapted for this purpose. Even if the entire corpus were available in machine-readable form, it would still be impossible, as Table 2 shows, to represent all the variables. Some of these lacunae are less serious than others. For example, although North German literary texts are not well represented until the seventeenth century, it is

Table 2 Distribution of Heidelberg Corpus texts according to region, type and date (see section 3.3 for abbreviations)

	NG	WCG	ECG	NUG	WUG	EUG	Enclaves
Rewi.							
14c.	(3)	4 (25)	4 (17)	3(5)	3 (36)	15 (11)	2 (2)
15c.	1 (3)	1 (25)	2 (19)	2(7)	6 (44)	3 (17)	5 (2)
16c.	–	2 (19)	6 (13)	3 (5)	2 (38)	2 (12)	(3)
17c.	(1)	(15)	(5)	(2)	(28)	(7)	(1)
Chron.							
14c.	–	1 (1)	1	–	1 (1)	–	(1)
15c.	–	4 (1)	5	3 (1)	7 (5)	8	(1)
16c.	1	1 (2)	1	(2)	16 (4)	3	(1)
17c.	(1)	2	–	2	2	–	(1)
Lit.							
14c.	–	1	–	2	3 (1)	2	–
15c.	–	4 (1)	3	2(4)	7 (6)	6 (3)	–
16c.	–	4 (1)	2	2 (1)	8 (5)	–	–
17c.	1	–	1	2	3	–	–
Did.							
14c.	2	1(2)	(4)	–	(3)	1 (2)	–
15c.	–	(3)	2	2 (4)	4 (11)	2 (6)	–
16c.	(7)	(2)	(1)	(1)	7 (5)	(1)	–
17c.	–	–	–	–	–	–	–
Theol.							
14c.	–	3 (2)	4 (5)	–	8 (2)	4 (1)	–
15c.	–	2 (3)	1 (3)	3 (1)	9 (3)	4 (5)	–
16c.	(7)	(3)	4 (1)	1 (1)	5 (1)	(1) 1	–
17c.	–	1	–	–	–	1	–
Erb.							
14c.	–	1	(1) 1	1	2	–	–
15c.	–	–	(1) 1	(1)	1	3 (4)	–
16c.	1	1	1	2	2	–	–
17c.	–	–	1	–	1	–	–
Real.							
14c.	–	1	–	1	2	1	–
15c.	1	1	1 (1)	1	3	5 (4)	–
16c.	–	1	(1)	1 (1)	2	4 (2)	–
17c.	–	–	1	1	–	–	–
Wb.							
14c.	–	–	–	–	–	–	–
15c.	–	1	1	1	2	(1)	–
16c.	2	1	1	1	4	–	–
17c.	–	–	–	–	2	–	–

Note Numbers of texts not uniquely representing a given category are in brackets probable that fourteenth- and fifteenth-century texts from this region would not be particularly informative on the question of the development of High German (HG), as the majority of centres went over to HG only during the sixteenth century. In a similar way, the cluster of West Upper German (WUG) dictionary texts represents the dominance of this area in the production of dictionaries. Finally, it is unclear at this stage of research exactly which variables will be relevant. As there is a good deal of overlap between some of the Heidelberg categories – for example, didactic and religious texts often deal with similar subject matter – it remains to be seen whether the distinction, even when it can be unambiguously made, will be significant for syntax and word formation. It is therefore unwise simply to take over the Heidelberg classification in the new corpus. In addition, new texts must be found to fill the slots in the matrix, so that each category is represented by a number of sources.

Another problem is the comparative rarity of texts uniquely representing one field in the matrix. Most span a number of time periods; some span dialect areas; and with yet others it has been impossible to determine the global text-type satisfactorily. These problem texts are indicated by chevrons in brackets.

2.1 The diachronic axis

The diachronic axis is one particularly problematic aspect of the Heidelberg corpus. A large number of the Heidelberg corpus texts are datable, but, as far as the distribution of texts over the period is concerned, the corpus reflects the editorial interests of preceding generations of scholars rather than changes in real language production. As is clear from Figure 1, the fifteenth century appears to be over-represented and the seventeenth century under-represented. This apparent under-representation is more serious when one considers that many of the seventeenth-century texts only partially represent the period – they provide evidence for other periods as well – and that the glossaries appended to them are necessarily less comprehensive than those for earlier centuries, as the texts are more accessible for modern readers (Reichmann, *FWB* 1: 57). Even though this imbalance can be compensated for by statistical methods, and is indeed a weakness in the corpus which we shall address again below, it is worth noting that the later period is represented, partly through a sub-set of the secondary sources (*FWB*: 225–85), by a number of compendious dictionaries which function both as a control and rich source of data.[6] The importance of dictionaries in extending compositional word formation patterns (WFPs) has already been shown using data from Dasypodius' dictionary (West 1993).

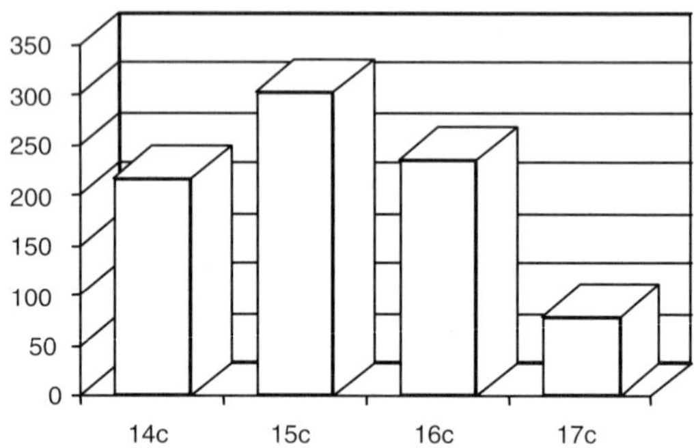

Figure 1 Datable texts in the Heidelberg corpus

2.2 The diatopic axis

As far as diatopic variation is concerned, the grouping corresponds to the major dialect areas listed below and their associated main centres of production (see König 1994: 98–9; von Polenz 1994: 181–2).

- Low German (LG) – Lübeck, the second largest German city in the Middle Ages, Magdeburg, Hamburg, Rostock; Cologne and Wittenberg also printed in Low German;
- West Central German (WCG) – Cologne, the largest German city in the Middle Ages, Mainz, Marburg, Worms, Speyer, Frankfurt, Trier, later also Hanau and Heidelberg;
- East Central German (ECG) – Leipzig, Erfurt, Wittenberg, Dresden, Jena, Eisleben;
- West Upper German (WUG) – Strasbourg, by far the earliest and most significant centre, Basel, Freiburg, Augsburg, Hagenau, Zürich, Ulm;

- North Upper German (NUG) – principally Nuremberg, but also Würzburg;
- East Upper German (EUG) – Vienna, Ingolstadt, Munich, Regensburg, Altdorf.

In addition, German was printed in enclaves in Eastern Europe. The relative significance of each of these areas in the Heidelberg corpus is expressed in Figure 2.

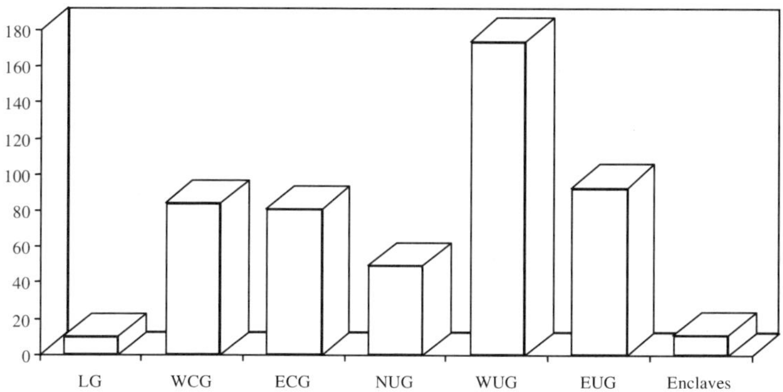

Figure 2 The representation of dialects in the Heidelberg corpus

At first sight, it would appear that WUG is grossly over-represented, but one must bear in mind that the contribution of each area to German written output was uneven and also variable over time. For example, König (1994: 90) shows the relative contribution of the WUG, EUG, NUG, WCG and ECG dialect areas to book production during the sixteenth and seventeenth centuries: WUG falls from just under forty per cent in the first half of the sixteenth century – no doubt due to the pre-eminent position of Strasbourg in printing – to just over twenty per cent in the second half of the century, a position it maintained for the seventeenth century as well. The 'market leader' at the end of the period is ECG, which climbs steadily in significance from just over twenty per cent at the beginning of the sixteenth century to just under forty per cent at the end of the seventeenth, reflecting the growing importance of Leipzig, Wittenberg and Dresden. Particular text-types may originate predominantly from a particular region. Of the seventy-one manuscripts which form the basis of the *Liber ordinis rerum* (*LOR*) edition (Schmitt 1983: xiii–lxviii), three are LG, two are WCG, one is undifferentiated CG, two are ECG, and four are WUG, whereas fifty-six are EUG. It is probable that, as far as the UG dialect areas are concerned, the Heidelberg corpus is representative enough, whereas LG, especially at the end of the period when the LG cities had adopted High German for administrative purposes and Berlin was becoming an important centre, requires further data.

2.3 The text-type axis

Text-typical variation has been the subject of a number of studies in recent years. For example, Schwitalla (1976) distinguishes four *Sinnwelten/Funktionsbereichen* 'conceptual/functional spheres': Alltagswelt, Religion, Wissenschaft, Dichtung ('practical/every-day, religious, scientific/learned, literary texts'). The Heidelberg corpus distinguishes the following, also essentially thematic, categories (Reichmann 1989: 54–5): legal and economic (*Rewi: rechts- und wirtschaftsgeschichtliche Texte*), chronicles and reports (*Chron.: chronikalische und berichtende Texte*); literary (*Lit.: unterhaltende und literarische Texte*); didactic (*Did.: didaktische Texte*); ecclesiastical and theological (*Theol.: kirchliche und theologische Texte*);

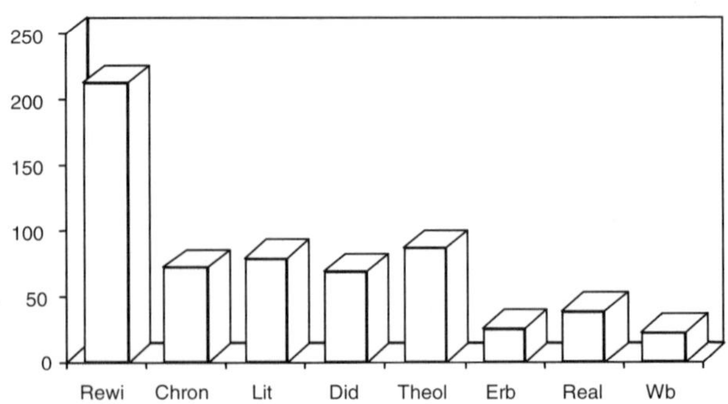

Figure 3 The representation of text-types in the Heidelberg corpus

devotional (*Erb.: erbauliche Texte*); factual (*Real.: Realientexte*), and dictionaries (*Wb.: Wörterbücher*).

However, this scheme, represented in Figure 3, takes no account of the medium – i.e. poetry vs. prose – nor of the number of speakers – i.e. dialogues vs. monologues. As these variables have been shown to be significant in the texts of Hans Sachs (West 1995), there is some reason to suppose that they may be significant over the whole corpus.

3 The Newcastle corpus

The Newcastle corpus will therefore attempt on the one hand to represent features not accounted for by the Bonn corpus and on the other to supplement the range of texts in the Heidelberg corpus to take account of the sixteenth and seventeenth centuries and the output of Central German presses. Bearing in mind that the primary aim of the project is to complete volume Q–SR of the *Frühneuhochdeutsches Wörterbuch*, efforts to date have been directed towards the parts of the Heidelberg corpus which are not in machine-readable form. A number of these texts have therefore been scanned and used to supplement the Bonn corpus, which forms the core of the electronic element in our text base. Most of these additions require post-editing and checking before they can be used even for compiling the dictionary. This process is ongoing. Not all texts are suitable for a variety of reasons. Some are facsimiles, and others are in *fraktur*, and thus are, at the present time, beyond the capability of the scanning software available to us. With others, the typeface is damaged to such an extent that post-editing has had to be postponed. Yet other texts have been entered manually either in whole or in part.

Once the texts are declared 'clean', they can be marked up for analysis. This involves coding for references, non-standard characters, and basic parsing information. The following paragraphs outline the conventions used and then the new work in ENHG syntax and word formation is described.

3.1 Reference coding

The Bonn corpus uses fixed references: a three digit code to indicate the part of the corpus, then the dialect area and finally the time period, followed by additional information on page and line numbers. This method has been adopted for the extended corpus. It will be observed from Table 1 that the Bonn corpus is split into two sub-corpora (designated 1 and 2 respectively by the first digit), leaving eight digits and the entire alphabet in position one and five digits in position two for additional coding (more will probably not be necessary). The first position can now be used to identify additional sub-corpora as they become relevant for our research. The second position can be used to identify Low German: 16 and 26 would then indicate WLG and ELG respectively. The third digit indicates the time period: here, eight of the available ten digits are used, leaving '9', which could be used for the period after 1750, and '0'. This system consequently leaves room for expansion while retaining the references in the Bonn corpus and allowing for the coding of additional variables such as text-type.

3.2 Text coding

The text coding problems associated with ENHG texts revolve around the character set, language mixing, parsing and grammatical tagging. As far as the character set is concerned, ENHG has a much wider range of symbols than the modern language and these are not standardized. The character set used must therefore be flexible enough to retain all the information of the original texts while still being able to be used on as wide a range of machines as possible. At Newcastle, Oxford Concordance Program (OCP) has been used for the analysis of individual texts and groups of texts but other programs, such as WordCruncher, which was used in Bonn, could be employed equally well. ENHG regularly mixed German and Latin, but other languages are also encountered, for example in dual-language dictionaries. Finally, additional characters are needed for parsing and grammatical tagging.

4.2.1 The character set

The first problem with the Bonn corpus is that it was compiled using punched cards and upper case letters only. This restriction is no longer necessary, as both current machines and programs can deal with both upper and lower case, so the code '*A' for <A> as opposed to 'A' for <a> can be dispensed with. A small program has been used to re-code the corpus using upper and lower case, thereby liberating the '*' sign for use elsewhere. However, despite the temptation to use a more elaborate character set, including <ü>, <ö>, <ß> and other characters, it was decided, so that the corpus can be used as widely as possible, to restrict the corpus and its tags to the ASCII character set. The Bonn corpus also used a code '2' to indicate umlaut: thus <Nürnberg> is encoded 'N2URNBERG'. However, umlaut can just as easily be encoded under the superscript system, so <Nürnberg> becomes 'Nu>"rnberg', releasing the digit '2' for other purposes.

Symbol	**Function**	**Examples**
<	superscript	m**u<**"ssen 'm**ü**ssen' m**u<e**ssen 'mùssen' habe<- 'habe'
'	ligatures	dis'z 'diß'

Of course, it should be remembered – and we shall have to make this point again below – that merely representing the information in the original does not necessarily absolve the user from interpreting the data. Umlaut is a case in point. We know that the phonological changes must have taken place prior to the Old High German period, with some subsequent analogical levelling (Keller 1978: 163), also evidenced in the modern dialects (Chapman 1994). However, it was not regularly marked until the late sixteenth century in German, and even when it was indicated in writing, a variety of orthographical devices were employed, including superscript <e>, superscript <i>, acute accent, and diaeresis. In the case of [uː] and [ʊ] vs.[yː] and [ʏ], the matter is further complicated by the fact that <v> was used beside <u> in initial position, so that NHG <über> can easily be encountered as ENHG <vber>, as well as <uber>, with any of the diacritics mentioned above.

3.2.2 Grammatical coding

The problems facing grammatical coding derive firstly from the non-standardized texts themselves. In NHG, or any other standard language, we are lulled into thinking that word-forms and orthographical words are one and the same thing. Thus a NHG orthographical word <Stadt> is the word-form {stadt}, reflecting the singular of {STADT}. ENHG offers us a more realistic picture, as the orthographical realization of word-forms is variable.

	NHG	**ENHG**
LEXEME	{STADT}	{STADT}
Word-form	{stadt}	{stadt}
orthographical word	<Stadt>	<stat>, <stad>, <statt>, <stadt>, etc.

Problems also derive from the nature of German itself as an inflected language with a significant amount of lexical conditioning, so that the coincidence of any grammatical and lexical morphemes may produce a set of unpredictable forms. For example, the realization of {PLURAL} and {STADT} is easily dealt with at a word-form level, in so far as the set of possible plural forms using either umlaut or umlaut and {-e} – {städt} / {städte} – are triggered by the lexeme {STADT}, and the distribution of these forms is conditioned mainly by regional factors. However, this masks significant problems at the level of orthographical word, where we have for all practical purposes an open set of forms: {<stet>, <stedte>, <stàdt>, …}. The case of {STADT} is a simple example. Verbs have a much larger set of word-forms, reflecting not only number, but person, tense, mood and voice, and a correspondingly larger set of orthographical realizations. There are three basic lexically conditioned inflectional types (strong, weak and preterite present), with the past tenses of the strong forms being lexically conditioned also (e.g. *ich liege* vs. *ich lag* 'lay', but *ich biege* vs. *ich bog* 'bend'), and a significant set of the weak verbs as well, especially in the earlier period (e.g. *ich sende* vs. *ich sante* 'send', but *ich blende* vs. *ich blen(de)te* 'blind'). Dialect forms also complicate matters: *ich liege* may have a past tense *ich log* 'I lied' if it corresponds to NHG *ich lüge* in addition to the form given above.

To begin to solve these problems, significant distributional categories have been coded in the Bonn corpus using a variety of symbols placed before the encoded orthographical words concerned. This has the advantage of partly lemmatizing the word-forms, as '+' for instance has a higher ordinal value than '&' in the ASCII character set.

Symbol	Function	Examples
+	noun	ein &scho<ene ***+Historia***
&	adjective	ein **&scho<ene** +Historia
$	verb	Darumb **$spricht** er [...]
^	adverb	Jch $will euchs **^reichlich** $vergelten

The Bonn team also developed an automatic lemmatizing routine using the consonants of the root and disregarding prefixes such as {ge-}, {be-}, etc. (Lenders and Wegera 1983). Suppletive forms (e.g. *ich bin* 'I am' vs. *ich war* 'I was') can then be accessed individually, as there are relatively few of them. In the analysis of Dasyopodius' dictionary (West 1989: 39–41), the lemma form was specified in every case, with additional coding for case and number.

NSg masc	+LEMMAA	**NSg fem**	+LEMMAI	**NSg neut**	+LEMMAQ
A	+LEMMAB	**A**	+LEMMAJ	**A**	+LEMMAR
G	+LEMMAC	**G**	+LEMMAK	**G**	+LEMMAS
D	+LEMMAD	**D**	+LEMMAL	**D**	+LEMMAT
NPl	+LEMMAE	**NPl**	+LEMMAM	**NPl**	+LEMMAU
A	+LEMMAF	**A**	+LEMMAN	**A**	+LEMMAV
G	+LEMMAG	**G**	+LEMMAO	**G**	+LEMMAW
D	+LEMMAH	**D**	+LEMMAP	**D**	+LEMMAX

So the nouns from the first entry –

> A1. A PRAEPOsitio cum ablatiuo significat Von. Interdum post, ut à partu, Nach der geburt. à coena, Nach dem nachtmal. Ita, Secundus à rege. Der oberst nach dem kœnig.

were coded '+GEBURTL_geburt'; '+#NACHTMALD_nachtmal'; '+KÖNIGD_ko<enig', which allowed easy access to number and case forms.

However, both the Bonn programs and the Dasypodius procedure suffered from the drawback of assuming that grammatical features such as number, case, tense, person, etc., are expressed at word level. However, as Durrell (1990) has shown in the case of the noun phrase, these features are expressed at phrase level. The use of periphrastic verb forms to indicate tense, phase, mood and voice makes this analysis obvious in the case of the verb phrase. A fresh approach has significant implications for the description of ENHG syntax (see below).

3.2.3 Word formation coding

A number of studies have used the Bonn corpus to investigate word formation. For instance, Prell and Solms (1987) used the Bonn corpus to investigate methodological problems and look at deadjectival formations and verbs with prefix {zer-}; Nitta (1987) addressed the problem of secondary compounds. Several features of ENHG word formation present researchers with problems.

Again, the orthographic variability of the allomorphs is significant. For example, the formative {heit} commonly appears as <heit>, <hait>, <heyt>, and <hayt>; {nis} appears as <nis>, <niss>, <nisse>, <nus>, <nusse>, <nús>, <nússe>, etc. Such variants may have regional significance. For example, the <a>-variants of {heit} are characteristic of Upper German, whereas the <e>-variants are usual elsewhere (*FG*: 57–8). With <nis>, the <i>-variants are characteristic of Central German and Alsatian, whereas the <u>-variants are East Upper German, East Alemannic and Swabian (Besch 1967: 225–8). However, the variants in a single text, or a group of texts, are unlikely to preclude the strategy of specifying the endings in a precise enough way to allow them to be analysed. Using OCP, for example, where '*' stands for any number of letters including none, and '@' stands for any one letter, the formula

+*@@@heit* +*@@@heyt* +*@@@hait* +*@@@hayt*

would pick out nouns where the sequence specified does not begin within the first three letters, but may be followed by an ending. It would therefore exclude nouns such as '+scheit', but include forms such as '+kranckheyten'.

The identification and marking of nominal compounds is another area of difficulty, primarily because orthographical univerbation did not become regular until the closing phase of the period. For most of the period, it is quite possible for compositional elements to be written separately. So while the need to preserve features of the original text dictates that we should not normalize this practice, it would be useful to be able to access compounds in the same way as any other nouns. The Bonn corpus solves part of the problem by marking the orthographical space between compositional elements with the hatch symbol '#', as in the example given below

1350018V040[...] das es ein +leibs#u<ebung
1350018V050$wer / auff das sie [...]

but does not mark compounds written together in any special way. The Newcastle solution is to code orthographically unified compounds as '+#' so that all compounds can be accessed together, regardless of whether they are written as one word or two in the original text. The pick command of OCP would therefore, using the formula '*#*', list both the example of {LEIBESÜBUNG} given above and the following one

1350018V080+Herr $lest solche +#leibsu<ebung fallen / [...]

which occurs a few lines further on. This involves a partial re-coding of the Bonn corpus, a slightly more intensive coding of the extended corpus than would otherwise be the case, and defining '#' as a letter. It can, of course, be omitted when printing if desired. The advantage of this approach is to go beyond seeing orthographical univerbation as the only means of accessing changes in the use of compounding in the ENHG period (Pavlov 1983). Even though it is a useful indication of the awareness of compounds as lexical items, the use of linguistic rather than orthographical criteria to identify compounds (West 1993) will provide more reliable data on the history of these important word formation patterns and again illustrates the responsibility of the researcher to analyse the material in a transparent way.

A slightly more difficult case is the treatment of so-called separable verbs. In the following example,

> 1350019V010Wer euch $auffnimbt / der $nimbt mich auff / rc.

'$auffnimbt' and '$nimbt ... auff' are both forms of {AUFNEHMEN}, but a concordance program such as OCP would list them separately. Various solutions are possible, ranging from the inclusion of the form under which the word is to be lemmatized in the text

> 1350019V010Wer euch $AUFNEHMEN_auffnimbt / der $AUFNEHMEN_nimbt mich auff / rc.

which would not involve programming, to simply tagging the separable prefix as such

> 1350019V010Wer euch $auffnimbt / der $nimbt mich %auff / rc.

so that a parsing program, on encountering a '%' sign would look back for a word-form tagged with '$'.

As far as the size and variety of the corpus is concerned, some questions of word formation, such as primary vs. secondary composition, and the relative frequency of compounds, can probably already be tackled using the Bonn corpus, as these are not directly dependent on individual lexical choices. Derivational WFPs, on the other hand, require a larger corpus. For example, is the choice between {SIECHTAG} and {SIECHTUM} of the same order as the choice between either of these and {KRANKHEIT} – i.e. do they all represent simple lexical choices? I suspect the answer is much more complex.[7]

3.2.4 Syntax coding

Work on ENHG syntax is extensive (this section is largely based on the surveys of Ebert and Erben),[8] but suffers from a number of problems. No definitive solutions are offered for syntax coding, as this is work for the future. Instead, a number of criteria are presented which any eventual system would have to fulfil.

First, treatments are generally traditional (*FG*: 313–492; Philipp 1980: 92–145), and, although this does not of itself invalidate the descriptions involved, it certainly multiplies the difficulties inherent in comparing ENHG with NHG. A syntactic description of ENHG should therefore use a dependency framework in order to facilitate comparison with NHG (Engel 1988) and MHG, for which some semi-compatible descriptions now exist (Maxwell 1982). As this model assumes that syntactic structures are partially lexically conditioned, a large corpus is needed to capture the structures over the range of lexical items involved, even though the sixteenth- and seventeenth-century dictionaries mentioned above can often provide basic data. Furthermore, only a large corpus will allow us to distinguish reliably between complements and adjuncts in a language only partially accessible to native-speaker intuition.

Second, and probably as a result of using the traditional framework, most descriptions use existing categorizations and therefore important features of the data are missed. For example, Ebert (*FG* 434–6) leaves the reader with the impression that sentences with a *Nachfeld* are comparatively rare, except when *Nachfeld* elements are clausal. However, the briefest perusal of ENHG texts will show that not only are prepositional phrases extrapolated (Ebert's examples consist of three of this type), but also subject complements, and accusatives, and others (Philipp 1980: 97):

subject complement:

1350028V180Solches $zeigt ^klar an das +Gleichnus'z von den +#Weingertnern [...]

accusative complement:

1330155X030[...] ein &andechtiger

1330155X040+man $hat ^ainsten $gehort von einer $sel ein &jemerlich +clag.

The problem appears to lie in the different approaches of the original Bonn group (Solms and Wegera) and Ebert with regard to corpus material. The parts of *Frühneuhochdeutsche Grammatik* which deal with inflectional morphology are based on the corresponding volumes of the *Grammatik des Frühneuhochdeutschen*, which exhaustively analysed a corpus in a transparent way. Even though one might quarrel with the word-based rather than phrase-based approach to morphology, it is certain that no material was left out because it was inconvenient and the statistics give a reliable picture of the relative frequency of phenomena in the corpus and (probably) in the language as a whole. By contrast, Ebert's syntax section of the *Frühneuhochdeutsche Grammatik*, is also based on a corpus but it is impossible to reconstruct how it has been used. Only when a sound empirical description of the ENHG verb phrase exists, both with regard to the number and type of possible constituents and their possible arrangements, can we begin to describe the development of the verb phrase towards NHG with any confidence.

Traditional categories are also used for parts of speech. Even the Bonn corpus falls down on this criterion, for it does not distinguish between adjectives and particles of various types. In the original coding of the extracts given above, for example, '^klar' was coded as an adjective, and '^ainsten' was not coded at all, despite the use of them both here as adverbs. As there is no agreement regarding the distributional classes of the parts of speech in NHG, it is perhaps unreasonable to expect this question to have been settled for ENHG, but even these few examples point up the need for further research.

What might the syntactic marking look like? I use the following short sentence from Michael von Beheim's *Evangelienbuch*, 1343 (Bechstein 1966) (Matt. 5.3) as an example:

> Sêlic sint di armen des geistes, wan daz himelrîche ist ir.

First, it would reflect the position of {SEIN} as nucleus of the sentence. The dependency framework usually employed for the description of NHG discovers sentence constituents – immediate constituent analysis – according to whether they can be moved to first constituent position (before the finite verb which is usually in position two), and then classifies these elements according to whether they depend on a sub-class of verb. On this basis, <Sêlic> would be an adjectival complement (Eadj) and <di armen des geistes> a subject complement (Esub); the *wan*-clause would be a causal adjunct (Icaus).

(Eadj%Sêlic) sint ({SEIN}<sub, adj>) (Esub%di armen des geistes), (Icaus%wan daz himelrîche ist ir).

A major problem with this approach is the unreliability of the criteria for immediate constituent analysis in the ENHG period, as the pattern which places the finite verb in second constituent position was less well developed than it is in the modern language. The evidence of a large corpus would allow us to gauge the significance of other patterns (e.g. *Spricht zu ihm einer seiner Jünger...* 'And one of his disciples said to him...')[9] so that we can put the problem into its proper context – verb initial statements do not appear to figure in Michael von Beheim's *Evangelienbuch*, two centuries older than Luther's 1545 text, for example. A corpus is probably also the only way to decide which constituents are, on the basis of their sub-class specificity, complements or adjuncts.

4 Outlook

This paper has outlined some past and current work with Early Modern German corpora in lexicography, and explored some possibilities for further research into morphology, word formation and syntax using the Newcastle corpus of texts. As we are still at the stage of collecting and marking up texts, the ideal of a corpus – possibly even an online corpus – flexible enough to reflect the many variables which determine the forms we find in Early Modern German is probably many years ahead. It remains to be seen whether a single corpus can provide data for both our main areas of interest, or whether it would be more convenient both for eventual end-users and ourselves to mark up two completely separate corpora. In the meantime, the nucleus of a corpus at our disposal is already beginning to revolutionize the way we view the task.

The first change in perspective relates to size. The Bonn corpus totalled about half a million words; by contrast the Newcastle corpus is expected to exceed forty-five million words in the foreseeable future. This huge increase in the amount of total available data has to be set against the axes of region, date and text-type, so that the entire data set would probably never be used at once. But we must still reckon with a very large number of examples being generated in response to any query. As McEnery and Wilson (1996) have recently pointed out, this in turn demands more sophisticated data retrieval software to sort out the examples into manageable chunks. In other words, a large data set means that we not only have to differentiate between occurrences of <man> 'man' from <man> 'one', but may also wish to determine the meaning and syntactic context before we interrogate the system. The second major change in perspective relates to encoding and standardization. The advent of SGML (Standard Generalized Markup Language) has provided us with a sophisticated but flexible set of guidelines for text encoding, which could not only allow the Newcastle texts to be employed more widely, but could also be used instead of the presently rather idiosyncratic syntactic and morphological tags.

To conclude, whatever the problems in the data, or keeping up with developments in coding and software, or ensuring compatibility with other corpora, one fact remains constant. A dead language such as Early Modern German has to be investigated on the basis of properly constructed corpus information, simply because it can be very misleading to rely on subjective knowledge of the modern language. The Bonn corpus provides just such a starting point, and additions from the Heidelberg corpus – supplemented by further texts to reflect the later periods and the importance of the north – offer us the chance to extend its scope so that the extraction of useful data regarding word formation and syntax will be a practical proposition for the first time.

Notes

1 See Hartweg and Wegera (1989: 18–20) for a discussion of the periodization problem.

2 The most important are listed by Gärtner and Kuhn (1984, 1985: 620–41).

3 I am indebted to Professor Besch and his colleagues for permission to use the Bonn corpus.

4 For background to the new *Frühneuhochdeutsche Grammatik* and *Grammatik des Frühneuhochdeutschen*, see West (1992; 1998).

5 See Biber et al. (1998: 248ff.) for a discussion of this issue.

6 See, for example, Henisch (1973), Stieler (1968–69), Frisch (1977), and Adelung (1970). Although this last item falls outside the ENHG period, the first edition was 1774–86 and reflects the lexicon of the end of the period.

7 See Besch (1967: 206–9) for an overview of the situation in the fifteenth century.

8 Ebert et al. (1987); now also the syntax section of *Frühneuhochdeutsche Grammatik*.

9 Philipp (1980: 95) taken from Luther's 1545 translation of the Bible.

References

Adelung, Johann Christoph (1970), *Grammatisch-kritisches Wörterbuch der Hochdeutschen Mundart mit beständiger Vergleichung der übrigen Mundarten, besonders aber der Oberdeutschen. Zweite vermehrte und verb. Ausgabe. Mit einer Einführung und Bibliographie von Helmut Henne* (Documenta Linguistica. II Wörterbücher des 17. und 18. Jahrunderts. Reprint of the 1793–1801 Leipzig edition). Olms: Hildesheim.

Bechstein R. (ed.) (1966), *Des Matthias von Beheim Evangelienbuch in mitteldeutscher Sprache 1343* (reprint of the 1867 Leipzig edition). Rodopi: Amsterdam.

Benecke, G. F., W. Müller and F. Zarncke (1963), *Mittelhochdeutsches Wörterbuch. Mit Benutzung des Nachlasses von Georg Friedrich Benecke ausgearbeitet von Wilhelm Müller und Friedrich Zarncke* (Reprint of the first edition (1854–56) Hirzel: Leipzig). Hirzel: Stuttgart.

Besch, W. (1967), *Sprachlandschaften und Sprachausgleich im 15. Jahrhundert. Studien zur Erforschung der spätmittelhochdeutschen Schreibdialekte und zur Entstehung der neuhochdeutschen Schriftsprache* (Bibliotheca Germanica, 11). Francke: Munich.

Besch, Werner, O. Reichmann and S. Sonderegger (eds) (1984–85), *Sprachgeschichte. Ein Handbuch zur Geschichte der deutschen Sprache und ihrer Erforschung*, 2 vols. de Gruyter: Berlin.

Biber, Douglas, Susan Conrad and Randi Reppen (1998), *Corpus Linguistics. Investigating language structure and use*. Cambridge University Press: Cambridge.

Bremer E. (ed.) (1990), *Vocabularius optimus*, 2 vols. Niemeyer: Tübingen.

Chapman, C. (1994), 'A diachronic argument against the Split Morphology Hypothesis – analogical umlaut in German dialects', *Transactions of the Philological Society* 92: 25–39.

Dammers, Ulf, Walter Hoffmann and Hans-Joachim Solms (1988), *Flexion der starken und schwachen Verben*, vol. IV of *Grammatik des Frühneuhochdeutschen. Beiträge zur Laut- und Formenlehre* edited by Moser, H., H. Stopp and W. Besch. Winter: Heidelberg.

Diefenbach, L. (1857); *Glossarium latino-germanicum mediae et infimae aetatis. E codicibus manuscriptis et libris impressis concinnavit L.D.* Sauerländer: Frankfurt am Main.

Diefenbach, L. (1867), *Novum glossarium latino-germanicum mediae et infimae aetatis. Beiträge zur wissenschaftlichen Kunde der neulateinischen und der germanischen Sprachen.* Sauerländer: Frankfurt am Main.

Diefenbach L. and E. Wülcker (1965), *Hoch und niederdeutsches Wörterbuch der mittleren und neueren Zeit. Zur Ergänzung der vorhandenen Wörterbücher insbesondere der des Brüder Grimm* (Reprint of the 1885 edition.). Olms: Hildesheim.

Deutsches Rechtswörterbuch. Wörterbuch der älteren deutschen Rechtssprache. In Verbindung mit der Akademie der Wissenschaften der DDR hrsg. v. der Akademie der Wissenschaften zu Heidelberg (1914–83), vols 1–7. Weimar.

Durrell, M. (1990), 'German noun inflections: synchrony and diachrony', *German Life and Letters* 43: 113–24.

Ebert, H., H. and J. Erben (1987), 'Forschungsbericht zur Syntax des Frühneuhochdeutschen', *Zeitschrift für deutsche Philologie* (Sonderheft) 106: 149–77.

Engel U. (1988), *Deutsche Grammatik*. Groos: Heidelberg.

Frisch, Johann Leonhard (1977), *Teutsch-Lateinisches Wörter-Buch. Mit einer Einführung und Bibliographie von Gerhard Powitz* (Documenta Linguistica. II Wörterbücher des 17. und 18. Jahrunderts. Reprint of the 1741 Berlin edition). Olms: Hildesheim.

FG= Frühneuhochdeutsche Grammatik, edited by R. P. Ebert, O. Reichmann, H.-J. Solms and K.-P. Wegera (1993). Niemeyer: Tübingen

FWB= Frühneuhochdeutsches Wörterbuch, edited by R. A. Anderson,

U. Goebel and O. Reichmann. Vol. 1. (1989), Einführung, a – äpfelkern, edited by Oskar Reichmann. de Gruyter: Berlin, New York; Vol. 2. (1993), apfelkönig – barmherzig, edited by Oskar Reichmann. de Gruyter: Berlin, New York; Vol. 3 (1995), Fasc. 1. barmherzigkeit – befremden, edited by Oskar Reichmann. de Gruyter: Berlin, New York.

Gärtner K. and P. Kuhn (1984–85), 'Indices und Konkordanzen zu historischen Texten des Deutschen; Bestandsaufnahme, Typen, Herstellungsprobleme, Benutzungsmöglichkeiten' in W. Besch, O. Reichmann and Stefan Sonderegger (eds), *Sprachgeschichte. Ein Handbuch zur Geschichte der deutschen Sprache und ihrer Erforschung*, 2 vols. de Gruyter: Berlin.

Götze A. (1971), *Frühneuhochdeutsches Glossar* (Kleine Texte für Vorlesungen und Übungen, 101; reprint of the 7th edition, Berlin 1967; first edition 1912). de Gruyter: Berlin.

Grimm, J. and W. Grimm (1984), *Deutsches Wörterbuch*, 33 vols (Reprint of the first edition 1854–1971. Revised version prepared by the Akademie der Wissenschaften zu Göttingen). deutscher taschenbuch verlag: Munich.

Grubmüller, K., B. Schnell, H.-J. Stahl, E. Auer and R. Pawis (eds) (1988ff), *Vocabularius Ex quo. Überlieferungsgeschichtliche Ausgabe*, 5 vols. Niemeyer: Tübingen.

Hartweg F. and K.-P. Wegera (1989), *Frühneuhochdeutsch. Eine Einführung in die deutsche Sprache des Spätmittelalters und der frühen Neuzeit*. Niemeyer: Tübingen.

Henisch, Georg (1973), *Teutsche Sprache und Weißheit. Thesaurus lingue et sapientiae Germanicae* (Documenta Linguistica. II Wörterbücher des 17. und 18. Jahrunderts. Reprint of the 1616 Augsburg). Olms: Hildesheim.

Hoffmann, W. and Friedrich Wetter (1985), *Bibliographie frühneuhochdeutscher Quellen. Ein kommentiertes Verzeichnis von Texten des 14. – 17. Jahrhunderts (Bonner Korpus) mit einem Geleitwort von Werner Besch* (Europäische Hochschulschriften, Reihe I, 869). Lang: Berne, Frankfurt and New York.

Kästner, H. and B. Schirok (1984–85), 'Die Textsorten des Mittelhochdeutschen' in Werner Besch, O. Reichmann and S. Sonderegger (eds), *Sprachgeschichte. Ein Handbuch zur Geschichte der deutschen*

Sprache und ihrer Erforschung, 2 vols. de Gruyter: Berlin, 1164–79.

Kehrein, J. (ed.) (1965), *Kirchen- und religiöse Lieder aus dem zwölften bis fünfzehnten Jahrhundert* (Reprint of the 1853 edition, Schoeningh: Paderborn.). Olms: Hildesheim.

Keller, R. E. (1978), *The German Language*. Faber: London.

König, W. (1994), *dtv-Atlas zur deutschen Sprache*. deutscher taschenbuch verlag: Munich.

Lenders, W. and K.-P. Wegera (eds) (1983), *Maschinelle Auswertung sprachhistorischer Quellen*. Niemeyer: Tübingen.

Lexer, M. (1872–78), *Mittelhochdeutsches Handwörterbuch*, 3 vols. Hirzel: Leipzig.

Maxwell, H. (1982), *Valenzgrammatik mittelhochdeutscher Verben* (Europäische Hochschulschriften, 1/504). Lang: Frankfurt am Main/Bern.

McEnery T. and A. Wilson (1996), *Corpus Linguistics* (Edinburgh Textbooks in Empirical Linguistics). Edinburgh University Press: Edinburgh.

Moser, V. (1929), *Frühneuhochdeutsche Grammatik. I. Band: Lautlehre. 1. Hälfte: Orthographie, Betonung, Stammsilbenvolkale*. Winter: Heidelberg.

Moser, V. (1951), *Frühneuhochdeutsche Grammatik. III. Band: Lautlehre 3. Teil: Konsonanten, 2. Hälfte (Schluß)*. Winter: Heidelberg.

Nitta, H. (1987), 'Zur Erforschung der "uneigentlichen" Zusammensetzungen im Frühneuhochdeutschen', *Zeitschrift für deutsche Philologie* (Sonderheft) 106: 400–16.

Pavlov, M. (1983), *Zur Ausbildung der Norm der deutschen Literatursprache im Bereich der Wortbildung (1470–1730). Von der Wortgruppe zur substantivischen Zusammensetzung*. Akademie Verlag: Berlin.

Philipp, G. (1980), *Einführung ins Frühneuhochdeutsche*. Quelle & Meyer: Heidelberg.

Prell, H.-P. and H.-J. Solms (1987), 'Zur Wortbildung des Verbs', *Zeitschrift für deutsche Philologie* (Sonderheft) 106: 89–116.

Reichmann, Oskar (1989), 'Lexikographische Einleitung' in *FWB* I: 10–164.

Schade, O. (ed.) (1966), *Satiren und Pasquille der Reformationszeit*, 3 vols (Reprint of the second edition, Hannover, 1863). Olms: Hildesheim.

Schmitt P. (ed.) (1983), >Liber ordinis rerum< (Esse-Essencia-Glossar), 2 vols. Niemeyer: Tübingen.

Schwarz, A (1984–85). 'Die Textsorten des Althochdeutschen' in Werner Besch, O. Reichmann and S. Sonderegger (eds), *Sprachgeschichte. Ein Handbuch zur Geschichte der deutschen Sprache und ihrer Erforschung*, 2 vols. de Gruyter: Berlin, 1052–60.

Schwitalla, J. 'Was sind Gebrauchstexte?', *deutsche sprache* 4 (1976): 20–40.

Solms, Hans-Joachim and Klaus-Peter Wegera (1988), *Flexion der Adjektive*, vol. VI of *Grammatik des Frühneuhochdeutschen. Beiträge zur Laut- und Formenlehre* edited by H. Moser, H. Stopp and W. Besch. Winter: Heidelberg.

Stieler, K. (1968–69), *Der Teutschen Sprache Stammbaum und Fortwachs. Oder Teutscher Sprachschatz [...]. Mit einer Einführung und Bibliographie von Gerhard Ising*, 3 vols (Documenta Linguistica. II Wörterbücher des 17. und 18. Jahrunderts. Reprint of the 1691 Nuremberg edition). Olms: Hildesheim.

Tauber, W. (1983), *Der Wortschatz des Hans Sachs. I: Untersuchungen. II: Wörterbuch* (Studia Linguistica Germanica 19 and 20). de Gruyter: Berlin.

von Polenz, P. (1994), *Deutsche Sprachgeschichte. Vom Spätmittelalter bis zur Gegenwart. II: 17. und 18. Jahrhundert*. de Gruyter: Berlin.

Wegera, K.-P. (1987), *Flexion der Substantive*, vol. III. of *Grammatik des Frühneuhochdeutschen. Beiträge zur Laut- und Formenlehre* edited by H. Moser, H. Stopp and W. Besch. Winter: Heidelberg.

West, J. (1989), *Lexical Innovation in Dasypodius' Dictionary* (Studia Linguistica Germanica, 24). de Gruyter: Berlin.

West, J. (1992). Review of Wegera (1987), Dammers et al. (1988) and Solms and Wegera (1988) in *Zeitschrift für deutsche Philologie* 111: 144–54.

West, J. (1993), 'Zu den Kompositionstypen im Wörterbuch des Dasypodius' in Klaus J. Mattheier, Klaus-Peter Wegera, Walter Hoffmann, Jürgen Macha and Hans-Joachim Solms (eds), *Vielfalt des Deutschen. Festschrift für Werner Besch*. Lang: Frankfurt, pp. 209–24.

West, J. (1995), 'A preliminary approach to word formation in the works of Hans Sachs and some of his contemporaries' in R. Aylett and P. Skrine (eds), *Hans Sachs and Folk Theatre in the Late Middle Ages. Studies in the History of Popular Culture.* Mellen: Lewiston, pp. 167–86.

West, J. (1998), Review of Ebert et al. (1993) in *Modern Language Review* 93: 264–6.

Wetekamp, S. (1980), *Petrus Dasypodius, Dictionarium latinogermanicum et vice versa.* (1535) [sic] *Untersuchungen zum Wortschatz* (Göppinger Arbeiten zur Germanistik, 282). Kümmerle: Stuttgart.

Rights and obligations in legal contracts: corpus evidence

Anne Wichmann and Jane Nielsen

This paper describes a study of 'contractual modalities' in German legal contracts; that is, the way in which **rights** and **obligations**, those modalities central to the function of contracts, are expressed. The study is based on a corpus of fifteen contracts covering a variety of subjects, and comprising 25 423 running words of text.[1] In it we show that the expression of modality is more complex than standard grammars imply. Our findings are of interest for the study of modal meaning in general, and in particular for the specialist legal translator engaged in the sensitive task of translating legally binding documents such as contracts.

1 Data

The data on which this study is based forms part of a larger corpus of German legal texts, still in preparation. The entire corpus will contain one million words of text in the field of contract law. It is planned to complement three existing machine-readable corpora of Danish, French and English contract law, compiled from 1987 to 1989 at the Business Schools of Aarhus and Copenhagen (Faber and Lauridsen 1991). These special-domain corpora comprise six text-types (or their equivalent in each language) in approximately even distribution: statutes, working papers and law reports, judgments, contracts, legal textbooks, articles in law journals. The observations described here are derived from the contracts contained in an already completed section of the new German corpus. The issues involved in compiling the corpus are described more fully in Nielsen (1997). The contracts are authentic, and were made available in anonymized form by a number of lawyers (mainly attorneys/*Rechtsanwälte*, but also one notary public/*Notar*) in the jurisdiction of Erlangen Local Court (*Amstgericht Erlangen*). In the view of these lawyers, the contracts were typical of those they frequently dealt with, and of those in the business community in general. They include the following areas of contractual agreement:

- employment contracts (senior management)
- conditions of purchase, delivery and payment (standard contractual terms)
- licensing agreements (for industrial products)
- purchasing agreements (e.g. building land)
- rental agreement for commercial property
- business partnership agreements
- contracts between performing artists and artists' agent

For obvious reasons all names, dates and other identifiers have been omitted.

2 The nature of contractual modalities

Unlike many other discussions of modality, this study is not restricted to the use of modal verbs. The starting point for the analyisis was any expression, implicit or explicit, of a right, limited right, obligation or limited obligation in the given contracts. Contractual obligations include **obligation** *(Pflicht)*, which may occur in the form of a **promise** *(Versprechen)*, **liability** *(Haftung)* and to a certain extent **necessity** *(Notwendigkeit)*. Examples 1–4 illustrate these:

1 Grundsätzlich **hat** die Geschäftsführerin den Urlaub in Natura **zu** nehmen.

2 Wegen der Personenbezogenheit dieses Vertrages **sichert** der VERTRIEBSPARTNER ... **zu**, daß er während der Dauer des Vertragsverhältnisses die Mehrheit des Kapitals nicht an einen Dritten übertragen wird.

3 Sofern wir auf Grund des Eigentumsvorbehaltes Ware zurückneh-

men, ist der Vertragspartner zur spesenfreien, frankierten Rückgabe verpflichtet und **haftet für** Minderwert und entgangenen Gewinn.

4 Alle Änderungen und Ergänzungen dieses Vertrages **bedürfen** zu ihrer Wirksamkeit der Schriftform.

Contractual rights include **permission** *(Erlaubnis)*, **entitlement** *(Anspruch),* and to a certain extent also **possibilty** *(Möglichkeit)*, since what is possible often equals what is permitted within a contractual context. See examples 5–8.

5 Will der Vermieter das Grundstück verkaufen, so **darf** er oder/und sein Beauftragter die Mieträume zusammen mit den Kauflustigen während der Geschäftszeit betreten.

6 Herr... **hat Anspruch auf** einen Jahresurlaub von 35 Arbeitstagen.

7 Soweit wir in Verzug kommen, ist der Käufer oder sonstige Vertragspartner **berechtigt,** eine angemessene Nachfrist zu setzen.

8 Bis zum Eingang der geforderten Vorschußbeträge **kann** das Schiedsgericht seine Tätigkeit aussetzen.

The categories of limited rights and obligations contain two degrees of limitation, that of restriction, typically marked by *nur* ('only'), and, at its most extreme, that of exclusion (in the case of rights, generally prohibition) marked by a form of negation (examples 9–11).

9 Mängelrügen ***können*** **nur** berücksichtigt *werden*, wenn sie uns spätestens innerhalb 14 Tagen nach Wareneingang in schriftlicher Form durch eingeschriebenen Brief angezeigt *werden*.

10 Der Vermieter **ist nicht verpflichtet**, aber berechtigt, alle Glasscheiben und Spiegel zu versichern.

11 ...**ist nicht berechtigt**, an den Vertragsschutzrechten Unterlizenzrechte ohne Zustimmung von ... zu vergeben und **ist nur berechtigt**, die Vertragsprodukte in ihrem eigenen Betrieb herzustellen.

It should be noted that the categories of limited rights and obligations are based on a restriction or negation of the modality, as in *nur/nicht berechtigt/verpflichtet, x zu tun.* This is to be distinguished from a restriction or negation of the proposition modified by the modal expression, as in *berechtigt/verpflichtet, x nicht zu tun.* The latter constructions are regarded as clear rights or obligations.

In addition to distinguishing between limited and unlimited modalities we also make here a pragmatic distinction between what is performative and therefore actually constituting a right or obligation, and what is non-performative and therefore merely describing or referring to rights and obligations already (or to be) laid down elsewhere, as, for example, *zu treffenden* in example 12 below.

12 Bei starkem Frost ist die Wasserleitung sachgemäß zu entleeren. Der Mieter hat daneben für die Entleerung der Toilettenbecken, Abortspülkästen und sonstiger Einrichtungen zu sorgen. Abwesenheit entbindet den Mieter nicht von den **zu treffenden** Frostschutzmaßnahmen

3 Common modal expressions

The vehicles for the expression of contractual modalities can be grammatical or lexical. Those considered relevant for this study, derived largely from Helbig and Buscha (1989), are as follows:

1 modal verbs
2 *werden*
3 modal infinitive (*hat zu tun*, *ist zu tun*)
4 *Gerundiv*
5 deverbal expressions ending in *–bar* etc.
6 lexical expressions

So-called 'modal particles' (*doch, ja* etc.) convey a different kind of modality – including the attitude of the speaker to the proposition – and occur rarely in formal written texts. They are therefore not included here.

3.1 Modal verbs and *werden*

Those verbs counted as modal by Helbig and Buscha (1989: 131ff) are *dürfen, können, mögen, müssen, sollen* and *wollen*. In their view, the verbs *dürfen* (and, to some extent, *können*) express a permission, the difference being one of style. The use of *können*, they claim, is restricted to informal contexts; thus one might expect that only *dürfen* will occur in the formal language of contracts. *Müssen* and *sollen* both express an obligation but differ regarding the source of authority. *Müssen* is regarded as conveying objective necessity or obligation while *sollen* is taken to indicate an external force in the form of a person, society or moral principle (1989: 134). Both verbs therefore have the potential to express contractual obligations, and will be considered here together with *nicht brauchen,* as a possible negation of *müssen*.

Whether or not *werden* should be included in the category of modal verbs in German is controversial. Vater (1975) argued for it to be included in the category, while more recently Thieroff (1992: 119ff) argued that *werden* +infinitive should be classified as future tense. Given that it has at least the potential to express modality in certain contexts, the verb *werden* was included in this study but treated as a category on its own, separate from verbs conventionally regarded as modal.

3.2 The modal infinitive and *Gerundiv*

The term 'modal infinitive', adopted from Gelhaus (1977), refers to constructions of either *haben* or *sein* followed by *zu* and an infinitive, as in the following examples and their paraphrase taken from Helbig and Buscha (1989, page number given in brackets):

13 Die Arbeit **ist** in 3 Tagen kaum **zu schaffen**. (=Die Arbeit kann in 3 Tagen kaum geschafft werden.) (130)

14 Die Arbeit **ist** unbedingt in einer Woche zu **erledigen**. (=Die Arbeit muß unbedingt in einer Woche erledigt werden.) (130)

15 Ich **habe** mit dir **zu reden** (=Ich muß mit dir reden.) (128)

16 Was **hast** du **zu berichten**? (= Was kannst du berichten?) (128)

Both of these expressions can carry modal meaning. The *haben* construction has an active meaning and the *sein* construction has a passive meaning, so that the *sein* construction is the more impersonal of the two, particularly when the agent is deleted.

The term *Gerundiv* is used by Helbig and Buscha (1989: 186, 589), and also by others, to mean the present participle used attributively with *zu*, as in:

17 Der Brief ist abzuholen – der abzuhholende Brief (Der Brief kann/ muß abgeholt werden) (186)

The *Gerundiv* is, as the example shows, a derivation of the construction *sein+zu*+infinitive, and is therefore an alternative to a construction consisting of the modal verbs *müssen* or *können* and a passive infinitive, and can be classified as a passive paraphrase with the modal meaning of necessity or possibility.

3.3 Adjectives ending in *–bar* etc.

Another type of passive paraphrase with modal meaning includes the deverbal adjectives in *–bar*, *-lich* or *–fähig*, as in the following examples:

18 Der **Wunsch ist erfüllbar**. (=Der Wunsch **kann** erfüllt werden.) (186)
19 Seine Schrift **ist leserlich**. (=Seine Schrift **kann** gelesen werden.) (186)
20 Der Aufsatz **ist erweiterungsfähig**. (=Der Aufsatz **kann** erweitert werden.) (186)

3.4 Lexical expressions

These can be grouped into three categories. Firstly there is a group of verbs, such as *sich verpflichten*, which indicate the speech act being performed and are therefore performative. Other verbs in this category include *erklären, versichern* and *vereinbaren*. The second and largest category includes items belonging to a variety of classes and which denote an obligation or necessity. These include *Aufgabe sein, bedürfen, bereit sein, gehalten sein*, *-pflichtig*, and *verpflichtet sein*. The third group contains expressions restricted in use to a legal context and expressing special types of legal obligations. These include *haften (für), Gewähr leisten*, and *Beweislast*.

4 Method of analysis

The linguistic phenomena which can be accessed using most available automatic retrieval methods depend on the nature of the data. Raw, unannotated data lends itself to lexical searches only; grammatical annotation allows global searches for categories such as modal verb, but an automatic tagging of the material was not possible. For the purpose of this analysis the data was therefore annotated manually, using a set of tags designed for the purpose. Four levels of tags were created, each designating an aspect of the modal expression. Firstly the tag indicated whether the expression was performative or not, and secondly whether it was explicit or not. Thirdly the tag encoded the type of expression used (modal verb, lexical expression etc.), and finally the kind of modality being expressed (right, limited right, etc.). The tag-set is shown in Table 1 below. All subsequent examples cited in this paper (21 onwards) are reproduced in their tagged form.

Table 1 The four categories constituting the tag-set

I	II	III	IV
#> contractual modality, performative #< contractual modality, non-performative	**E** explicit **I** implicit **Q** questionable	**1** modal verb **2** *werden* + infinitive **3** modal infinitive **4** *Gerundiv* **5** *–bar* etc. **6** lexical expression **7** other	**a** obligation **b** limited obligation **c** right **d** limited right **f** fuzzy

Once the data have been annotated, automatic searches were possible using simple concordancing software. (We were able to use the Longman MiniConcordancer, although it was not designed for languages other than English, by minimal editing of the text. This involved replacing umlauts with 'e' and 'ß' with 'ss'.)

5 Frequency distribution of modal expressions

There are approximately three times as many performative expressions of modality in these contracts (seventy-four per cent) as there are non-performative expressions (twenty-six per cent). This is to be expected, since it is in the nature of contracts to establish rights and obligations rather than to refer to existing ones. Of the non-performative expressions, nearly ninety per cent are expressed lexically. A large proportion of these are compound words ending in, for example, *-recht*, *-anspruch*, or *-verpflichtung*, as in the following examples:

21 …wird#>E2a, sofern sich bei der Fertigung von Paletten Verbesserungen ergeben, diese Verbesserungen unverzüglich … mitteilen und … das **Recht** #<E6c einräumen, derartige Verbesserungen in den von … GmbH vorgesehenen Ländern zum **Patent**#<E6c anzumelden. Sollten auf diese **Patente**#<E6c entsprechende **Schutzrechte**#<E6c erteilt werden, räumt … an diesen **Rechten**#<E6c … eine ausschließliche **Lizenz**#<E6c wie an den **Vertragsrechten**#<E6c gem. § 1 ein #>Ia.

22 Stehen jedoch außergewohnliche gewichtige Gründe, die im Geschäftsablauf der Gesellschaft liegen, dem Urlaubsantritt entgegen, so ist#>E3a der **Urlaubsanspruch**#<E6c abzugelten. Der **Abgeltungsanspruch**#<E6c bemißt sich nach der Höhe eines monatlichen Grundgehaltes#>If.

23 Übernahme von Bürgschaften mit Ausnahme von geschäftsüblichen, soweit die **Bürgschaftsverpflichtung**#<E6a DM 5.000, – im Einzelfall übersteigt oder durch das Eingehen der **Bürgschaftsverpflichtung**#<E6a das Volumen derartiger Bürgschaften DM 25.000, – übersteigen würde;

In fact, as the high density of occurrence in example 21 suggests, these expressions are not evenly distributed over the corpus, but occur particularly in the two licence agreements in the corpus. For this reason the remaining analysis will concentrate on the expression of rights and obligations in the performative sense, i.e. those rights and obligations which are laid down by the contract and not those which are simply referred to as already existing.

The relative frequency of the expressions under investigation (see section 3 above) is set out in Table 2. This shows that the most commonly used vehicle for expressing a contractual modality, taking rights and obligations together, is lexical expressions, closely followed by implicit expressions of modality. These two categories account for nearly sixty per cent of the cases registered. Approximately a further thirty per cent of cases are of modal verbs or modal infinitives. The *werden* construction is relatively unimportant, and the remaining possible expressions are rare.

Table 2 Rank order of expressions of contractual modalities

Rank	Expression	Frequency (abs.)	Frequency (rel.)
1	lexical	(301)	(30.9%)
2	implicit	(269)	(27.6%)
3	modal infinitive	(152)	(15.6%)
4	modal verb	(135)	(13.9%)
5	*werden*+infin.	(50)	(5.1%)
6	*Gerundiv*	(13)	(1.3%)
7	*–bar* etc.	(12)	(1.2%)
8	other	(2)	(0.2%)

So far the analysis has conflated the different contractual modalities to give an overall view. In what follows we will consider rights and obligations separately, and show that the modal expressions are not evenly distributed across them. The analysis shows that these contracts focus on what parties are obliged to do rather than what they are entitled to do. In Tables 3, 4, 5, and 6 the expressions used in the four categories of (limited) rights and obligations have been ranked according to frequency. They show that lexical expressions especially, but to a lesser extent also implicit expressions, are central to the realization of all four categories. Modal verbs are not dominant in any category. Either they are used only infrequently or the other expressions are used just as often.

Table 3 Rank order of expressions of an obligation

Rank	Expression	Frequency
1	implicit	(165)
2	lexical	(152)
3	modal infinitve	(149)
4	*werden*+infin	(50)
5	modal verb	(27)
6	*Gerundiv*	(12)
7	-*bar* etc.	(4)
8	other	(2)

Table 4 Rank order of expressions of a limited obligation

Rank	Expression	Frequency
1	lexical	(37)
2	implicit	(15)
3	modal infinitive	(3)
4	modal verb	(2)
5	*Gerundiv*	(1)
6	–	
7	–	
8	–	

Table 5 Rank order of expressions of a right

Rank	Expression	Frequency
1	lexical	(69)
2	modal verb	(60)
3	implicit	(40)
4	*-bar* etc.	(7)
5	–	
6	–	
7	–	
8	–	

Table 6 Rank order of expressions of a of a limited right

Rank	Expression	Frequency
1	modal verb	(45)
2	lexical	(43)
3	implicit	(8)
4	*-bar* etc.	(1)
5	–	
6	–	
7	–	
8	–	

6 The most frequent expressions of modality in contracts

6.1 Modal verbs

Modal verbs play a particularly minor role in the expression of obligation, which is most commonly presented implicitly, by a modal infinitive, or lexically. They do, however, play a role in the expression of rights and limited rights. The distribution of modal verbs in the corpus is shown in Table 7.

Table 7 The absolute and relative frequencies of the modal verbs used in the performative sense and their distribution among contractual modalities

	Obligation	Limited obligation	Right	Limited right	Total
dürfen	–	–	7	29	36
	–	–	5.2%	21.5%	26.7%
können	–	2	54	15	71
	–	1.5%	40.0%	11.1%	52.6%
müssen	17	–	–	–	17
	12.6%	–	–	–	12.6%
sollen	10	–	–	1	11
	7.4%	–	–	0.7%	8.1%
Total	27	2	61	45	135
	20.0%	1.5%	45.2%	33.3%	100.0%

Contrary to expectations, the modal verb most closely associated with permission, *dürfen*, is used far more infrequently than its counterpart, *können*, described by Helbig and Buscha (1989: 131f) as mainly informal and colloquial. *Können* is also the most frequently used modal verb overall. The following examples are typical of *können* used to express a right:

24 Die in § 6 Ziff. 2 a, b, des zwischen ... und dem VERTRIEBSPARTNER abegschlossenen Partnerschaftsvertrages vereinbarte

Verpflichtung#<E6a zum wiederkehrenden Bezug der Vertragsprodukte **kann**#>E1c der VERTRIEBSPARTNER schriftlich widerrufen.

25 Bei unbefugter#<E6d Untervermietung **kann**#>E1c der Vermieter verlangen, daß der Mieter sobald wie möglich, spätestens jedoch binnen Monatsfrist, das Untermietverhältnis kündigt. Geschieht dies nicht, so kann#>E1c der Vermieter das Hauptmietverhältnis ohne Einhaltung einer Kündigungsfrist kündigen. Dieses Recht#<E6c **kann**#>E1d der Vermieter nur binnen eines Monats geltend machen, nachdem er von der unbefugten#<E6d Untervermietung Kenntnis erlangt hat.

The significant preference for *können* over *dürfen* to express rights in these contracts may be explained by a parallel difference between 'can' and 'may' in English (Palmer 1979: 150). According to Palmer the difference lies in the involvement of the speaker. 'May' signals that the permission is granted at least in part by the speaker and is therefore subjective, whereas 'can' signals that the speaker merely reports a permission granted by someone else and is therefore objective. It could be that *können* is the more neutral and objective of the two German modals, conveying as it does an objective possibility or right as laid down by the law, while *dürfen* may convey a permission granted by one of the contractual parties rather than objectively by the law. This distinction is particularly evident in the expression of limited rights. *Dürfen* is typically used to express rights dependent on the consent of the other party, and hence in conjunction with *ohne*, *nur mit Genehmigung*, *Einwilligung*, *Zustimmung von,* whereas *können* excludes, or especially restricts, a right on legal grounds. See example 26:

26 Der VERTRIEBSPARTNER **darf**#>E1d sein Geschäft ohne Genehmigung#<E6d durch ... **weder** vermieten, untervermieten, **noch** verpachten.

6.2 The modal infinitive

The modal infinitive is the third most frequently used expression of contractual modality (see Table 2). It is particularly prominent as an expression of obligation, and there is also a clear tendency to use the *sein* construction rather than the construction with *haben*. This preference is ascribed to the passive meaning of the *sein* construction, which focuses on the obligation to be fulfilled rather than on the obligor, and is thus more impersonal. The use of the modal infinitive in German contracts contrasts interestingly with the distribution of 'to have to' and 'to be to' in a parallel set of English contracts (Nielsen and Wichmann 1994). The English corpus revealed only one example of 'to have to', and no examples of 'to be to'. This is important when considering translation equivalents. A concurrent investigation into the distribution of modal verbs in the English contracts showed a marked frequency of the verb 'shall'. This means that while the similarity of the German and English infinitives might lead a translator to render *ist schriftlich zu begründen* as 'is/has to be in writing', a more authentic translation would be 'shall be in writing'.

6.3 Lexical expressions

As is evident from Table 2, the use of a lexical expression is overall the most common way of defining rights and obligations in the contracts, followed by implicit expressions and the modal infinitive. Lexically expressed contractual modality constitutes 30.9 per cent, nearly one third, of all contractual modalities. These lexical expressions can be divided into three categories: performatively used verbs, general expressions of rights and obligations, and more specialized legal terms. These are set out in Table 8, which also reflects the overall trend in the corpus for rights to be expressed less frequently than obligations.

Table 8 Lexical expressions of rights and obligations

	rights	obligations
performative	2	45
general	57	79
restricted	10	28
total	69	152

6.3.1 Obligation

First of all there is the group of verbs, typically *sich verpflichten* as in examples 27 and 28, which may be characterized as performative. Through the statements *der Lizenzgeber verpflichtet sich* ... and *der Mieter verpflichtet sich*, in examples 27 and 28 respectively, the licensor and the lessee declare their obligation:

27 Der Lizenzgeber **verpflichtet**#>E6a **sich**, die Dienstleistungsmarke während der Dauer des Vertrages auf eigene Kosten aufrechtzuerhalten und gegen etwaige Angriffe Dritter zu verteidigen.

28 Erhöhungen dieser Betriebskosten kann#>E1c der Vermieter umlegen. Der Mieter **verpflichtet**#>E6a **sich** hiermit, die Zahlung seines entsprechenden Anteiles zu übernehmen.

Performative verbs are typically associated with the first person subject, but here they are used with a third person subject and often, as in example 28, accompanied by *hiermit*, the insertion of which may generally be used as a test for whether a verb is being used performatively or not. *Sich verpflichten* may be described as the performative exponent of an obligation as a speech act, and accounts for thirty-six of the forty-five occurrences of performative verbs (eighty per cent) in the contract corpus. The remaining nine occurrences are distributed amongst the verbs *anerkennen, erklären, versichern, zusichern* and *vereinbaren*. (See Table 9.)

Table 9 Performative verbs expressing obligation

Sich verpflichten	36	80%
anerkennen	9	20%
erklären		
versichern		
zusichern		
vereinbaren		
	Total: 45	

The second, and largest, category of items conveying an obligation includes verbs, nouns and adjectives which are general terms denoting obligation/necessity. These are set out in Table 10.

Table 10 General expressions of obligation

verplichtet	39	49%
bedürfen	17	22%
Aufgabe sein	23	29%
-bedürftigkeit		
bereit sein		
gehalten		
obliegen		
-pflichtig		
Sache sein		
verantwortlich sein für		
verbindlich		
Voraussetzung		
vorgeschrieben		
zuständig		
	Total: 79	

The most common of these are *verpflichtet*, accounting for thirty-nine out of seventy-nine occurrences (forty-nine per cent) and *bedürfen* (seventeen out of seventy-nine, or twenty-two per cent). These are illustrated in examples 29 and 30. Most of the remainder occur only once or twice.

29 Die Parteien **verpflichten**#>E6a **sich** vielmehr, die unwirksame Bestimmung durch eine wirksame Regelung zu ersetzen, die dem wirtschaftlichen Zweck der unwirksamen Bestimmung am nähesten kommt.

30 Alle Änderungen und Ergänzungen dieses Vertrages **bedürfen**#>E6a zu ihrer Wirksamkeit der Schriftform.

The final category consists of a small set of expressions, listed in Table 11, which are largely restricted in usage to a legal context. The most common, *haften für* and *fällig* are illustrated in examples 31 and 32.

Table 11 Specialized expressions of obligation

haften (für)	13
fällig	9
Beweislast	7
einstehen für	
Gewähr leisten/übernehmen	
schulden	
	Total: 29

31 Eine etwaige Schuld des ausscheidenden Gesellschafters gegenüber der Gesellschaft ist#>E3a sofort zur Zahlung **fällig**#>E6a und in gleicher Weise zu verzinsen.

32 Im Falle einer Kündigung ohne Einhaltung einer Kündigungsfrist durch den Vermieter **haftet**#>E6a der Mieter **für** den Ausfall an Miete, Nebenabgaben und sonstigen Leistungen.

6.3.2 Rights

Only twelve different lexemes are used for the expression of rights, adding up to a total of sixty-nine occurrences. The term can be categorized in the same way as for the expression of obligation – performatively used verbs, general expressions and more specifically legal terms. There are only two examples of a verb laying down a right performatively, once with *wird ... ermächtigt*, as in example 33, and once with *wird ... gestattet*, as in example 34.

33 ...**wird** ab sofort **ermächtigt**#>E6c, die Grundstücke zu betreten,

bezüglich der Vertragsgrundstücke Bauvoranfragen und Baugenehmigungen#<E6c zu beantragen, Nachbarunterschriften einzuholen, Bauvorbereitungen aller Art zu treffen, auch Vermessungsanträge zu stellen und sonstige Handlungen vorzunehmen, die der beabsichtigten Erschließung und Bebauung der Grundstücke und dessen Durchführung dienen.

34 Dem Erwerber **wird** jedoch **gestattet**#>E6c, bis zum ... von den unter Ziff. 3.2. genannten Grundstücken eine Fläche von insgesamt bis zu 40.000 m2 ausschließlich an die noch zu gründende Kalksandstein ... zu verkaufen, die das unter Ziff. 5.4. beschriebene Kalksandsteinwerk errichtet#>Ia und nach Fertigstellung betreiben wird#E2a.

The most common general lexemes expressing rights are the related expressions *berechtigen, berechtigt (sein)* and *das Recht haben*, illustrated in examples 35 and 36, which together make up seventy-five per cent (forty-three out of fifty-seven) of the lexemes in this category. The other expressions, listed in Table 12, occur very infrequently.

Table 12 General lexemes denoting rights

berechtigen *berechtigt sein* *das Recht haben*	43	75%
gestattet (sein) *die Möglichkeit haben* *sich vorbehalten* *zulässig (sein* *zustehen*	14	25%
	Total: 57	

35 Der Lizenznehmer **ist berechtigt**#>E6c, die Dienstleistungsmarke nicht nur auf seinen Drucksachen, Werbeschriften und dergleichen zu verwenden, er **hat** auch **das Recht**#>E6c, die Dienstleistungsmarke auf den von ihm benuzten Kraftfahrzeugen anzubringen.

36 Fälle höherer Gewalt oder sonstige von uns oder unseren Zulieferanten nicht verschuldete Umstände insbesondere Verkehrs- oder Betriebsstörungen, Ausstände und Aussperrung, Mangel an Rohstoffen und dergleichen **berechtigen**#>E6c **uns**, die Lieferung um die Dauer der Behinderung und einer angemessenen Ablaufzeit hinauszuschieben oder wegen des nicht erfüllten Teils vom Vertrag zuruckzutreten, ohne daß der Käufer Schadensersatzansprüche #<E6c geltend machen kann#>E1d.

The more specifically legal terms used in the corpus to express rights are *Anspruch (auf) -anspruch*, and *Eigentum,* illustrated in examples 37 and 38.

37 Herr ... **hat Anspruch auf** #>E6c einen Jahresurlaub von 35 Arbeitstagen.

38 Entwürfe, Zeichnungen, Modelle, Organisationspläne und dergleichen die von uns ausgearbeitet und abgegeben werden **bleiben unser Eigentum**#>E6c.

To summarize, by far the most common lexical expressions of obligation in this corpus are *sich verpflichten* and *verpflichtet sein*, while common legal terms referring to specific kinds of obligation are *haften für* and *fällig*. The most common lexical expressions of rights are *berechtigen / berechtigt*, and *das Recht haben*.

7 Implicitly expressed contractual modality

The grammatical and lexical expressions of modal meaning which have been described above all indicate modality in a more or less explicit manner. During the analysis it became clear, however, that the contracts laid down a number of rights and obligations using none of these explicit markers. In fact the second most frequent way of expressing rights or obligations in this corpus is to use no modal expression at all. These we refer to as implicit contractual modalities. All occurrences of implicit contractual modalities are expressions using the present tense, usually active, as in examples 39–45, and sometimes passive, as in examples 46–7.

39 **Herr ... legt** in die Gesellschaft die von ihm in ... betriebene orthopädische Praxis mit allen Aktiven und Passiven **ein** #>Ia:

40 Gegen diese Vereinbarung zurückgesandte Ware **lagern wir** sach- und fachgerecht **zu Lasten** des Käufers#>1a ein#>Ia.

41 Aufrechterhaltung der von der .. .gewünschten Schutzrechte#<E6c **werden von der** ... einschließlich der Patentanwaltskosten **getragen**#>Ia.

42 **Jeder Gesellschafter hat soviele Stimmen**#>Ic mit wieviel Prozent er am Gewinn beteiligt ist.

43 **Die Agentur erhält** als Gegenleistung für ihre nach diesem Vertrag zu erbringenden#<E4a Leistungen eine Vergütung#>Ic, welche sich nach den Einnahmen des Künstlers aus den jeweiligen Engagements mittelt.

44 Die **Zurücknahme** bereits in Betrieb- oder Gebrauch genommener Gegenstände **kommt nicht in Betracht**#>Ib.

45 **Keller und Böden sind kein Aufbewahrungsort für** leicht entzündliche und feuergefährliche Stoffe wie Papier, Packmaterial, Benzin, Öl usw.#>Id.

46 **Gewinn und Verlust werden den Gesellschaftern** im Verhältnis ihrer Gesellschaftsbeteiligungen zugeteilt#>If, derzeit also 51 % für Herrn ... und 49 % für Herrn ...

47 **Dem Mieter werden** für die Mietzeit die **hauptsächlichen Schlüssel** sofort – bei Einzug – übergeben#>If.

An explanation for the redundancy of modal expressions was suggested by Trosborg (1995) and Dietrich (1992), and is fundamentally a pragmatic one. Trosborg was concerned primarily with the acts performed by statutes, but by applying her argument to contracts, we can claim that the text of a contract may be regarded as a 'master speech act' (see Fotion 1971), which could be expressed as 'we hereby agree the following'. The very nature of a contract is performative, and implies that the propositions contained in it are the agreed rights and obligations of the relevant parties, subject to certain felicity conditions including the signatures of the parties. If this is so, we can regard propositions expressed using the present tense, which in other contexts would merely constitute statements of fact, as expressing the rights or obligations inherent in the contract which contains them. Explicit modal markers of rights and obligations are therefore largely redundant within the context of a contract.

8 Conclusion

The analysis of rights and obligations in a corpus of German contracts reveals a different pattern of usage from that which is generally associated with the expression of modality. The most frequent way of defining rights and obligations is not to use modal verbs, but to use either an explicit lexical expression such as *verpflichtet* or *berechtigt,* or to use nothing but the present tense of the verb and let the rest be implied by the context. The modal verbs, the prototypical vehicle of modality, are not even the most frequent grammatical expression, but are surpassed in frequency by the modal infinitive, *haben /sein ... zu.*

While the advantages of a machine-readable corpus are clear, there are also certain limitations if, as in this case, the search is for semantic categories, rather than for grammatical categories which can be tagged automatically or for individual lexical items. The manual tagging needed for this study would not be practicable for a larger corpus. Given the fairly restricted and specialized domain of legal contracts the findings reported here cannot be claimed to be representative of the expression of modality in general, nor of the expression of modality in legal texts. None the less we feel that our observations have important implications for the study of legal language, and in particular for the work of specialized translators.

Notes

1 The study described here is presented in detail in Nielsen (1997)

References

Dietrich, R. (1992), *Modalität im Deutschen. Zur Theorie der relativen Modalität.* Westdeutscher Verlag: Opladen.

Faber, D. and K. M. Lauridsen (1991), 'The compilation of a Danish-

English-French corpus in contract law' in S. Johansson and A. B. Stenström (eds), *English Computer Corpora. Selected Papers and Research Guide*. Mouton de Gruyter: Berlin and New York, pp. 235–43.

Fotion, N. (1971), 'Master speech acts', *Philosophical Quarterly* 21: 232–43.

Gelhaus, H. (1977), *Der modale Infinitive. Mit einem dolkumentarischen Anhang uber die im gegenwartigen Schriftedeutsch gebrauchlichen 'bar' - Ableitungen* (Working papers of the Institut für Deutsche Sprache, Mannheim, volume 35.) Gunter Narr: Tübingen.

Helbig, G. and J. Buscha (1989), *Deutsche Grammatik: ein Handbuch für den Ausländerunterricht.* Verlag Enzyklopädie: Leipzig.

Nielsen, J. N. (1997), 'The expression of rights and obligations in German contracts', unpublished MPhil thesis, University of Central Lancashire, Preston.

Nielsen, J. N. and A. Wichmann (1994), 'A frequency analysis of modal expressions in German and English legal texts', *Hermes*: *Journal of Linguistics* 13: 145–55.

Palmer, F. R. (1979), *Modality and the English Modals.* Longman: London and New York.

Thieroff, R. (1992), *Das finite Verb im Deutschen: Tempus-Modus-Distanz* (Studies in German Grammar, volume 40). Gunter Narr: Tübingen.

Trosborg, A. (1995), 'Statutes and contracts: an analysis of legal speech acts in the English language of the law', *Journal of Pragmatics* 23: 31–53.

Vater, H. (1975), 'Werden als Modalverb' in J. P. Calbert and H.Vate (eds)r, *Aspekte der Modalität* (Studies in German Grammar, volume 1). Gunter Narr: Tübingen, pp. 71–148.

Inflected and periphrastic subjunctive verb forms in German newspaper texts of the 1960s and 1990s

Nic Witton

Introduction

This investigation[1] compares the usage and distribution of the *würde*+infinitive (periphrastic) and Subjunctive II (inflected) constructions of selected verbs in German newspaper and news magazine texts of the 1960s and 1990s. The purpose of the investigation was to establish whether there has been a shift over this period between these functionally largely equivalent[2] forms. It takes as its starting point the seminal studies of Siegfried Jäger (1971) and Karl-Heinz Bausch (1979). These studies are important because, like the present investigation, they were able to be based on large amounts of text accessible in machine-readable corpora. Jäger used selected literary and non-literary printed texts from the Mannheimer Korpus 1,[3] while Bausch used the Freiburger Korpus[4] of transcribed spoken German texts, both housed at the Institut für Deutsche Sprache[5] in Mannheim.

Jäger devotes only a few pages of his book (Jäger 1971: 251–7) to the relationship between the *würde*+infinitive and Subjunctive II constructions. Despite the fact that his results show that the former occurs between two-and-a-half and three times as frequently as the latter (1971: 257), he still considers Subjunctive II to be the standard form and ventures the opinion that it is doubtful whether the *würde*+infinitive construction will supplant it.[6] His investigation also indicates that the Subjunctive II form is most frequently used in conjunction with certain verbs.[7]

Bausch's study shows that in spoken standard German, it is the *würde*+infinitive construction which is the norm, and that the Subjunctive II construction is a sociolinguistically marked variant influenced by grammars and style manuals.[8] Like Jäger, his data also indicates that the use of Subjunctive II is largely restricted to a small number of frequently used verbs.

Table 1 Subjunctive II usage of selected verbs as a percentage of all lexical Subjunctive II occurrences (Taken from Bausch 1979: 203)

GESCHRIEBENE SPRACHE [WRITTEN LANGUAGE]		GESPROCHENE SPRACHE [SPOKEN LANGUAGE]	
(Jäger 1971a)	%		%
kommen	12,46	*kommen*	24,49
geben	7,83	*geben*	15,65
wissen	7,47	*gehen*	10,20
stehen	5,69	*wissen*	8,16
lassen	5,69	*tun*	6,12
finden	5,33	*stehen*	4,08
gehen	4,64	*finden*	2,72
liegen	4,64		
tun	3,20		

He notes that in Jäger's corpus, which consists mainly of literary texts, the verbs *kommen, geben, wissen, stehen, gehen, finden, tun* alone make up 46.62 per cent of all occurrences of lexical (i.e. non-auxiliary) verbs in Subjunctive II form (Bausch 1979: p. 203). The evidence from his corpus shows that in the spoken language, the tendency for the *würde*+infinitive construction to predominate and for Subjunctive II to be restricted to a small number of frequently used verbs is even more pronounced: the same list of verbs accounts for 71.42 per cent of all occurrences (1979: p203).

Aim of this investigation

The question of the productiveness of the *würde*+infinitive and Subjunctive II constructions can only be answered, Bausch points out (1979:

206), by a contrastive analysis of corpora of written standard German. He cautions that account must be taken of the special status of the print media, subject as they are to monitoring by editorial staff influenced by prescriptive, normative grammars (1979: 206; 263 n. 324).

Having regard firstly to Bausch's and Jäger's results, which show that the use of Subjunctive II is in the main restricted to a relatively small number of frequently occurring verbs, and secondly, to Bausch's warning about the print media, it seemed that an appropriate test of whether the *würde*+infinitive construction was tending to replace Subjunctive II in written standard German would be to contrast the usage of these two constructions in German newspaper articles from the 1960s and the 1990s in relation to the verbs highlighted in the two studies, since these two parameters (the print media and high frequency verbs) are presumably the last domains where a shift away from the written norm favoured by the grammars towards the spoken norm is likely to take place.

Application of information technology: data collection, analysis and classification, evaluation of results

Data

The machine-readable corpora of the Institut für Deutsche Sprache (IDS) offered the opportunity to undertake such an analysis. Jäger had used only a selection of the newspaper articles held in the Mannheimer Korpus 1, so the range was broadened to include all of them and newspaper articles from *Die Welt* held in the Bonner Zeitungskorpus.[9] These together represent the entire holdings of the Institute for the 1960s and comprise 3109 texts totalling 1 933 089 words from *Die Welt* (1965–66), the *Frankfurter Allgemeine Zeitung* (1966), and the *Bild-Zeitung* (1967).[10]

For the 1990s, the holdings of the Institute from the weekly news magazine *Der Spiegel* of 1994 and the daily newspaper *Mannheimer Morgen* of 1995 were chosen as examples of two different types of print media with differing target audiences. It was not possible to compare the same publications as for the 1960s since these are not held. The 1994 *Spiegel* corpus comprises 6685 texts totalling some five million words, and that of the 1995 *Mannheimer Morgen* 36 920 texts totalling half a million words.

Data collection

A feature of the IDS COSMAS software is its lemmatization function: if a search word is prefixed by the symbol & (e.g. *&finden*), the system generates all the forms of the word (e.g. *finde, findest, findet*, etc.) in a list for the user to choose from. Once the choice has been made, only the forms selected are searched for. Normal concordancing wildcards such as * and ? are also available. In addition to searches for various forms of words, the system allows sophisticated specifications of collocational arrangements. For example, the search request: *würde* /s0 kommen* will find all instances of *würde, würdest, würden, würdet* occurring in the same sentence as *kommen*.

The output, too, can be customized to the individual user's requirements. For example, amongst others, it can take the form of a single-line KWIC (Key Word In Context) concordance or of a text extract consisting of one or more words or sentences before and/or after the search item. For this investigation, an output was chosen of one sentence before and one after the sentence containing the search item, as this was found to provide enough context for the function of the item to be determined.

Users can also combine various corpora or sections of various corpora into a single 'virtual corpus'. For this investigation, the 1960s corpora were combined into one (K60), while the others, *Der Spiegel* (S94) and the *Mannheimer Morgen* (M95) were left as individual corpora. Later, for the tabulation of the results, the individual newspapers making up the K60 corpus were separated out again. For each corpus, searches were conducted for occurrences of the *würde*+infinitive and Subjunctive II constructions of *finden, geben, gehen, kommen, lassen, liegen, stehen* and *tun* and the output from the searches was stored in computer files, one per verb per construction per corpus.

Analysis and classification

For his purposes, Bausch merely totals the occurrences of each construction (*würde*+infinitive and Subjunctive II). Jäger does a partial classification, listing the distribution of the two constructions in relation to the functions of indirect speech, conditional sentences and unreal comparison ('as if') clauses (Jäger 1971: 251). However, finer distinctions need to be made if one is to determine not only if a shift has occurred between the two constructions *per se*, but also if a shift or shifts have occurred in their distribution over their various functions.

In tabulating the total occurrences of the two constructions, all 2499 instances extracted from the corpora were used. But for the analysis of the functional distribution, because of the disparate sizes of the corpora (see above under *Data*), a roughly equivalent number of occurrences from each corpus was examined: all 219 occurrences from the smaller K60 corpus and a random selection comprising every fourth occurrence from M95 and S94, making 281 and 221 occurrences respectively.

To facilitate the analysis, a database was set up to record the function of each occurrence. The software used was dBase IV and ancillary programs were written in its accompanying programming language to assist in analysing the data and to speed up the process of entering the results of the analysis. The corpus text extracts containing the occurrences were held in separate text files, not in the database. The time and effort that would have been required to transfer each extract into the relevant database record[11] was rendered unnecessary by combining a dBase program with one written in QuickBASIC 4.5 so that each record in the database could be linked to the relevant extract in the text files. The database record and the extract containing the occurrence to which the record referred could then be viewed simultaneously in two windows on the screen.

A separate database was set up for each corpus. When the analysis of the K60 corpus was complete, three further databases were extracted from it representing the *Bild*, *Welt* and *FAZ* data.

Evaluation

To facilitate the compilation and evaluation of the results, four further computer programs were written. Their basic functions were to search through the databases and count the instances of each function category. The first program counts the main categories for all the verbs together. The second counts the main and sub-categories for all the verbs together. The third counts the main categories for each of the verbs separately and the fourth counts the main and sub-categories for each of the verbs separately.

These programs were designed so that their output is in the form of text files in comma-separated value format. This format can be utilized as input for a spreadsheet program. In this instance Microsoft Excel (1985–86) was used to express the findings in the form of tables and graphs.

Categories

For the most part, traditional classification categories and sub-categories were found to be appropriate for the data and were employed. In the following, each category or sub-category is followed by an instance from one of the corpora and the relevant section is underlined.

Note:

- Only those categories are listed which actually occurred in the data.
- All can be realized by either the *würde*+infinitive construction or Subjunctive II unless otherwise indicated.

1 Result clauses

Sub-categories:

1. *Result clauses of explicit condition clauses*
MMM/511.31973: Mannheimer Morgen, 30.11.1995, Politik; Die schwere politische Last der NATO
Es soll verhindert werden, daß waffentechnische Ungleichgewichte, wie sie in den Kriegsjahren bestanden haben, fortdauern. Sollte nichts erreicht werden, dann käme es zu Waffenlieferungen der USA an die bosnische Seite. Doch dies wäre die letzte, von niemandem gewollte Alternative.

2. *Result clauses of implicit or lexical conditions* (Jäger 1971: 200)
S94/H22.02578: Vergebens gelockt, S. 21
Ein Zweikampf der Lager als Folge der Herzog-Wahl – hier

Union plus FDP, dort SPD und Grüne – wäre Kohl und Kinkel nur recht. *Dann* käme es zur ideologieträchtigen Polarisierung, hinter der sich die wirklichen Probleme gut verstecken lassen. In der FDP wächst allerdings das Unbehagen über Kinkels eindeutige Fixierung auf die Koalition mit der Union. [My italics]

2 Condition clauses

Sub-categories:

1. *Introduced by* wenn *or similar conjunctions*

MMM/506.02275: Mannheimer Morgen, 09.06.1995, Lokales; Was meinen Sie dazu?

„Ich habe ja auch Mitschüler und Freunde, die in den Jugendmannschaften mitspielen. Es wäre toll, wenn der Verein in die erste Bundesliga kommen würde. Die ganze Mannschaft hat es verdient."

2. *No conjunction, verb in first position*

BZK/W69.01049, WELT 28.05.69, S.02, POLITIK

Seit seinem glanzvollen Empfang in Washington fühlt sich König Hussein sicher, daß die Israelis nicht wagen würden, die Grenze zu überschreiten und die Batterien auszuheben, denn täten sie es, so würde der Sicherheitsrat sofort zusammentreten, und die Verurteilung Israels wäre gewiß.

3. *Clauses functioning as implicit conditions*

MMM/506.01220: Mannheimer Morgen, 02.06.1995, Feuilleton; Scharfzüngiger Entertainer

Für die einen ist Marcel Reich-Ranicki, der heute seinen 75. Geburtstag feiert, ein „furchtbarer Kunst-Richter", für die anderen ein famoser Entertainer, über den Walter Jens einmal schrieb: „Man stelle sich vor, es gäbe den Mann nicht... Mein Gott, wäre das langweilig."

3 Future in past narrative[12] (only *würde*+infinitive construction)

(Zifonun et al. 1997: F2 3.2; Hammer 1991: 285: §14.3.3(b))

MMM/506.00410: Mannheimer Morgen, 03.06.1995, Un-

terhaltung; Wie aus Michi ein Michael wurde
Sein Vater nickte, seine Mutter nickte, stolz, geschmeichelt, und zu guter letzt nickte auch ich. Es war geschehen, aus Michi war ein Michael geworden, ein Junge, der seinen Weg gehen würde mit einem festen Ziel vor Augen und einer kleinen Erinnerung im Herzen, vielleicht an diese und jene Gelegenheit, bei der hinter Michael noch drei Ausrufezeichen standen...

4 Hypothetical sentences or clauses

Sub-categories:

1. *Hypothetical statements*
S94/H40.04910: Zitate, S. 298
Inzwischen ist der Junge herangewachsen, und seine Generation wurde vom SPIEGEL einer Basisumfrage unterworfen: Nur für 10 % aller Jugendlichen ist Demokratie nichts Wertvolles, 19 % aber würden nichts für ihre Verteidigung tun, nicht einmal – wie 11 % unserer Jugend – Wände bemalen, 19 %, die nicht bereit sind, etwas ihnen Wertvolles zu schützen? 19 % Demokratiephlegmatiker?

2. *Wishes*
MMM/512.34502: Mannheimer Morgen, 14.12.1995, Lokales; Weihnachten wird längst vorbei und ...
... bis hin zum Urlaub, dessen Erholung schon lange flöten ist, wenn die Raten noch immer nicht abgezahlt sind. Wenn es dann doch wenigstens „nur" um zehntausend Mark ginge. Es ist schlimm, wie sich vor allem junge Menschen ihr Leben verbauen, indem sie ohne jede wirtschaftliche Vernunft Geld ausgeben.

5 Politeness

Sub-category: *Polite questions*
BZK/W69.01231.2, WELT 23.06.69, S.06, POLITIK
Frage: Gäbe es für Sie nicht ein durchaus plausibles Motiv, die theoretische Möglichkeit einer Koalition mit der CDU/

CSU wieder in Erinnerung zu bringen?
Scheel: …

6 Sentence-adverbial clauses

(Zifonun et al. 1997: H1 7.3)

Sub-categories:

1. *Comparative ('as if') clauses*

S94/H08.00938: „75 B, also eher klein"

Lillehammer ist in Alarmbereitschaft. Sogar David Hurley, Star der Paparazzi, dem es als erstem gelungen war, die Brüste der Claudia Schiffer zu fotografieren, wird in der Meute von über 1500 Medienschaffenden vermutet, die über das Amphitheater hergefallen sind, als fänden dort die Hochzeit von Boris Becker und der Weltwirtschaftsgipfel zeitgleich statt.

2. *Purpose and comitative*[13] *clauses*

MMM/510.25128: Mannheimer Morgen, 23.10.1995, Lokales; Elternsprecher: Mehr Geld für die Schulen

Die gleichen Probleme stellten sich bei Großgeräten für Physik und Chemie oder aber im Bereich Anschaffung von Computern. In diesen Bereichen müssen nach Auffassung von Scharff trotz der knappen finanziellen Mittel große Anstrengungen unternommen werden, damit die Schulen in Ludwigshafen „wieder wenigstens auf einen minimalen, aber vernünftigen Stand der Technik" kommen würden.

S94/H45.05502: WUNDERSAMES NICHTS, S. 202

Die (begrenzte) Wirksamkeit einiger Methoden konnte so tatsächlich belegt werden – etwa die der Chirotherapie gegen Kreuzschmerzen. Selbst die Homöopathie bestand mittlerweile eine Reihe von Prüfungen, ohne daß sich die Wirkung mit den Mitteln heutiger Wissenschaft erklären ließe. Doch wie sollte bei Taiji oder Kunsttherapie, dem Malen und Gestalten zum Ausgleich innerer Verspannungen, die Placebo-Kontrolle aussehen?

3. *Causal clauses (Zifonun et al. 1997: H1 7.3.4.2) with verb first and* doch
S94/H47.05740: Über die rote Linie, S. 143
Oder sollte er den offenen Schlagabtausch mit den Fanatikern wagen? Dann wiederum würde er einen verhängnisvollen Guerillakrieg beginnen, der ihn um sein Ansehen in der eigenen Bevölkerung bringen könnte, stünde er doch als Büttel der Israelis da. Immerhin gelten mehr als ein Drittel der Palästinenser in Gaza als Hamas-Sympathisanten.

7 Indirect speech: original condition or result clauses

Sub-categories:

1. *Result clauses of explicit condition clauses*
MK1/ZFA.00001, FRANKFURTER ALLGEMEINE ZEITUNG, Mittwoch, 1. Dezember 1965, S. 1
Wie zu hören war, lehnte Stewart es ab, die Pläne für ein atomares Mitspracherecht innerhalb der Nato zugunsten eines Ost-West-Paktes zur Verhinderung der Verbreitung von Atomwaffen aufzugeben. Die Kontrolle über die Anwendung von Atomwaffen, erklärte er, würde weiterhin bei den gegenwärtigen Atommächten liegen, selbst wenn sich die Nato entscheiden sollte, eine neue multinationale Verteidigungsmacht zu schaffen.

2. *Result clauses of implicit or lexical conditions*
BZK/W64.01357, WELT 09.11.64, S.02, POLITIK
Das betreffe vor allem den Vorschlag aus den Kreisen der anderen Ressorts, für alle Sozialversicherten nicht mehr Mindestsätze, sondern sogenannte Regelsätze einzuführen, die mit den Arztgebühren der Ersatzkassen übereinstimmen und unter denen *dann* die Mindestsätze für Unbemittelte und Fürsorgeempfänger liegen würden. Auch sei noch offen, ob die Höchstsätze das Zehnfache oder das Sechsfache der Mindestsätze ausmachen sollten, [my italics]

3. *Condition clauses introduced by* wenn *or similar conjunctions*
MMM/508.11765: Mannheimer Morgen, 07.08.1995, Loka-

les; Ein Treffen bei „L'Art" – Musik, Kunst und Gespräch Musik vom „Trio Aquarela", die Kunst hautnah, das Miteinander – Günther Berlejung, Manfred Graf, Gisela Hachmann-Ruch sorgten sich um das künstlerische Ambiente; Original-Druckplatten und Objekte kamen zum Verkauf. Hans-Jürgen Mayer hatte es betont, es wäre schön, wenn es weitere solche Veranstaltungen gäbe. Und Michael Cordier unterstrich, man müsse nur wollen – es koste nur Engagement, weniger Geld.

4. *Condition clauses: no conjunction, verb in first position*
MK1/ZFA.00530, FRANKFURTER ALLGEMEINE ZEITUNG, Samstag, 4. Dezember 1965, S. 4
Im Potsdamer Abkommen hätte man beschlossen, Deutschland als eine Einheit zu behandeln und ihm einen Friedensvertrag zu geben. Ginge man diesen Weg, so würden die Schwierigkeiten mit den Grenzen vermieden. Die britische Regierung erkenne an, daß die Russen gewisse Befürchtungen gegenüber den Deutschen hegten.

8 Indirect speech: hypothetical sentences or clauses

Sub-category: *Hypothetical statements*

MK1/ZFA.03010, FRANKFURTER ALLGEMEINE ZEITUNG, Dienstag , 21. Dezember 1965, S. 1
Die Zeitung hatte Erhard unterstellt, er wolle mit dem erhofften Abkommen für die Bundesrepublik ein Miteigentum an einer Atomstreitmacht gewinnen, die aus sechs amerikanischen und vier britischen Polaris-U-Booten bestehen solle. Das Abkommen solle auf deutschen Wunsch bis zu den Wahlen für die französische Nationalversammlung Anfang 1967 geheim bleiben, bei denen voraussichtlich keine gaullistische Mehrheit mehr zustande käme. Dies würde die französische Gegnerschaft zu atomaren Vorhaben der Bundesrepublik verringern.

9 Indirect speech: Sentence-adverbial clauses

Sub-category: *Purpose clauses*

MMM/511.27301: Mannheimer Morgen, 06.11.1995, Regionales; Bio-Botschaft reift zwischen den Rebzeilen
Umkehr auf sozial-, umwelt- und generationsverträgliche Pfade predigte Hans Joachim Roos von der evangelischen Kirche Hessen-Nassau. Es gelte die Rahmenbedingungen zu ändern, damit die Folgekosten „bei den Irrwegen" nicht mehr zu Lasten der Allgemeinheit, sondern des Endprodukts gingen.

10 Indirect speech: Subjunctive II where Subjunctive I would be indistinguishable from indicative

MK1/ZFA.01065.1, FRANKFURTER ALLGEMEINE ZEITUNG, Mittwoch , 8. Dezember 1965, S. 4
Statt dessen habe, wie Berichte wissen wollen, Apel die Wirtschaft der Zone aus dieser eisernen Umklammerung Moskaus, ähnlich, wie andere Volksdemokratien das praktizieren, langsam herauslösen wollen und sich dadurch etwas größeren Bewegungsspielraum in Richtung Westeuropa, aber auch Westdeutschland, schaffen wollen. Aus diesem Grunde stünden, heißt es, hinter dem Freitod Apels keineswegs nur wirtschaftliche Sachfragen, sondern vor allem auf lange Sicht bedeutsame politische Beweggründe.

11 Indirect speech: Subjunctive II where a Subjunctive I form is available

MMM/507.06112: Mannheimer Morgen, 03.07.1995, Wirtschaft; Bei Daimler-Benz werden Löcher größer
Dies erklärte gestern ein Sprecher des Stuttgarter Unternehmens… . Es sei jedoch zum jetzigen Zeitpunkt unmöglich, die Gesamtbelastungen von Daimler-Benz exakt zu beziffern, weil niemand die weitere Entwicklung des Dollarkurses kenne und zudem noch ein halbes Geschäftsjahr vor dem Konzern läge. Zu einem Bericht des Magazins „Spiegel", Daimler-Benz werde 1995 einen Verlust ausweisen, „der zwischen einer und zwei Milliarden Mark, näher an zwei

Milliarden“ liege, sagte der Sprecher, er wolle dies nicht dementieren.

12 Indirect speech: *würde*+infinitive where a Subjunctive II or Subjunctive I form is available

MK1/ZB3.01356, BILDZEITUNG, Freitag, 10. März 1967, S. 4
Mit dem vierten Zug der zweiten Kompanie des Luftlandejägerbattaillons 19 lagerte er am Westufer des Flusses. Er war Stabsoberjäger. Als der Feldwebel sagte, er würde jetzt zum Arzt gehen und käme bald wieder, hatte Dietrich Julitz vorübergehend die Befehlsgewalt über den Zug.

13 Indirect speech: Subjunctive II or *würde*+infinitive in place of future form

Subjunctive II

MMM/506.01086: Mannheimer Morgen, 01.06.1995, Lokales; Enge auf dem Advokatenmarkt
Daß einzelne Advokaten ein so schlechtes Auskommen finden, daß sie nächtens Taxi fahren oder sich als Bar-Mann etwas dazu verdienen, ist dem Präsidenten der Anwaltskammer noch nicht zu Ohren gekommen.
Wer sich ständig weiterbilde, sich zum Beispiel der Europäisierung des Rechts anpasse, fände sein Auskommen, meint Zimmermann. Außerdem habe der Bedarf an juristischer Dienstleistung gewaltig zugenommen, weil immer mehr Lebensvorgänge reglementiert und „justiziabel“ gemacht würden

würde+infinitive

BZK/W69.00904, WELT 10.05.69, S.19, SPORT
Stastny will seine endgültige Mannschaft erst kurz vor dem Spiel benennen – , dann werden in dieser Vorstellung gleich sechs Mann der Bayern-Elf zu finden sein. Man würde sich dadurch allerdings nicht beirren lassen, meint der deutsche Mannschaftskapitän Willi Schulz, denn im Spiel käme es nur

darauf an, daß das Trikot stimmt. Am 21. Mai im Qualifikationsspiel gegen Zypern werden viele schöne Tore erwartet. Diesmal in Nürnberg erwartet man vor allem einen Sieg. Ein Tip?

14 Indirect mental processes[14]

Sub-categories:

1. *Inner Monologue (first person narrative) and* Erlebte Rede *(third person narrative);*[15] *no introducing verb; future reference*[16]

MK1/ZB7.02946, BILDZEITUNG, Nr. 169 , Montag , 24. Juli 1967, S. 3

„Sie" kommt eine Viertelstunde vor der verabredeten Zeit. Fröhlich, selbstbewußt und offenbar wohlhabend. Würde ich hier die vom Computer versprochene Übereinstimmung finden? Wir trinken, rauchen, gehen spazieren und erzählen, erzählen ...

BZK/W69.01236, WELT 23.06.69, S.07, SONSTIGES

Rasch legte sie alles wieder an Ort und Stelle, ließ den Koffer an seinem üblichen Platz zurück und ging nach unten, Lev anrufen. Sie müßte das Telefon hier benutzen. Die schreckliche alte Frau und ihr feixender Polizist im Postamt würden sie nie im Leben telefonieren lassen. Felix Zauner durfte sie Levs Geheimnummer nicht preisgeben; das wäre für ihre eigene Zukunft der schlimmste und folgenschwerste Fehler, der ihr hätte unterlaufen können.

2. *Introduced by a mental process verb;*[17] *future reference*

BZK/W64.00115, WELT 20.01.64, S.09, WIRTSCHAFT

Hongkongs Arbeitskosten betragen nur einen Bruchteil der Aufwendungen in den westlichen Ländern. Die *Hoffnung*[18] der deutschen Baumwollverarbeiter, daß sich mit dem Zug zur höheren Qualität Hongkong langsam, aber sicher abhängen ließe, hat sich als Trugschluß erwiesen. [My italics]

MMM/512.34270: Mannheimer Morgen, 13.12.1995, Politik; Hat sich Schmidbauer am Atom die Finger verbrannt?

> Der BND, so der Kern seiner Aussage, habe schon Monate vor der Aktion gewußt, daß der Stoff erst in Rußland besorgt werden mußte. Mehr noch: Mindestens acht Tage vor dem Schmuggel *sei* auch der politischen Spitze *klar gewesen*, daß der Stoff per Flugzeug aus Moskau kommen würde. Rafa: „Wir alle wußten, was wir taten." [My italics]

Note:
Jäger (1971: 174, 182–4) points out that in this function of the subjunctive – in contrast to indirect speech – Subjunctive II can never be replaced by Subjunctive I. This also applies to the parallel *würde*+infinitive construction, i.e., it too cannot be replaced by *werde*. The use of *werde* would indicate an original verbal, not mental, process.

Results

This investigation was designed to test the hypothesis that between the 1960s and the 1990s the *würde*+infinitive construction, which Bausch's study had shown to be the norm in spoken standard German, would have made inroads on the entrenched position of Subjunctive II in written standard German. It was decided to examine:

a) the print media, which are conservative because of the normative influence of grammars (Bausch 1979: 206), and
b) a group of frequently used verbs, which are resistant to change because of the familiarity born of frequency.

Note:
The following findings do not list all the categories examined. They present only those results which are in some way noteworthy.

A. *würde*+infinitive vs Subjunctive II

1 Overall usage

The investigation showed that *in relation to these verbs and in the newspapers analysed*[19] there has actually been a *decrease* in the use of *würde*+infinitive compared with Subjunctive II:

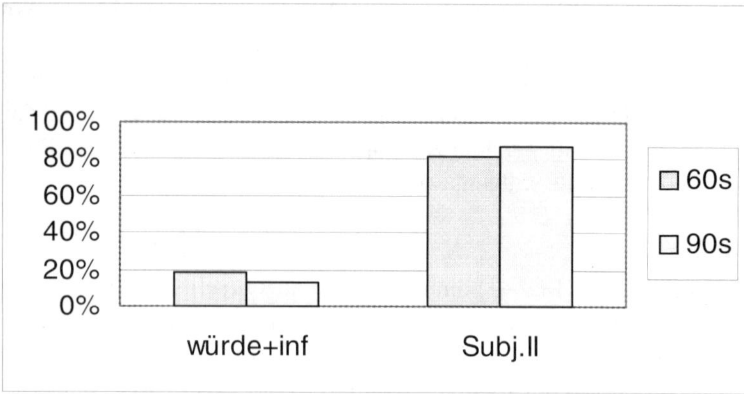

Figure 1 Overall usage (selected verbs)

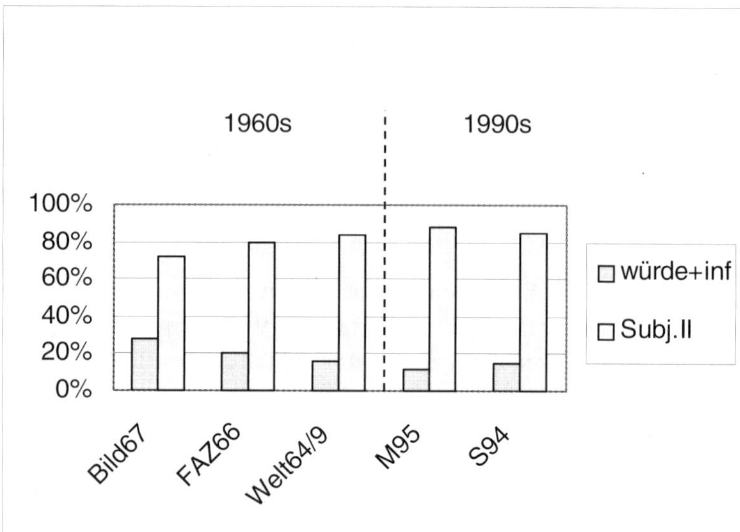

Figure 2 Overall usage (selected verbs) by newspaper

It will be noted that the highest level of usage of the *würde*+infinitive construction is in the *Bild-Zeitung*. This is in line with its style, which can be expected to be closer to spoken German than that of the other publications.

2 Conditional clauses

As long ago as the 1960s, the old punning dictum that the use of the *würde*+infinitive construction in *wenn*-clauses was '*Würde-los*' had been relaxed (DUDEN 1995: 581), and the 1995 edition of the DUDEN *Grammatik* even mentions a desire for variety as a justifiable reason for its use (DUDEN 1995: 775). It is striking, then, that there is virtually no use of *würde*+infinitive in *wenn*-clauses in the data. The only instance is perhaps an anomaly, since the context would not lead one to expect an irreal form:[20]

> MMM/507.09055: Mannheimer Morgen, 21.07.1995, Lokales; Heiser begrüßt Modell zur Bauförderung
> Angedacht ist, die Finanzämter auch als Wohnungsbauförderungsstelle einzurichten. Die neue Förderpraxis will dann zusätzlich Mittel gewähren, wenn die zu zahlende Einkommensteuer unterhalb des Förderbetrages von insgesamt 40 000 Mark bzw. 5000 Mark pro Jahr liegen würde. Die alte Regelung des Paragraphen 10-e des Einkommensteuergesetzes macht die Förderhöhe weitgehend von der Steuerprogression des Bauherrn abhängig.

The print media are obviously continuing to observe the tenor of the relevant sections in reference grammars, namely that in *wenn*-clauses Subjunctive II is to be preferred to *würde*+infinitive in the case of strong verbs unless the Subjunctive II form is an uncommon one.

3 Result clauses

Although the use of the *würde*+infinitive construction in result clauses has traditionally been less subject to stricture than in conditional clauses, the data again show a *decrease* in usage in the case of the verbs under examination. Here too, then, the preference advocated by grammarians for Subjunctive II forms in the case of common strong verbs still prevails. Note that in the sample investigated, the levels of usage by the *Bild-Zeitung* and *Der Spiegel* are the same.

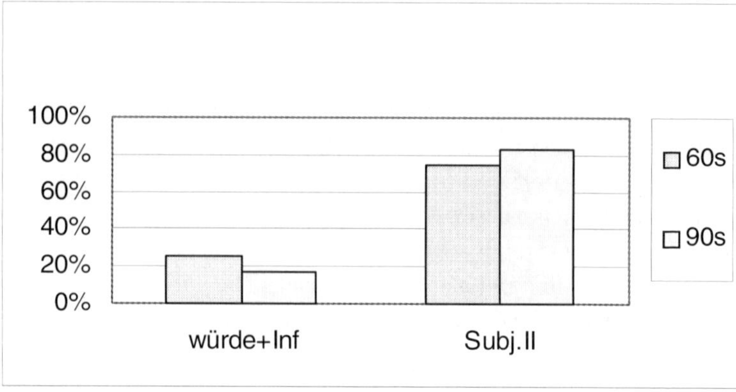

Figure 3 Result clauses (selected verbs)

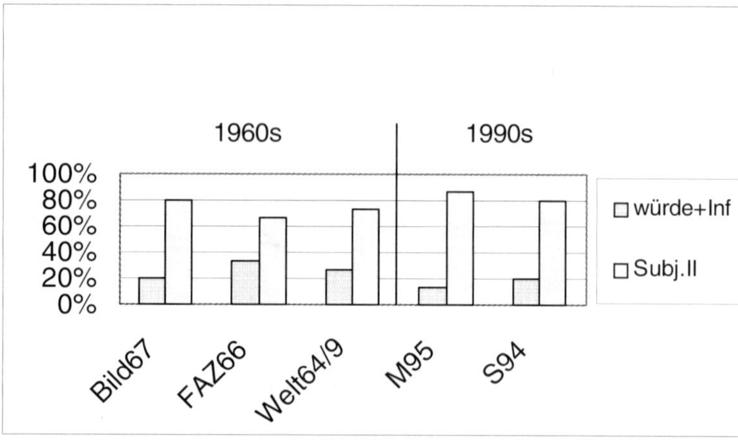

Figure 4 Result clauses (selected verbs) by publication

Table 2 Result clauses (selected verbs)

Totals		*würde*+Inf %	Subj.II %
	1960s	**25.9**	74.1
	1990s	**17.0**	83.0

Table 3 Result clauses (selected verbs) by publication

	Publication	*würde*+Inf %	Subj.II %
1960s	Bild67	**20.0**	80.0
	FAZ66	**33.3**	66.7
	Welt64/9	**27.0**	73.0
1990s	M95	**12.8**	87.2
	S94	**20.0**	80.0

4 Indirect Speech: würde+infinitive where a Subjunctive II or Subjunctive I form is available

This possibility was only realized in a handful of cases, but again showed a slight decrease.

Table 4 würde+infinitive where a Subjunctive II or I is available

Publication	%
Bild67	3.1
FAZ66	2.0
Welt64/9	0.0
Average 1960s	0.9
M95	0.7
S94	0.5
Average 1990s	0.6

Two examples:

MMM/510.24705: Mannheimer Morgen, 20.10.1995, Wirtschaft; Direktbank nicht billiger
Zu den Kosten der Direktbanken schreibt „Finanztest", üblich sei die Abrechnung zu einem Pauschalbetrag, der mindestens

alle Buchungen, Daueraufträge und die EC-Karte abdecke. Die Preise der Anbieter würden dabei weit auseinandergehen und zwischen 5 DM und 12,50 DM liegen. Neben möglichen Provisionen an fremden Geldautomaten können bei Direktbanken die Telefonkosten der Kontoführung durch Ferngespräche ins Geld gehen.

MK1/ZFA.00338, FRANKFURTER ALLGEMEINE ZEITUNG JAN./FEBR. 1966, D-Ausgabe, Freitag, 3. Dezember 1965, S. 4
An Hand einer Darstellung der Entwicklung in dieser Zeit werde deutlich, daß Moskau nicht einen Friedensvertrag wolle, sondern die Spaltung. Wenn man eine solche Darstellung geben würde, „dann fällt in der Welt bei einigen der Groschen".

If it were the case that the written standard German as used in the print media were tending toward the predominance of the *würde*+infinitive construction, one would expect to find far more examples of this type.

B. Distribution

Table 5 Result clauses with and without explicit condition clause

würde+*inf*	With explicit condition %	With implicit condition %	**Subj.II**	With explicit condition %	With implicit condition %
Bild67	13.3	**6.7**		40.0	**40.0**
FAZ66	0.0	**33.3**		16.7	**50.0**
Welt64/9	5.4	**21.6**		32.4	**40.5**
Average 1960s	6.9	**19.0**		32.8	**41.4**
M95	2.6	**10.3**		28.2	**59.0**
S94	9.1	**10.9**		30.9	**49.1**
Average 1990s	6.4	**10.6**		29.8	**53.2**

1 Result clauses

It is perhaps surprising to see that, both in direct and indirect speech, by far the greater number of result clauses are those *without an explicit condition clause* (see Tables 5 and 6).

Table 6 Result clauses with and without explicit condition clause (indirect speech)

würde+*inf*	With explicit condition %	With implicit condition %	**Subj.II**	With explicit condition %	With implicit condition %
Bild67	0.0	**0.0**		0.0	**0.0**
FAZ66	11.1	**55.6**		0.0	**33.3**
Welt64/9	0.0	**28.6**		0.0	**71.4**
Average 1960s	6.3	**43.8**		0.0	**50.0**
M95	0.0	**11.1**		16.7	**72.2**
S94	12.5	**25.0**		12.5	**50.0**
Average 1990s	3.8	**15.4**		15.4	**65.4**

Note that the *Bild-Zeitung* is again the odd one out.

The conditions can be either implicit or lexical. Two examples:

> lexical (here realized by the prepositional phrase beginning with *bei*):
> BZK/W64.01524, WELT 21.12.64, S.09, WIRTSCHAFT
> Das ergibt schon 5,2 Mrd. DM in fünf Jahren. Bei angenommenen Einbußen von 700 Mill. DM jährlich nach Inkrafttreten der Getreidepreissenkung 1967 kämen bis 1970 weitere 2,1 Mrd. DM hinzu. Einschließlich der in jedem Fall fälligen deutschen Zahlungen an den EWG-Agrarfonds und der voraussichtlichen Mindereinnahmen bei Abschöpfungen ergibt sich schnell ein Betrag in der Größenordnung von 8,3 Mrd. DM in fünf Jahren.

implicit:
S94/H04.00376: "ICH BIN OHNE NACHSICHT", S. 26
Kohl weiß, daß sich Nachforschungen nicht auf Wehner beschränken lassen. Es würde ans Tageslicht kommen, wie weit sich CDU-Politiker wie Lothar Späth oder Walther Leisler Kiep oder auch Richard von Weizsäcker mit der SED-Seite eingelassen und wie viele Interna sie aus der Bonner Politik erzählt haben. Über Weizsäcker zum Beispiel ist bekannt, daß er in Gesprächen mit DDR-Kichenvertretern höchst abfällig über Kanzler Kohl geredet hat.

2 Indirect speech: Subjunctive II where a Subjunctive I form is available

Despite considerable variation of usage between the publications, the average level of usage has not significantly changed. Table 7 indicates the rate of occurrence of a Subjunctive II form of the verbs examined, expressed as a percentage of the total occurrences of Subjunctive I and II of these verbs in third person singular indirect speech.

Table 7 Rate of occurrence of Subjunctive II form of verbs

	%
Bild67	25.0
FAZ66	0.6
Welt64/9	8.0
Average 1960s	**4.8**
M95	3.4
S94	7.1
Average 1990s	**4.1**

As in the corresponding use of *würde*+infinitive where a Subjunctive II or Subjunctive I form is available (see above, A.4), the *Bild-Zeitung* again has the highest rate of occurrence, in keeping with its less formal style.

3 Indirect speech: Subjunctive II or würde+*infinitive in place of future form*

This possibility only appeared in *Die Welt* and the *Mannheimer Morgen* and only in a handful of cases.

> MMM/510.19260: Mannheimer Morgen, 06.10.1995, Wirtschaft; Endspurt der Kapitalanleger
> Auch die finanzkräftigeren Haushalte in den großen Städten, die bisher als Hauptinteressenten für den Kauf von Eigentumswohnungen galten, könnten wegen fehlender steuerlicher Anreize künftig ausfallen. Gerade der Personenkreis, der im Mittelfeld der Einkommenspyramide liege und als wichtigste Stütze des Eigenheimbaus gilt, würde künftig nicht mehr zum Zuge kommen. Das gelte auch für die Erwerber von Altbauwohnungen.

> MMM/510.22961: Mannheimer Morgen, 10.10.1995, Politik; „Die Situation könnte besser sein"
> Fraktions-Vize Rudolf Dreßler schwant Böses mit Blick auf die heutige Sitzung der SPD-Fraktion. Er befürchte, daß viele ihrem Unmut freien Lauf ließen, sagt Dreßler, aber: „Es gibt keine Alternative zu Scharping."

(In the second example, one would have expected the *würde*+infinitive construction as a replacement for the future form 'lassen werden,' which is not uniquely subjunctive).

4 stünde vs. stände

Although, as early as 1970, Schulz and Griesbach (1970: 21) described *stünde* as hardly in use,[21] judging by the data examined for this investigation there has been an *increase* in its use between the 1960s and the 1990s, again demonstrating the inherent conservatism in the print media and in the use of high-frequency verbs, since this trend goes against the general linguistic tendency toward analogic regularization.

Table 8 Usage of *stünde* vs. *stände*

stünde/-n		stände/-n	
	%		%
Bild67	66.7	Bild67	33.3
FAZ66	100.0	FAZ66	0.0
Welt64/9	86.4	Welt64/9	13.6
Average 1960s	**88.6**	**Average 1960s**	**11.4**
M95	92.2	M95	7.8
S94	95.5	S94	4.5
Average 1990s	**93.3**	**Average 1990s**	**6.7**

Conclusion

This comparison of a selection of print media from the 1960s and the 1990s has shown that there has been no shift from the conservative use of Subjunctive II towards the spoken German norm of the *würde*+infinitive construction, at least in the case of the eight frequently used strong verbs whose usage was examined. On the contrary, there is evidence for a shift in the opposite direction. This is not to say that the move towards the spoken German norm has not taken place elsewhere in written German, but not in this constellation of frequently used verbs and the print media. The latter are apparently still following the recommendations of grammarians rather than common practice in the spoken standard.

This investigation has also highlighted the role of information technology in corpus linguistics, not merely at the data-gathering stage but in facilitating the analysis process.

Interactive information resource

The databases, the occurrence files and the ancillary computer programs are more than just a vehicle for carrying out this investigation: they represent an interactive information resource for students and researchers. Users can browse through the databases and, when viewing a record of particular interest, can call up the relevant occurrence and its immediate context. Alternatively, a dBase command ('set filter') can be utilized so that only certain records are presented, e.g., only cases of *wenn*-clauses containing a *würde*-form. These can then be viewed as described above. As a further enhancement, a program was written which extracts from the occurrence files all the instances covered by the filter command and saves them together with the information in their database records in a single text file for later perusal or use.

Opportunities for further research

Facilities for corpus linguistic research such as offered by the Institut für Deutsche Sprache are now within the reach of institutions like universities and of individual researchers. This is because of the expansion of the Internet (World Wide Web), the availability of suitable concordancing software and the ever-expanding hard disk capacities and microprocessor speeds of personal computers which allow the storage and manipulation of quantities of data for which only a short time ago a mainframe computer was required.

Data

The World Wide Web offers a wide range of text-types from the German-speaking countries which includes numerous newspapers and magazines but – importantly for further research in the area of this investigation – also comprises fields as diverse as government, politics, business, financial institutions, religion, the arts, culture, popular science, the environment, advertising, communications and media, schools and universities, leisure activities and hobbies, food and beverages, dining and restaurants, nutrition and health, tourism and travel, transportation, towns and cities, and states and provinces.[22] In addition, there are a number of discussion or mailing lists where the language of communication is German and where the text type can be either relatively formal or closer to that of the personal letter.[23]

Material available on the World Wide Web can be downloaded according to a specific plan in order to build up corpora of particular text-types (though one should always check the copyright status of such material). In some cases, large amounts of contemporary data are available from websites which archive material or provide information.

Software

There is now quite a variety of concordancing software available for the personal computer.[24] Some of these can handle letters with accents or diacritics. Other features desirable for the type of research exemplified by this investigation would be the ability to search batches of text files and output search results to a file rather than to working memory, so that both the processing of data and the storage of results is not limited by the memory capacity of the computer. Further, the capability to output search results not only in the form of KWIC concordances, but also in full sentences or paragraphs.

Areas of investigation

Bausch states that in order to be able to make reliable assertions about the productiveness of the Subjunctive II and *würde*+infinitive constructions, one needs to determine which verbs occur in which of the two forms and with what frequency, and also which of the two is chosen in contexts where both are structurally possible (Bausch 1979: 203–6). The present investigation represents a diachronic study of this in regard to a restricted number of verbs in a particular text type. Using the facilities described above, a synchronic study such as proposed by Bausch could be carried out for text-types other than the print media and for a wider selection of verbs both strong and weak.

Within the print media, the availability of material through the World Wide Web would also make possible a synchronic comparison of usage between different newspapers and magazines.

Notes

1 The data for this investigation was gathered from the machine-readable corpora of the Institut für Deutsche Sprache in Mannheim (see note 5 below for contact details for the Institute) in the second half of 1996, using the Institute's COSMAS system. At this point, I would like to thank the staff of the Institute for their friendly and expert assistance, in particular Prof. Gerhard Stickel (Director), Frau Eva Teubert (Librarian), Dr Irmtraud Jüttner (the

COSMAS adviser), Prof. Dieter Herberg and Dr Wolfgang Teubert.

2 Thus in: Zifonun et al. (1997: F2 3.2); DUDEN (1995: 774–5); Weinrich (1993: 245); Engel (1991: 422–3); Flämig (1991: 409); Hammer (1991: 237); Helbig and Buscha (1991: 191). See also Jäger (1971: 202).

3 This corpus comprises 293 texts from the years 1950–67, totalling approximately 2.2 million words and consisting of literary texts, memoirs, scientific and popular scientific texts, trivial literature and articles from newspapers and magazines (al-Wadi 1994: 257).

4 Transcriptions of recordings of discussions, interviews, lectures, reports, stories and media reporting from 1968 to 1974 totalling approximately 700 000 words (al-Wadi 1994: 257).

5 Institut für Deutsche Sprache, Postfach 101621, D-68016 Mannheim, Germany. Web site: <http://www.ids-mannheim.de>. Tel.: +49 621 15810; Fax: +49 621 1581200.

6 'Ob die *würde*-form die Vollverbform verdrängt, erscheint fraglich' (Jäger 1971: 257).

7 Jäger, *Konjunktiv*, p. 256.

8 Bausch (1979: 206). See, for example, DUDEN (1995: 775), where a list of instances is presented where the *würde*+infinitive construction may be used instead of Subjunctive II, implying that the latter is the standard form – and this despite the claim made on p. 2 of the foreword that the grammar covers both spoken and written standard German (see p. 2 of the foreword). However, 'proximity to the spoken language' has been added to the list of instances. *Hammer's German Grammar* (1991: 237) bases its whole presentation on Bausch.

9 A representative selection of texts from the newspapers *Neues Deutschland* (GDR) and *Die Welt* (GFR) from the years 1949, 1954, 1959, 1964, 1969 and 1974, comprising 10 840 texts totalling approximately 3 million words (al-Wadi 1994: 257).

10 Jäger (1971: 20) erroneously has 1966.

11 The 'records' of the database are analogous to the cards of a card index.

12 This may appear similar to *Erlebte Rede* ('interior monologue': see below), but is different in that it is not indirect mental process.

13 Typically *wobei* and *ohne daß* clauses (Zifonun et al.1997: H1 7.3.9.1).

14 Cf. Käte Hamburger's 'Verben der inneren Vorgänge': '*denken, sinnen, glauben, meinen, fühlen, hoffen u.ä*' quoted in Jäger (1971: 301).

15 Mainly literary narrative forms used to express a person's thoughts, feelings, etc. See Zifonun et al. (1997: F2 3.4.2.4) and DUDEN (1995: 756ff. (§1320)).

16 Note that DUDEN (1995: 756) does not mention Subjunctive II as a possible means of expressing futurity in *Erlebte Rede*. Cf. Jäger (1971: 180–2) (§4.19.10)) and Kaufmann (1976: 153).

17 This is not the same thing as indirect speech. See Jäger (1971: 174–8)

(§4.19.3 – 4.19.13)), Zifonun et al. (1997: F2 3.4.2). Note also the distinction made by Halliday (1994) between 'Verbal processes … processes of saying' (§5.5.2) and 'Mental processes: processes of sensing' (§5.3).

18 This nominalization of the mental process verb *hoffen* has a function in relation to the following clause equivalent to that which the verb itself would have had.

19 See above under **Data**. The term 'newspapers' is used for simplicity to avoid having to refer each time specifically to the weekly news magazine *Der Spiegel.*

20 It does not seem to be a case of differing levels of probability (DUDEN 1995: 772, 1336).

21 The DUDEN is more cautious (1995: 124).

22 The following websites are good starting points: <http://www.isu.edu/~nick-crai/german.html>; <http://www.ualberta.ca/~german/Jump_Stations.html>; <http://www.uncg.edu/~lixlpurc/german.html>.

23 A few of these are listed at <http://www.ualberta.ca/~german/Jump_Stations.html>.

24 An excellent source of information on this topic can be found on Tim Johns' web page at: <http://web.bham.ac.uk/johnstf/timconc.htm>.

References

al-Wadi, Doris (1994), *COSMAS Benutzerhandbuch*. Institut für Deutsche Sprache: Mannheim.

Bausch, Karl-Heinz (1979), *Modalität und Konjunktivgebrauch in der gesprochenen deutschen Standardsprache.* Sprachsystem, Sprachvariation und Sprachwandel im heutigen Deutsch. Max Hueber Verlag: Munich.

dBase IV (1988). Ashton-Tate: Torrance, California.

DUDEN (1995), *Grammatik der deutschen Gegenwartssprache*, 5. (5th edn, completely revised and enlarged). Dudenverlag: Mannheim/Leipzig/ Vienna/Zurich.

DUDEN (1966), *Grammatik der deutschen Gegenwartssprache*, 2. (2nd edn, enlarged and corrected). Dudenverlag: Mannheim/Vienna/Zurich

Engel, Ulrich (1991), *Deutsche Grammatik.* Julius Groos Verlag: Heidelberg.

Flämig, Walter (1991), *Grammatik des Deutschen.* Akademie Verlag: Berlin.

Halliday, Michael (1994), *An Introduction to Functional Grammar*, 2nd edn. Edward Arnold: London/Melbourne/Auckland.

Hammer, A. E. (1991), *Hammer's German Grammar and Usage*, 2nd edn, rev. by Martin Durrell. Edward Arnold: London/New York/Melbourne/Auckland.

Helbig, Gerhard and Joachim Buscha (1991), *Deutsche Grammatik.* Ein Handbuch für den Deutschunterricht. Verlag Enzyklopädie-Langenscheidt: Leipzig/Berlin/Munich.

Jäger, Siegfried (1971), *Der Konjunktiv in der deutschen Sprache der Gegenwart.* Untersuchungen an ausgewählten Texten. Max Hueber Verlag: Munich/ Pädagogischer Verlag Schwann: Dusseldorf.

Kaufmann, Gerhard (1976), *Die indirekte Rede und mit ihr konkurrierende Formen der Redeerwähnung*. Max Hueber Verlag: Munich.

Micro-OCP (Oxford Concordance Program), Version 2 (1988). Oxford University Press: Oxford.

Microsoft Excel (1985–96). Microsoft Corporation: Seattle.

QuickBASIC v.4.5 (1985–88). Microsoft Corporation: Seattle.

Schulz, Dora and Heinz Griesbach (1970), *Grammatik der deutschen Sprache*. Max Hueber Verlag: Munich.

Tribble, Chris and Glyn Jones (1990, *Concordances in the Classroom. A resource book for teachers*. Longman: Harlow.

Weinrich, Harald (1993), *Textgrammatik der deutschen Sprache*. Dudenverlag: Mannheim/Leipzig/Vienna/Zurich.

Zifonun, G., L. Hoffmann, B. Strecker et al. (1997), *Grammatik der deutschen Sprache*. de Gruyter: Berlin/New York.

Index